ISLAM AND THE MODERN MUSLIM WORLD

G W Choudhury
Adjunct Professor
Columbia University

Scorpion Publishing Ltd
London

First published in 1993 by Scorpion Publishing Ltd,
Victoria House, Buckhurst Hill, Essex, England.

ISBN 0 905906 43 8

Typeset in Linotype Bembo

Printed in Wales by Charter Press Ltd., Rhuddlan

Dedication

To the loving memory of my parents, Fatema and Golam Mowla, and with the most affectionate feelings to my wife Dilara, my sons Pappu and Sayeed, and their wives, my 'daughters', Lipi and Jui respectively.

Preface

Since I wrote my first book on Islam in 1990, I have been teaching a course on 'Islam and Modernisation' at Columbia University, New York. In the meantime, I also wrote a book on the life and eternal message of the Prophet of Islam—one cannot write a book on the Prophet Muhammad without thorough study and research on Islamic sources.

These two factors, teaching at Columbia for the last four years and my research for the book on the Prophet Muhammad, have enabled me to do extensive research and reading on Islam, mainly at Columbia University's libraries; I also visited during this period a number of Muslim countries, including Pakistan and Saudi Arabia, to do empirical research on Islam.

I am happy to be able to complete my work on *Islam and the Modern Muslim World*.

In expressing my appreciation and thanks for being able to produce this volume on Islam, I must first mention the unique opportunity of teaching at my *alma mater*, Columbia University, New York. I am now an Adjunct Professor at the School of International and Public Affairs of Columbia University. Professor Ainslee T Embree took the initiative in introducing this course on Islam at Columbia University and appointing me as an Adjunct Professor. I must thank him sincerely. Subsequently, the Associate Dean, Robin Lewis, has been of great help to me to continue my assignment at Columbia and thereby helping me to write this book. He has never been tired of extending his helping hand towards me. Associate Dean, Steven A Cohen, was also very helpful to me. I must also express my thanks to Assistant Dean, Mrs Dorothy chambers.

The author also acknowledges his deep appreciation of the

following, which have been of great help in preparing this work and also his recent book *The Prophet Muhammad: His Life and Eternal Message* (1993); Fazhur Rahman Ansari, *The Quranic Foundation, The Structured Muslim Society* (Karachi, 1977); Muhammad Asad, *The Principles of State and Government* (Gibraltar, 1980); Jophn Esposito, *Islam, the Straight Path* (New York, 1989) and *The Islamic Threat: Myth or Reality* (New York, 1992); A K Brohi, *Islam in the Modern World* (2nd ed., Lahore, 1975); and Abul A'la Mandudi, *Towards Understanding Islam* (Leicester, 1977) and his other valued works.

I must also thank the Islamic Affairs Division of the Royal Embassy of Saudi Arabia in Washington for their financial grant. 'In this connection I would especially mention the generous attitude of His Highness Prince Muhammed Bin Faisal Bin Turki and his special Assistant Dr Ibrahim Fafanah. I am really grateful for their continuous support.

I must also thank Scorpion Publishing Ltd of London, England, for their ready willingness to publish my book. I must thank Mr Leonard Harrow, General Editor of Scorpion, for his help at every stage of publication; Mr Alan Ball of the publishing company also deserves my thanks and appreciation.

Last, but not least, I must mention the affectionate encouragement I received from my family: my wife Dilara, my two sons, Pappu and Sayeed and my two 'new daughters'—Lipi and Jui (wives of Pappu and Sayeed); without their affection it would not have been possible for me to work over a period of four years. They endured my countless hours of work at the libraries and in my study; Dilara also accompanied me to Pakistan and Saudi Arabia.

I wish to make it clear that the views expressed in this book are entirely mine and do not belong to anyone who helped me in writing the book. I sincerely hope that this book will lead to a better and correct understanding of Islam and its spirit, which is the prime objective of my work.

Golam W Choudhury
Columbia University
New York
September 1993

Contents

Introduction

An author has always some objective in writing a book. I have no hesitation in stating that my prime objective of this book is my honest desire to project Islam in its proper prospective and spirit.

In recent years, Islam has been grossly misinterpreted in many quarters, in particular since there has been a resurgence of Islam in the 1970s. Some of the concepts of Islam, such as *jihad* (sadly too often translated as 'holy war'), and its attitude towards non-Muslim minorities in a society where Islam is an important factor, are often misunderstood. Islam has been depicted as 'a religion of the sword', while in reality Islam is basically a religion of peace and universal brotherhood. 'Islam' is an Arabic word whose literal translation means peace and submission; and it is based on two words with the same root: *salam* meaning peace, and *silm* meaning submission to the will of God.

The contributions of Muslim reformists such as Sayyid Jamal al-Din al-Afghani, Shaykh Muhammad 'Abduh, and his follower Rashid Rida in the Middle East, and those of Shah Waliullah, Sir Sayyid Ahmad Khan and the poet-philosopher, Muhammad Iqbal, in the South Asian sub-continent, have been discussed. Their attempts to give Islam a dynamic interpretation in accordance with changed circumstances and their role in Muslim liberation movements against European colonial rule over the world of Islam have also been examined.

We then move to a discussion of the role of Islam as a nation-building force in the nationalist movements of the modern Muslim states which emerged after the Second World War following the liquidation of the European colonial empires.

As regards Islam's attitude towards other religions, we quote from the fundamental source—the Quran—which enjoins its followers: 'I worship not that which ye worship, nor will ye worship which I worship . . . to you be your way and to me mine.' This principle of 'unto you your religion, and unto me my religion' falsifies the inaccurate concept that Islam is intolerant or that it is 'the religion of the sword'. This is one of the finest principles of religious tolerance, formulated at a time in human history when religious toleration was in effect unheard of. We are not unaware of the many lapses of the noble and ideal principles of Islam in its history over the last fourteen centuries. We are also aware of the many shortcomings and limitations in many Muslim countries in the contemporary world: corruption, poverty, exploitation of the poor, illiteracy, discrimination and many other vices. However, that is not the fault or any deficiency of Islam and its ideals: there are also many limitations and shortcomings in many 'democratic' states, but these should not be attributed to democracy and its ideals. The Islamic community, *ummah*, we freely admit, has a long way to go in realizing and implementing the true spirit and meaning of Islam. We present the basic principles and fundamental message of Islam in the expectation that its followers will strive to achieve these broad ideals. We also expect that the message and principles of Islam, properly presented, should remove the centuries-old prejudices against Islam in the West.

Another sad development in recent years is that in certain quarters a new term has been frequently used which is 'Islamic fundamentalism'. What does it really mean? Are Islam and the West on a collision course? Is Islam a new threat to world peace and stability? Will there be a new cold war between the West and the Islamic world after the ending of the East-West one? These and similar issues have been examined and analysed in depth, and with as much objectivity as possible. In matters where one's own faith and religion are involved, one's impartiality may be questioned. However, these are, after all, facts and they may speak for themselves.

The book begins with a chapter on Islamic values and teachings—the five fundamental pillars, the unity of God (*tawhid*), etc. Then we go on to examine the concept of an Islamic state: what are its basic features and requirements? Is an Islamic state compatible with a modern democratic one? Do the citizens of an Islamic state enjoy any fundamental rights and the rule of law? This chapter is followed by a history of the growth of the Islamic political community from the time of the Prophet in the 7th century up to the present, including a study of the leading Muslim reformers in the 19th and 20th centuries.

There are two chapters dealing with the place of Islam in modern Muslim states. Reference has also been made to the Muslim minorities in India, in Central Asia under the demised Soviet empire and to the Muslims in China. In the subsequent chapters we have discussed the Islamic theory of international relations and the Islamic International Organisation, OIC (Organisation of the Islamic Conference). The concluding part of the book deals with resurgence of Islam and the concept of Islamic fundamentalism.

Chapter I
Fundamentals of Islam

Islam is an Arabic word whose literal translation means peace and submission [to the will of God]. *Islam* derives from two words with the same root: *salam* and *salm*. Professor Khurshed Ahmed explained the basic principles of Islam in this way: 'Islam stands for a commitment to surrender one's will to the will of God and thus to be at peace with the Creator and with all that has been created by Him. It is through submission to the will of God that peace is brought about. Harmonization of man's will with the will of God leads to the harmonization of different spheres of life under an all-embracing ideal.' He adds that Islam is a world view and an outlook on life. It is based on the recognition of unity of God and the Muslim's submission to the will of God. 'In it', he concludes, 'is embodied a framework for the conduct of the whole of human life.'[1]

Sayyid Abul A'la Mawdudi pointed out that in Islam man's entire individual and social life 'is an exercise in developing and strengthening his relationship with God. *Iman*, the starting point of Islam, Mawdudi continues, consists in the acceptance of this relationship by man's intellect and will. All those persons, he further added, 'who thus surrender themselves are welded into a community and that is how the Muslim society comes into being. It is an ideological society, radically different from those which are founded on the basis of race, colour or territory.'[2]

The central theme of Islam is the unity of God or *tawhid*. Tawhid has been given greatest emphasis in the Quran. In order to understand Islam one has to understand the various dimensions of *tawhid*. Dr Fazlur Rahman Ansari has elaborately explained the doctrine of *tawhid.* We have reproduced Dr Ansari's explanation of *tawhid*, in my previous book *Islam and the Contemporary World.*

Tawhid is an all-pervading principle which governs all the fundamental domains of human faith and action. 'As such', Ansari tells us, 'it is vitally necessary to understand it in all its dimensions in order to understand the basic Quranic approach to vital human problems.

'The Quranic concept of unity which, at the level of psychological, moral and social phenomena, assumes the form of the principle of integration, provides the guidance which can save mankind from disaster. Because Allah has created all human beings with a plan and a purpose, and has endowed them with the status of His vicegerency, and has created the world so that human beings can act in it in accordance with their status, the only goal worth the name, which every human being should by his very nature pursue, is the fulfilment of his destiny as the vicegerent of Allah—wherein he attains harmony with Allah, who is the Source of all life, light, power, happiness and beatitude. This only goal is, in fact, the comprehensive goal to which the pursuit of all partial goals should bear reference; and for that purpose all the immediate goals of human activity—and every healthy activity must be included in the empire of human action—should be pursued in an integrated and balanced manner, harmonizing every one of them with the rest, and all together with the comprehensive goal, or the ultimate goal'.[3]

A Muslim must believe in unambiguous terms and without any reservation that God is One and that there is no God but He. This belief in the unity of God is the basic foundation of the Islamic creed. It means complete surrender and submission to God. The Quran which was revealed to the Prophet Muhammad stresses the fact of the unity of God and the devotion to worship to Him. Muslims express their faith in the existence of God, in various expressions and forms; for instance it is said:

> God is the Mighty and The Almighty. He is The Willer of existing things and the things which will exist: and nothing Happens except with His Will. He is The Knower of all that can be known. His knowledge encompasses the whole universe which He has created and he alone sustains. He comprehends even suggestions of the mind and the concealed secrets in the inner most part of the breasts of men. God is Living: neither passing away nor does death overtake Him. He is The All Hearing of all audible things. His Hearing is not affected by distance and he hears even the sound of the creeping ant upon a rugged rock. He is The All Seeing; and light and darkness do

not affect the degree of His Seeing visible things. And He speaks with an eternal Speech not resembling the speech of created things. God's Might, Will, Knowledge, Life, Hearing, Seeing and Speech are inherent attributes in Him and not a thing or things apart from Him.

God is The Just, The Wise, The Merciful, The Compassionate, The Beneficent, The Eternal, The Creator, The Omni-Present and The Lord of the universe. There is no god but God.[4]

What Constitutes a Mu'min *(True) Muslim?*

What is the real meaning of a true Muslim ? 'Muslim' means : 'the human being who :(a) accepts the ideal of total surrender to God; and (b) pursues that ideal actively'. He remains a formal Muslim so long as he does not cross from (a) to (b) (Surah 49: 14). He starts on the road to being Muslim in the proper sense when he crosses into (b). He becomes a genuine Muslim only when he undertakes comprehensively the active pursuit of the ideal of total surrender to Allah, which, though it proceeds gradually, definitely implies the practical affirmation of faith (*iman*) through its translation into requisite action (*al-'amal al-salih*), elevating him finally to the rank of the *mu'min* (i.e. the Faithful, or the Believer in the true sense) (Surah 49: 15).[5]

God

The existence of God, Allah, as the creator and sustainer of the universe and of man, and particularly as the Giver of guidance for man, and He who judges man, individually and collectively and metes out to him merciful justice, is the most important and fundamental message of the Quran, which is called the 'guidance of mankind' (*hudan li'l-nas*). The Quran gives the attributes of Allah as infinitely merciful, and stresses His infinite majesty. Reference to God occurs 'well over 2,500 times in the Quran (not to count terms such as al-Rabb, the Lord, and al-Rahman, the Merciful[6] . . . The main points to be drawn from these numerous references to Allah are that:

1 Everything except Allah is contingent on Allah, including the entirety of nature.

2 Allah, with all His might and glory, is essentially the All-Merciful.

> 3 Both these aspects necessarily entail a proper relationship between Allah and man.[7]

The Quran again and again points out that Allah gives meaning and life to everything. 'He is all-enveloping, literally infinite and He alone is infinite.' The Quran lays down:[8]

> He is God other than whom there is none. He is knower of the unseen and the seen, the merciful, the compassionate. He is the God other than who there is none, the sovereign, the Holy, the one with peace and integrity, the keeper of the faith, the protector, the mighty, the one whose will is power, the most supreme, glory be to Him . . . He is the creator; the maker, the fashioner, to whom belong beautiful names; whatever is in the heavens and the earth sings His glories. He is the mighty one, the Wise one.(Surah 50: 22-24).

The Quran further lays down:

> And who other than Him made the earth a firm abode (for you) and set rivers traversing through it and put firm mountains therein and sealed off one sea from the other? Is there then a God beside God?
> And who other than Him responds to the distressed one when he calls Him and He relieves of the distress and who has made you (mankind) His vicegerents on earth? Is there then a God beside God?
> . . . And who other than Him guides you in darkness of the land and sea? And who sends forth winds heralding his mercy (rain)? Is there then a God beside God . . . ? (Surah 27: 60-64)

These verses from the Quran stress God's supreme power and lordship over mankind and the universe; they equally emphasize Allah's mercy and forgiveness. In the Quran it is repeatedly stressed that God is merciful and forgiving. It is said: 'He has imposed the law of mercy upon Himself' (Surah 6: 12) and 'My mercy comprehends all'. 'For those who genuinely repent, God transmutes their lapses into goodness' (Surah 25: 70).[9]

Muslims are noted for expressing their devotion, love, and unqualified faith in God in various ways and quite frequently; almost daily they invoke God's mercy and forgiveness by reciting some verses of the Quran which are full of praises, of the greatness, kindness, and forgivingness of God. We shall refer to 'Five pillars of Islam ' in our following pages of this chapter. Before we do so we would like to refer to those verses of the Quran which Muslims quite often utter to strengthen their bonds with God and also to seek His favours.

As Schimmel says:

> Certain surahs are thought to possess special blessing power, *barakah*, thus, Surah 36, *Yasin*, is usually recited for dying or dead people. Specific verses are used for the decoration of buildings, artistically penned tablets, or talismans. The most famous among these verses is the Throne Verse (Surah 2: 255), which can be found on walls and weapons, on fabrics and tiles, on agate bezels and woven in wall hangings because of its beauty and protecting power:
>
> God—there is no god but He, the Living, the Self-subsistent. Slumber seizeth Him not, neither sleep. To Him belongeth whatsoever is in the Heavens and whatsoever is in the Earth. Who is there that shall intercede with Him save by His Will? He knoweth what is present with men and what shall befall them, and nought of His knowledge do they comprehend, save what he willeth. His Throne is as wide as the Heavens and the Earth, and the keeping of them wearieth Him not. And He is the High, the Mighty One.
>
> Only one brief prayer was chosen as a kind of introduction—the *Fatihah*, 'the Opening'—which roughly corresponds in use to the Lord's prayer in Christianity, though is probably more frequently recited:
>
> Praise belongs to God, the Lord of the worlds, the Merciful, the Compassionate, the Lord at the Day of Judgement. Thee we worship and Thee we ask for help. Guide us on the straight path of those whom Thou showest kindness, not those on whom thy Wrath rests nor those who go astray.[10]

The last surah (*al-Nas*) of the Quran which is almost daily used in five time prayers is a touching appeal to God to protect human beings from evil-doings and evil thinking. It says, 'I seek refuge with the Sustainer of men, the Sovereign of men . . . from the evil of the whispering, elusive tempter who whispers in the hearts of men, from all temptations (to evil) by invisible forces as well as men'.

Explaining this verse of the Quran, Mohammad Asad in his most illuminating work, *The Message of the Quran*, tells, 'We are told to seek refuge with God' for controlling temptations from evil invisible forces emanating from the blindness of our own hearts, from our gross appetites etc'.[11]

Man is weak, feeble, subject to many undesirable forces, greed etc. So they need God's help and protection to lead a truly right path.

Frithjof Schoun's *Understanding Islam* is regarded as a classic book on Islam and one of the best works on the meaning of Islam. His principal theme is that 'Islam is the meeting between God and man', and from this he expounds the Islamic view of life, the role of the Prophet and the Quran. Schuon begins with the statement that 'Islam is the meeting between God as such and man as such.' God 'as such' he explains as God envisaged, not as He manifested himself in a particular way at a particular time but independently of history and inasmuch as He is what he is and also as by His nature he creates and reveals. Man, as such, Schuon tells, means a theomorphic being endowed with an intelligence capable of conceiving of the Absolute and with a will capable of choosing what leads to the Absolute. According to Schuon, these two doctrines of the Absolute and of man are to be found respectively, in the two 'testimonies' of the Islamic faith, the first, *la ilaha illallah,* concerning God and the second, *muhammad rasulallah,* concerning the Prophet.

The idea of predestination is strong in Islam but, as Schuon points out, it does not invalidate the idea of man's relative freedom: 'Man is subject to predestination because he is not God but he is free because he is made in the image of God. God alone is absolute freedom but human freedom, despite its relativity—in the sense that it is 'relatively absolute'—is not something other than light . . . To sum up: Islam confronts what is immutable in God with what is permanent in man.' Schuon repeats, as other interpreters of the Islamic message have pointed out, that Islam hangs on two statements: first, there is no divinity of reality or absolute outside the only divinity or reality or absolute (*la ilaha illallah*); and second, Muhammad, the glorified, the perfect, is the envoy, the mouthpiece, the intermediary, the manifestation, the symbol of the Divinity (*muhammad rasul allah*).[12] These, as we have already stated, are the fundamentals of the faith: *shahadah*.

Five Pillars of Islam

Apart from the *tawhid*, being the central theme of the Islamic principles, we may now refer to five obligatory duties which the followers of Islām are duty-bound to perform in their daily life.

These are known as 'Five Pillars of Islam'.They are the framework of the Muslim life: (i) Faith (ii) Prayer (*Salat*) (iii) Fasting in the month of Ramadan (iv) *Zakat* (Social security for the poor and the needy (v) *Hajj* (Pilgrimage).

The declaration of faith (i) is called *Shahadah*, a simple formula which all the faithful pronounce in Arabic, the first part is *la ilaha illa llah'*—'there is no god except God'; *ilaha* (god) can refer to anything which we may be tempted to put in place of God—wealth, power, and the like. Then comes *illa llah*: 'except God', the source of all creation. The second part of the *Shahadah* is *Muhammad rasulu 'llah*: Muhammad is the messenger of God'. A message of guidance has come through a man like ourselves.[13]

Prayer

Salat is the name for the obligatory prayers which are performed five times a day, and are a direct link between the worshipper and God. There is no hierarchical authority in Islam, and no priests, so the prayers are led by any learned person who knows the Quran, chosen by the congregation. These five prayers contain verses from the Quran, and are said in Arabic, the language of the Revelation, but personal supplication can be offered in one's own language. Daily five time prayer is an act of purification of both body and soul. A reputed scholar Annemarie Schimmel has explained the significance of prayers in a brilliant way: 'The belief in the purifying power of ritual prayer is intense. The Prophet compared it to a stream of water that washes of sins five times a day. The performance of prayer at the prescribed time constitutes ideally a means of educating Muslims to punctuality, cleanliness and since there is no ranking in the mosque, equal participation in the life of the community. Prayer can also lead to ecstasy experiences and when one observes a praying Muslim who is oblivious of anything and he seems to have drawn himself as it were, out of this world to stand humbly before the Lord. One realizes best whence Islam derives its vital strength.[14]

Many orthodox Muslim *'ulama'* put too much stress on forms of prayers, such as dress, cleanliness of the place of worship and other trivial things, but the real stress should be the condition of mind, devotion to God. Everyday Muslims are required to perform five times in which a particular surah (*Fatihah*) has to be recited; which means, among other things, a vow to God to show the followers of Islam the 'straight path'.

Now what is the 'straight path' that Muslims seek from Allah? The Quran emphasizes the concept of a 'straight path' (Surah 1: 5), which in the very nature of the case denotes the shortest and the most direct path. This path has been defined as the pursuit of the law of the ideal human nature (Surah 30: 30), which bears the glory of the impact of what God calls His 'spirit' (*ruh*) (Surah 32: 9). The path of religion consists, therefore, not in mysterious dogmas and magical rites but in the fulfilment of human destiny in accordance with the demands of the ideal human destiny in accordance with the demands of the ideal human nature and man's status of vicegerent of God (which God has bestowed on man). That necessitates, in its turn, constant exercise in respect of:

1 Acquisition of control by the higher self over the lower self, which always forms the greatest obstacle in the pursuit of all idealistic yearnings—spiritual, moral,intellectual, social and aesthetic—in order to build up human personality in harmony with the demands of ideal human nature.
2 Understanding human personality, nature and history in order to pursue harmony in human society.
3 Efforts in service to and reform of society for the practical establishment of harmony in the social order.
4 The subjugation of nature through the power of knowledge in order to bring nature into harmony with ideal human aspirations.
5 Submission to God, who is the basis of all existence, the source of all excellence and the fountainhead of all virtues, thereby to establish harmony with Him, which alone bestows the capability to achieve true human destiny.[15]

The Quranic message puts all its stress not on the rituals but on the spirit of true religion. In Surah *Fatihah*, with which Muslims are to begin their prayers five times a day—one of the fundamental ingredients of Islam—enjoins man to seek guidance from Allah, the merciful. Now if the followers of Islam do not merely bow to the west or to the east five times a day to fulfil one of the Five Pillars of Islam but really bow before God to seek guidance, to seek the 'straight path', Allah will surely guide man to the true path; and once man really follows the 'straight path' there is no reason why man will not be able to attain those higher ideals and objectives of the Quranic message. This is the secret of the success of the Quranic message and this is what makes the message universal and eternal. All through Surah *Fatihah* runs the note of warning, which indeed sounds throughout the Quran, that it is not mere profession of a creed but righteous conduct which is religion. True religion consists in the surrender of man's will and purpose to the will and purpose of the Lord of Creation.

The *Zakat*

One of the most important principles of Islam is that all things belong to God, and that wealth is therefore held by human beings intrust. The word *zakat* means both 'purification' and 'growth'. Our possessions are purified by setting aside a proportion for those in need, and like the pruning of plants, this cutting back balances and encourages new growth.[16]

Each Muslim calculates his or her own Zakat individually. For most purposes this involves the payment each year of two and a half percent of one's capital.

A pious person may also give as much as he or she pleases as *sadaqah* (charity) and does so preferably in secret. (Although, this word can be translated as 'voluntary charity' it has a wider meaning.) *Zakat*, the third of the five pillars of Islam, is placed after *Salat* (prayer) in order of merit—*iman* (faith) being the first. The utmost importance of *Zakat* in Islam is borne out by the fact that the Quran mentions *Salat* and *Zakat* together in at least thirty-two places as two of the foremost duties of the Muslims after the affirmation of *iman* (faith). The Quran refers to *Zakat* as follows:

> The likeness of those who spend their wealth in Allah's way is as the likeness of a grain which groweth seven ears, in every ear a hundred grains. Allah, giveth increase manifold to whom He will. Allah is all-embracing, all-knowing.
>
> Those who spend their wealth for the cause of Allah and afterward make not reproach and injury to follow that which they have spent, their reward is with their Lord and there shall be no fear come upon them, neither shall they grieve (Surah 2: 261-2).

According to the Quran only those people who pay their Zakat dues willingly and regularly intend to purify their hearts, to do good, to be blessed with divine wisdom and mercy and to win Allah's forgiveness, eternal peace of mind and bliss. The Quran says : 'O Prophet, accept propitiatory offerings from their possessions to cleanse and purify them' (Surah 9: 103). We find the words *Yutun az-Zakat* in the Quran, which means that those who pay *Zakat* pay a share of their wealth for purifying their souls.

We may consider the system of *Zakat* as an Islamic 'Social security system'. Sayyid Mawdudi is emphatic that 'Zakat, the alms-giving, is no less important than performing Salat (Prayer). Indeed, those who refuse to pay Zakat fall outside the pale of Islam . . . Zakat sustains the edifice of Islam.'[17]

Schimmel elaborates the significance of *Zakat* by pointing out, 'The third pillar is *Zakat*, the alms tax. As its root *zky* shows, it was meant originally as self-purification and considered as a 'loan to God'. The law regulated exactly the payable amount; the income should be used, according to Surah 9:60, for the poor, the needy, the tax collector; for those whose religious zeal needs to be strengthened; for slaves who want to buy themselves out of slavery; for debtors who by financing good works have become impoverished; and finally *sabil Allah*, 'in the way of Allah', that is for different purposes such as helping needy travellers, or building useful structures such as public fountains. *Zakat* is also used, as recently in Pakistan, to found religious schools. *Zakat*, correctly applied, appears to be a protective measure against both capitalism and communism, provided it is distributed by taxing the wealthy and supporting the needy. This is the opinion not only of modern Muslim thinkers (e.g. Iqbal, d. 1938), but also of Christian scholars such as Louis Massignon and Kenneth Cragg.[18]

Zakat is meant to reduce, not eliminate poverty, and the gap between haves and have-nots. It was introduced at a time when the concept of social security or social benefits were unheard of. It is a highly beneficial aspect of any fair, just, equitable economic system. It can be termed as one of the earliest, if not the earliest, step towards establishing a welfare state or society.

Fasting

Fasting may be termed as the fourth pillar. *Siyam*, fasting, may be described as abstaining from food, drink, sexual relations from sunrise to sunset in the month of Ramadan, which is the ninth month of the Islamic lunar calendar; due to the lunar calendar of the Islamic year, Ramadan rotates through the seasons.

Like prayers and other pillars of Islam, fasting is also not merely abstaining from food, drink etc. It is also primarily a spiritual ritual means for self-purification. By cutting oneself off from worldly comforts, a fasting person can appreciate the pinches of hungry people who cannot afford to eat regularly. It is also a spiritual exercise for self-purification, self-control and another illustration of man's unqualified submission to the Will of God.

Fasting sometimes becomes a hard task in the summer during the hottest days when one can not even drink a drop of water. Or in those countries like the UK or Canada in the summer when the sun does not set in less than 15 to 20 hours. Islam is, however, not a religion which would cause unnecessary hardship to its followers. So there are a number of concessions in respect of the month-long fast. For the sick, old, pregnant women, persons travelling, or during a war, fasting is not compulsory; it may be postponed or compensated for in some other ways

What is significant is the spiritual union between God and His creations through a process of self-control by abstaining from many comforts and pleasures of life. Mere abstention without mental purification, we consider, will be a mere fasting without the deep significance of *siyam*. Islam stresses again and again the condition of mind: spiritual purification. Fasting in the month of Ramadan is another method of such a procedure of self-purification and total submission to God.

Al-Hajj: Pilgrimage to Mecca

Pilgrimage may be termed the fifth of 'The five pillars of Islam.' *Hajj* (pilgrimage) requires a follower of Islam to make one trip to the House of God (Ka'ba) situated in Makkah in Saudi Arabia. In a sense, *Hajj* is the old custom of the Arab tribes to assemble once a year in Makkah which Islam has 'purified and spiritualized'. *Hajj* is to be performed in the last month of the Islamic calendar (*Zu 'l-Hijjah*); like Ramadan, it also rotates due to the lunar calendar of Islam and as such like fasting it becomes a very difficult exercise in the summer because of the extreme, hot climate of Saudi Arabia. But, millions of Muslims accept such physical discomforts gracefully, even death during the performance of *Hajj* is considered as a blessing of God.

Every year, about two million Muslims come to Makkah from different parts of the world. Thanks to the revolutionary improvement in the means of transport, notably air travel, the number of pilgrims is increasing in recent years.

It is a unique sight to see so many Muslims belonging to different countries, societies, cultures mingling and praying in the House of Allah and prescribed adjoining places like Arafat, Minna etc.

Everybody has to wear a single dress consisting of two pieces of special cloth (for men and for women dress is simple and dignified, ensuring chastity). The simple dress is meant to do away with any distinctions of status or position—king, prince, president, rich and poor—all stand together before God uttering the word *labbaka*, 'here I am at Thy service'.[19]

Hajj is an obligation which has to be performed once in the lifetime of a Muslim—but one may repeat it voluntarily. It is also not obligatory for the poor, invalids, or the sick. Again it illustrates Islam's flexibility and liberal features.

Like the other 'Five pillars of Islam' *Hajj* is basically a spiritual exercise on the part of Muslims to fulfil God's commands; to invoke His mercy, guidance, and kindness. God will judge the performance by the criteria of the condition of mind of the pilgrims.

Muslims feel a unique sense of sublimeness, humility, gracefulness, submission when they enter the Ka'bah as the present author may humbly testify from his personal experience. It also inculcates the sense of the spiritual bonds among the followers of Islam. Like, the other 'Five pillars of Islam' *Hajj* is also meant to strengthen Muslims' faith in one God and His teaching.

Commenting on 'The Five Pillars of Islam' Fazlur Rahman states: Islam 'envisages the establishment of a social order on earth based on a viable ethical foundation. It decisively rejects ethnicity, colour, tongue or territory as a valid base for human organization and unequivocally declares the consubstantiality of the entire human race. Virtue is the only valid basis for true human worth. To this end, the Quran established a brotherhood or community of Muslims whose members were expected to be imbued with that kind of virtue. The function of this community was to be median—that is to avoid and smooth out extremes—and above all, to promote communal good and prohibit evil 'in order to reform the earth and uproot corruption thereform'—morally, socially, politically and economically'.[20] The central theme of the Islamic message is: there is only one God; all men are equal; and man achieves dignity through knowledge. Islam gives the greatest emphasis to unqualified faith in Allah, reliance on His will and the realization that Allah is absolutely free. No religion has emphasized the transcendent aspect of Allah more than Islam.' Islam, as we have already elaborated, is based from beginning to end on the idea of unity (*tawhid*), for Allah is one; 'unity is the alpha and omega of Islam.'[21]

Islam has been more grossly misunderstood than perhaps any other religion. Frithjof Schuon, John Esposito, Annemarie Schimmel and others have done wonderful service in their presentation of the Islamic message, thereby dispelling many prejudices against Islam among both Westerners and those so-called 'modernized' Muslims who seem to have become alienated from their own tradition under the false concept of westernization. Islam is a dynamic religion and its principles are as 'modern' and applicable as any other doctrine or 'ism'. The sad aspect is that the Muslim intelligentsia has failed or does not want to face the challenges to Islam from modern history and science; even though Islam is quite capable of meeting these challenges. As A K Brohi tells us: 'What is really to be done is not so much a re-interpretation of Islam as to secure the application of its principles to the existing economic and political situation. What is wanted is an understanding of what the basic principles of Islam are and how they are to be applied to the existing conditions so that modern man may not live a life of discord and be continually at war with the harmonies of human life.'[22]

Fundamental Rights in Islam

Does Islam recognize any fundamental human rights? Some of the

Western scholars, mainly orientalist, are of the view that Islam speaks only of 'duties' and 'obligations' but of not of 'human rights'. Like many other aspects of Islam and Islamic principles, it is also a misinterpretation, if not vilification of Islam. Islam does recognize basic human rights. Human struggle for a free life in a free society has a long history behind it; from time to time, human rights have been sought to be defined in documents, such as the Magna Carta of 1215, The Habeas Corpus Act of 1679, the Bill of Rights of 1689, the American Declaration of Independence in 1776, and the French Declaration of the Rights of Man in 1789. Basic human rights, or what is termed fundamental rights, have gained an international recognition and status in the Declaration of Human Rights by the United Nations on 10 December 1948. Yet human aspiration for enjoyment of certain basic rights by everybody, irrespective of race, religion, colour, ethnicity, sex, language etc., is not over. The promotion of human rights or preventing violation of human rights is still a big challenge and a major issue facing the contemporary world.

Has Islam, a religion of nearly one billion, any contribution to provide and to safeguard human rights? Is Islam only a code of 'duties' and 'obligations' and has nothing positive about human rights? It is an issue which we must examine in our discussion on the fundamentals of Islam.

The Quran says, 'O Men, Behold, we have created you all out of a male and a female and have made you into nations and tribes so that you might come to know one another. Verily the noblest of you in the sight of God is the one who is most deeply conscious of Him. Behold, God is all-knowing, all-aware' (Surah 49: 13). While interpreting this verse Yousef Ali emphasised that all men are equal before God.

This injunction of the Quran is one of its fundamentals and one that must not be violated. It lays the foundation of equality of mankind—the edifice on which all concepts of human rights are based.[23]

Islam has laid down universal fundamental rights for humanity as a whole, which are to be observed and respected in all circumstances, irrespective of whether a person lives in or outside the territory of the Islamic state, and whether he is at peace or at war with the state. For example, human blood is sacred and may not be spilled without justification; it is not permissible to oppress women, children, old people, the sick or the wounded; a woman's honour and chastity must be respected in all circumstances; and the hungry must be fed, the naked clothed, and the wounded or diseased treated medically.

These, and a few other provisions, have been laid down by Islam as fundamental rights for every man by virtue of his status as a human being to be enjoyed under the constitution of an Islamic state.

The Universal Islamic Declaration of Human Rights was adopted at a conference of eminent Muslim scholars, jurists and representatives of Islamic movements and thought on 19 September, 1981, in Paris under the auspices of the Islamic Council, London; while making a forward to this declaration Mr Salem Azzam, Secretary General of the Islamic Council in London pointed out:

> Islam gave to mankind an ideal code of human rights fourteen centuries ago. Those rights aim at conferring honour and dignity on mankind and eliminating exploitation, oppression and injustice.
>
> Human rights in Islam are firmly rooted in the belief that God, and God alone, is the Law Giver and the Source of all human rights. Due to their Divine origin, no ruler, government, assembly or authority can curtail or violate in any way the human rights conferred by God, nor can they be surrendered.
>
> Human rights in Islam are an integral part of the overall Islamic order and it is obligatory on all Muslim governments and organs of society to implement them in letter and in spirit within the framework of that order.[24]

Islam as stressed in the Universal Islamic Declaration of Human Rights guarantees all familiar, well-recognised and widely-accepted basic civil, political and economic liberties as one finds in many post-World War II states where a lengthy list of fundamental rights are laid down in their constitutions. These rights are also laid down in the UN Declaration of Human Rights. Islam lays down these rights with usual qualification as one finds in almost all modern democratic constitutions. They include the following:

(i) All human beings shall be equal and none shall enjoy a privilege or suffer a disadvantage or discrimination by reason of race, colour, sex, origin or language.
(ii) Wherein all human beings are born free
(iii) Wherein slavery and forced labour are abhorred
(iv) Wherein conditions shall be established such that the institution of family shall be preserved, protected and honoured as the basis of all social life
(v) Wherein the rulers and the ruled alike are subject to, and equal before, the law
(vi) Wherein obedience shall be rendered only to those commands that are in consonance with the Law
(vii) Wherein all worldly power shall be considered as a sacred

trust, to be exercised within the limits prescribed by the Law and in a manner approved by it, and with due regard for the priorities fixed by it

(viii) Wherein all economic resources shall be treated as Divine blessings bestowed upon mankind, to be enjoyed by all in accordance with the rules and the values set out in the Quran and the Sunnah.

(ix) Wherein all public affairs shall be determined and conducted, and the authority to administer them shall be exercised after mutual consultation (*Shurah*) between the government and the People

(x) Wherein everyone shall undertake obligations proportionate to his capacity and shall be held responsible *pro rata* for his deeds

(xi) Wherein everyone shall, in case of an infringement of his rights, be assured of appropriate remedial measures in accordance with the Law

Right to Life

Human life is sacred and inviolable and every effort shall be made to protect it. In particular no one shall be exposed to injury or death, except under the authority of Law.

Right to Freedom

Man is born free. No inroads shall be made on his right to liberty except under the authority and in due process of the Law.

Right to Equality and Prohibition Against Impermissible Discrimination

(i) All persons are equal before the Law and are entitled to equal opportunities and protection of the Law.

(ii) All persons shall be entitled to equal wage for equal work.

(iii) No person shall be denied the opportunity to work or be discriminated against in any manner or exposed to greater physical risk by reason of religious belief, colour, race, origin, sex or language.

Right to Fair Trial

(i) No person shall be adjudged guilty of an offence and made liable to punishment except after proof of his guilt before an independent judicial tribunal.

(ii) No person shall be adjudged guilty except after a fair trial and after reasonable opportunity for defence has been provided to him.
(iii) Punishment shall be awarded in accordance with the Law, in proportion to the seriousness of the offence and with due consideration of the circumstances under which it was committed.

Rights of Minorities
(i) The Quranic principle 'There is no compulsion in religion' shall govern the religious rights of non-Muslim minorities.
(ii) In a Muslim country religious minorities shall have the choice to be governed in respect of their civil and personal matters by Islamic Law, or by their own laws.

Right and Obligation to Participate in the Conduct and Management of Public Affairs
(i) Subject to the Law, every individual in the community (*ummah*) is entitled to assumed public office.
(ii) Process of free consultation (*Shurah*) is the basis of the administrative relationship between the government and the people. People also have the right to choose and remove their rulers in accordance with this principle.

Right to Freedom of Belief, Thought and Speech
(i) Every person has the right to express his thoughts and beliefs so long as he remains within the limits prescribed by the Law. No one, however, is entitled to disseminate falsehood or to circulate reports which may outrage public decency, or to indulge in slander, innuendo or to cast defamatory aspersions on other persons.
(ii) Pursuit of knowledge and search after truth is not only a right but a duty of every Muslim.

Right to Freedom of Religion
Every person has the right to freedom of conscience and worship in accordance with his religious beliefs.

The Economic Order and the Rights Evolving Therefrom
(i) In their economic pursuits, all persons are entitled to the full benefits of nature and all its resources. These are blessings bestowed by God for the benefit of mankind as a whole.

(ii) All human beings are entitled to earn their living according to the Law.

Right to Social Security

Every person has the right to food, shelter, clothing, education and medical care consistent with the resources of the community. This obligation of the community extends in particular to all individuals who cannot take care of themselves due to some temporary or permanent disability.[25]

These rights are not properly implemented in most of the contemporary Muslim states just as UN Declaration of Human Rights are constantly and widely violated in practice. The eternal gap between theory and practice is applicable to Islamic provisions of basic human rights as in many other noble declaration and charter; it only reflects the short-comings and deficiencies of the contemporary world of Muslims.

Status of Women in Islam

'Islam sees a woman, whether single or married as an individual in her own right.' 'Woman in Islam can own and dispose of her property and earnings, maintain her own family name rather than taking her husband's one.' Women's dress is a source of misunderstanding but Islam enjoins 'both men and women are expected to dress in a way which is modest and dignified,' but it is true: 'The traditions of female dress found in some Muslim countries are often the expression of local customs'[26] rather than enjoining by Quranic injunctions; seclusion of women; wearing veils or maintaining purdah for instance, is the product of some imperial or rich elite customs rather than any Quranic injunction. So we must try to give an objective interpretation of the Quranic principles in their true perspective and meaning, taking also into account the circumstances prevailing at the time of such injunctions relating to women.

Women in a modern Muslim country are expected to play, and they do play, a significant role in political, social and economic spheres of life. Are they destined to be secluded from the society—they play an important role in the modern age—when there are Muslim women prime ministers, cabinet ministers, lawyers, doctors, journalists, university teachers etc? The correct picture of women in Islam is of vital importance in the context of Islam and modernization (not westernization),

There is considerable misunderstanding, sometimes deliberate misconception, about the status of women in Islam, particularly in Western society where it is widely held that women in Islam suffer from discrimination and occupy an inferior status compared to men. Nothing is further from the truth. Like many other aspects of Islam, the status of women has been grossly distorted by orientalists as well as by so called Muslim secularists who have no adequate or proper knowledge of the Quranic injunctions relating to status of the women of Islam.

Before we refer to any particular scholar or writer, let us begin our discussion by quoting from the original sources: the Quran and sayings of the Prophet Muhammad relating to the status of women in Islam. Here are a few verses from the Quran on this subject.

(i) 'He (God) it is Who did create you from a single soul and therefore did create his mate, that he might dwell with her (in love)' (Surah 7: 189).

(ii) 'The creator of heavens and earth: He has made for you pairs from among yourself' (Surah 42: 11).

(iii) 'And God has given you mates of your own nature and has given from your mates, children and grandchilds and has made provisions of good things for you' (Surah 16: 72).

(iv) The Quran provides clear-cut evidence that woman is completely equated with man in the sight of God in terms of her rights and responsibilities. The Quran says: 'Every soul will be (held) in pledge for its deeds' (Surah 74: 30).

(v) 'So their Lord accepted their prayers (saying): I will not suffer to be lost the work of any of you whether male or female' (Surah 3: 195).

(vi) 'Whoever works righteousness, man or woman, and has faith, verily to him we give a new life that is good and pure and we will bestow on such their reward according to the best of their actions' (Surah 16: 97).

(vii) The Quran refers to marriage as follows: 'And among His signs is this: that He created mates for you from yourself that you may find rest, peace of mind in them and he ordained between you love and mercy. Lo, herein indeed are signs for people who reflect' (Surah 30: 21).

(viii) The Quran enjoins its followers to be kind and compassionate to their wives: 'Consort with them in kindness, for if you hate them it may happen that you hate a ship wherein God has placed much good' (Surah 4: 19).

Surah 4 (*Nisa'*, or Women) deals specifically with women. It begins with an appeal to the solidarity of mankind, the rights of women and orphans and the implications of family relationship. It specifically recognizes the rights of women pertaining to marriage, (according to the Quran, women cannot be forced to marry anyone without their consent), property and inheritance. Women, as human beings, are entitled to a similar life, to honour and property. There is no discrimination in Islam on the grounds of sex, just as there is none on the grounds of race, colour, language, etc. Sex distinction, which is one of the mysteries of human nature, does not count in spiritual matters.

Commenting on Surah *Nisa'* in the Quran, Yousef Ali writes : 'Among the most wonderful mysteries of our nature is that of sex. The unregenerate male is apt, in the pride of his physical strength, to forget the all-important part which the female plays in his very existence and in all the social relationships that arise in our collective human lives. The wife through whom we enter parentage must have our reverence. Sex, which governs so much of our physical life and has so much influence on our emotional and higher nature, deserves our reverence in the highest sense of the term'.[27] With this higher concept of sex distinction, Islam defines the status of women. Husband and wife are so closely attached to each other they are treated as each other's garments (Surah 2: 187) which means that the relationship between husband and wife is based on mutual support, mutual comfort and mutual protection, fitting into each other as a garment fits the body.

A man's right to have more than one wife, i.e., polygamy, has been a source of great criticism and vilification of Islam by Western writers. But if one reads carefully the particular verse of the Quran relating to 'four wives', one will be inclined to agree that though polygamy is 'permitted' under some extraordinary circumstances, the trend in Islam is for monogamy. The unrestricted number of wives in the 'Time of Ignorance' in pre-Islamic society was strictly limited to a maximum of four provided the husband could treat all four wives 'with perfect equality in material things as well as in affection and immaterial things.' As this condition is practically impossible to fulfil, the real recommendation in Islam is for monogamy. Islam is a highly practical religion; so instead of leaving any scope for illegal sexual relationships, it is permitted to have more than one wife under strict conditions and under special circumstances. The Quran lays down: 'And if ye fear that he will not deal fairly to the orphans, marry of the women who seem good to you, twice, or thrice or four and if ye fear that ye can not do justice (to so many) then one (only) (Surah 4: 3).

This potent verse in Surah 4: 3 has given rise to many controversies and has more than one interpretation (like many other Surahs). However, a particular one deals with a very important issue which permits a male Muslim to have up to four wives in almost unrestricted ways, whoever he likes: young, attractive, wealthy; and for that matter for any sexual and worldly considerations or, more importantly, whether the man's choice of a second, third or fourth wife is restricted to orphans, widows or captives of war who are under his guardianship. This is a highly important issue facing the world of Islam today.

First, let us begin with a reference to the extraordinary circumstances when this Surah (4) was revealed, dealing with rights of women in general and in particular of orphans, widows, war prisoners etc. We shall have to refer to conditions in Arabia after the battle of Uhud in which Muslims lost many male members. When the Muslim community was left with many orphans, widows and captives, the ratio between male and female population in the newly born Muslim community in al-Madinah at that time was ten females to one male. The helpless women were under the care of Muslim males.

The Quran ensured their fair, dignified and proper treatment under the care of the male Muslims who happened to be their guardians. As Yousef Ali points out, 'their treatment was to govern by the principles of the greatest humanity and equity. The principles remain'.[28] Yusuf Ali adds, that the Quran enjoins the guardians of the orphans, etc., by saying 'Marry the orphans if you are quite sure that you will in that way protect their interest and their property with perfect justice to them'. The whole emphasis was against 'sexual intercourse without marriage'.[29] According to the Prophet's widow 'A'ishah 'this refers to the case of orphan girls whom their guardians wish to marry'.

The Quran as well as the practice of the Prophet of Islam strictly prohibited sexual intercourse without marriage. According to interpretations of some other eminent interpreters, who were successors of the Prophet's companions, such as Sayyid Ibn Jubayr and Qatabah, the main emphasis of this particular verse of the Quran was to protect the interest and dignity of the orphan's chastity, honour and prohibit sex without marriage.[30] That is why it is provided that in case a male guardian was tempted to treat these orphans, widows, etc, as mistresses, they had better marry and make them their legal partners in life. In that age of darkness when men could marry any number of women it was restricted to four. But there was a stricter provision against even the provision of four wives: 'if you have reason to fear that you might not be able to treat them with equal favour then (only) one.' This provision of treating four wives equally is so difficult to fulfil in reality, that Islam indeed encourages monogamy rather than polygamy.

Unfortunately, the provision of having four wives has been grossly misused. The view that Islam allows four wives for man in an unrestricted way is, we strongly believe, not correct. The provision of four wives was made in some extraordinary circumstances prevailing in Arabia after the battle of Uhud in the 7th century. Of course, we do not imply that any Quranic provision is meant for some local condition or for some specific time. The Quranic principles are universal and are applicable for all ages and in all circumstances. The occasion for a particular verse may be gone but the principle behind it is permanent. Now the Quranic principles are capable of being interpreted in more than one way. As Annimarie Schimmel in her thoughtful introduction of Islam points out 'possibilities of interpreting the Book (the Holy Quran) in the most diverse way seems to be a strong proof of its supernatural origin. As God's Words it has to be infinite as He Himself.'[31]

Our view about this so-called polygamy in the form of four wives is meant to protect the honour and chastity of dependent women and orphans or widows. If a male guardian of this category of helpless woman develops any illegal sexual desires towards them, then he better marry them to the maximum number of four and that also if he is absolutely sure that he will be able to treat all the four wives equally. It does not give unlimited licence to marry any or every women of a man's attraction or choice under any circumstances as this Quranic provision is being misused widely by Muslims, specially by the rich and the powerful ones. Allah does not, we firmly believe, give a man licence in the matter of marriage for one who has developed a sexual desire towards his dependents. So the choice of four wives is confined to orphans, widows who are dependents of that particular male guardian and not any and every man. Secondly, the man must be sure of equal treatment to all the four wives, a provision which we feel is almost impossible to implement. From a careful analysis of the Quranic provision relating to four wives we shall conclude that polygamy in the ordinary sense is not permitted. Islam puts great opprobrium on sexual relations outside marriage and as Islam is a highly pragmatic religion, it safeguards against illegal sexual relationship by providing for more than one wife in exceptional circumstances within a limited range of selection of four wives and with other highly restrictive clauses.

It is not a licence for free sex but a strict provision against illegal sex under any circumstances.

Another source of misunderstanding with regard to the rights of women in Islam is the fact that, though women are entitled to property and inheritance the Islamic law of inheritance gives women a lesser share of the property—a male shall have as much as the share of two females (Surah 4: 11). Why is there this difference? The Islamic law of inheritance allocates the shares of the property to different heirs according to individual circumstances. The inequality between male and female in respect of the shares of the property is based on the fact that in addition to what she inherits, she is entitled to a dowry from her husband over and above her maintenance allowance. Further, the male is given the responsibility of maintaining the family and the children.

Again we should exercise *ijtihad* (individual judgement) and *ijma'* (consensus) in interpreting such a Quranic provision. Women these days take an almost equal share in maintaining the family and children. Should this fact not be considered in interpreting this particular Quranic provision?

The position of women as mothers is very high in to the Islamic social system. According to Muhammad 'paradise lies underneath the feet of mothers.' Man is enjoined by the Quran to be mindful to his parents, particularly to 'the mother who bore him in pain and in pain did she give him birth' (Surah 46: 15).

The Prophet Muhammad was once asked by a man who should have the first claim to his respect and good treatment. The Prophet's reply was: 'Your mother.' The man asked:'Then who? The Prophet gave him the same answer three times and thereafter said, 'Then your father.' In his farewell pilgrimage message, the Prophet Muhammad asked his followers to be kind to women and pay heed to their rights. His words were: 'Ye people, ye have rights over your wives, and your wives have rights over you. Treat your women with kindness—verily, ye have taken them on serenity of God, and made them lawful unto you by the words of God.'[32]

The allegation that Islam does not give women a proper status and role are unfounded and are either based on lack of proper understanding of the Islamic social order or deliberately made to vilify Islam.

The Islamic social order, like its political and economic systems, is based on justice and fairplay to all—men and women, rich and poor, black and white. It is also based on universal brotherhood and fraternity. Islam and its political, social and economic systems can meet the challenges and problems of a modern nation state in the contemporary complex world. Those who advocate, 'Back to the

Quranic teaching,' are contributing to building up a world order which will bring peace, stability, progress and happiness to mankind as a whole.

Many of the present day Muslim countries do not come up to the real teaching and principles of Islam. Their loyalties to the Islamic message are merely lip service. The real situation in many parts of the Muslim world is sad and disappointing for the true spirit of Islam, and this has contributed to the misunderstanding and vilification of Islam. The critics of Islam point out the state of affairs in the Muslim world and reach the hasty conclusion that, whatever might be the theoretical aspects of the Islamic message, the reality among its followers belie those fine and broad principles. It is therefore a supreme duty for the leaders and intelligentsia of Muslim countries to make vigorous and sincere efforts to establish a world as enjoined by the Quran and as exemplified by the Prophet Muhammad. That is the only way to serve Islam.

Islamic Principles: Its Universal and Eternal Application

Muslims believe that the Quranic teachings quoted in the preceding pages are not meant for any particular period or age or for any particular country or any nation. The Quranic principles are eternal and they are applicable to all human races, in all ages and in all circumstances. These principles laid down in the Quran and given through the Prophet Mohammad are as applicable today in a modern, industrialized and enlightened society as they were in 7th century Arabia. The Quran is regarded as a book of *hidayat*, i.e., guidance for man. 'It is a book,' as A K Brohi rightly points out, 'that is available to all mankind—indeed, it addresses itself, by and large, to the totality of mankind. Its message is relevant to different peoples living in different parts of the world. Further, its message is valid for all time to come—in other words, it is not a Book that will ever be out of date.'[33]

We may substantiate the Muslim assertion that the Quranic message is eternal and universal by pointing out the fact the Quran is intended 'to guide' or 'to show the way',as the word *hidayat* implies, to those cherished values and ideals without which human life is not worth living. Human beings, as the highest creatures of God, have, or at least should strive for, certain higher and nobler values and ideals and how doest he Quran teach us to be the torch-bearer of these ideals? They include, among others:

(i) The equality, dignity and brotherhood of man.

(ii) The value of universal education, with an emphasis on the spirit of free inquiry and importance of scientific knowledge.

(iii) The principle of religious tolerance.

(iv) The liberation of woman and her spiritual equality with man.

(v) Freedom from slavery and exploitation of all kinds.

(vi) The dignity of manual labour.

(vii) The integration of mankind in a feeling of oneness, irrespective of differences of race, colour, sex, religion, language etc.

(viii) The principle of justice as the foundation of society.[34]

In a sense, these higher aims and objectives of human life have been expressed by many other religions, as well as many other philosophical doctrines and theories. But the Quran makes it obligatory for Muslims not only to preach these ideals but also to practise them in their daily life by following the 'Five pillars of Islam', not only in their forms but by adhering to the spirit of Islam. These obligations are repeatedly stressed in the verses of the Holy Book of Islam. These principles were further illustrated by the way of life practised by the Prophet of Islam, Muhammad

It is true that in the contemporary Islamic world many Muslim countries do not come up to these ideals. There are many shortcomings—corruption, tyranny, poverty, ignorance, injustice—in countries where the majority of the people are Muslims. Does this mean that there is anything inherently wrong in the Quranic message? Certainly not. A Muslim country is not an Islamic one unless its people and rulers adhere to the injunctions of the Quran. There are many countries in the world which are called 'democratic' but whose real political and socio-economic dynamics are far from the fundamental principles of democracy, but it does not follow that democracy itself is wrong or inherently defective. Similarly, for the critics of Islam to conclude from some contemporary Muslim countries' actual conditions that Islamic teaching is hollow would be grossly unfair to Islam and its fundamental teaching.

The Quranic message puts all its stress not on the rituals but on the spirit of true religion. In Surah Fatihah with which Muslims are required to begin their prayers five times a day—one of the fundamental ingredients of Islam—man is enjoined to seek guidance from God, the Merciful. Now if the followers of Islam do not merely bow to the west or to the east five times a day to fulfil one of the five pillars of Islam but really bow before God to seek guidance, to seek the 'straight path', God will surely guide man to the true path; and once man really follows the 'straight path' there is no reason why man will not be able to attain those higher ideals and objectives of the Quranic message. This is the secret of the success of the Quranic message and this is what makes the message universal and eternal. All through Surah Fatihah runs the note of warning, which indeed sounds throughout the Quran, that it is not mere profession of a creed but righteous conduct which is true religion. True religion consists in the surrender of man's will and purpose to the will and purpose of the Lord of Creation.

Islam and the Challenges of Science and Technology

Many Western scholars, mainly the 'orientalists', who claim to be experts and authorities on Islam, and Muslim secularists, trained in and oriented towards the West, consider Islam a major impediment to the modernization, in socio-political terms, of newly-independent Muslim countries. The study of modernization in Muslim countries 'is too often fraught with unwarranted dichotomies: tradition versus change, fundamentalism versus modernism, stagnation versus progress and development.'[35] This dichotomy is not inevitable: Islam is a dynamic religion which is quite capable of meeting the challenges of science and technology of the contemporary world. Impressed by the achievements of science and technology in the modern world, many psychologists and sociologists have expressed the view 'that religion had exhausted its usefulness and surrendered to science once and for all.'[36] 'This is alleged to be doubly true in the case of Islam, which is depicted by the orientalists as unscientific, unprogressive and static. The image of Islam that emerges from most books on Islam and Islamic history written by Western orientalists and their Muslim disciples is like this: 'Islam was revealed merely to put an end to idolatry and guide man to the worship of God alone . . . This, according to these people, was the sole purpose of Islam in human life! This being its historical mission, it has long since been fulfilled . . . Thus they conclude that Islam has served its purpose in this world; it has had its day but is no longer needed. It has nothing new to offer. We must,therefore, turn towards modern civilization and seek progress through it.'[37] Islam has been deliberately maligned and distorted by Western orientalists. Edward Said, in his book *Orientalism*, has spoken about these so-called 'authorities' on Islam by pointing out their preconceived misconception about Islam and its Prophet. He defines orientalism as 'a body of ideas, beliefs, clichés or learning about the East, and other schools of thought at large in the culture'. Said adds that the orientalists' consensus on Islam is its alleged 'latent inferiority' as compared to Western civilization.

He points out that 'books and articles are regularly published on Islam and the Arabs that represent absolutely no change over the virulent anti-Islamic polemics of the Middle Ages and Renaissance . . . The Muslim religion, called Islam, began in the seventh country. It was started by a wealthy businessman of Arabia, called Muhammad. He claimed that he was a prophet. He found followers among other Arabs. He told them that they were picked to rule the world.' Said then refers to von Grünebaum, a well-known European orientalist who emigrated to the United States; his remarks on Islam are: 'Islam is a unitary phenomenon, unlike any other religion or civilization and therefore it is anti-human, incapable of development, selfknowledge or objectivity as well as uncreative, and authoritarian.'[38] What a gross distortion of a religion which has taught justice, fair play, equality, universal brotherhood and the rule of law. Islam embodies all the essential ingredients of democracy, including tolerance of religion. Further, Islam, in the Quran, enjoins its followers to rise in revolt against those in authority if they rule unjustly, arbitrarily and against the teachings of God. It is true that as a general rule Muslims are asked 'to obey God, the Messenger and those who are in authority' (Surah 4: 59), but the Quran, also gives the right to resist or rebel.Indeed, according to the Quran, all messengers after the Prophet Noah were rebels against the established order. One of the criteria for the right to resist is what the Quran calls 'corruption on the earth' (*fasad fi' l-ard*), which can mean any state of affairs that leads to general lawlessness—political, moral or social—when national or international affairs are out of control.[39] Yet a leading orientalist, Bernard Lewis, commenting on Islamic concepts of revolution, writes, 'the Western doctrine of the right to resist bad government is alien to Islamic thought which leads to defeatism and quietism as political attitudes.'[40] We could cite many such unfair and unfounded concepts about Islam and its basic message from some of the Western scholars who seem to have failed to appreciate the true meaning and spirit of Islam.

There are, however, exceptions among Western scholars. The famous sociologist Jean Bridge eulogizes Islam 'for achieving a successful amalgam of the temporal with the spiritual into a harmonious system of thought blended with a practical code of life'.[41] Contemporary non-Muslim Western scholars like John Esposito and some others have done great service to Islam by projecting its true meaning and spirit. It would be, therefore, unfair to brand all Western scholars on Islam as anti-Islam or anti-Muslim. The present author is greatly appreciative of authors like John Esposito, Frithjof Schuon and several others of their works on Islam and its prophets.

A religion like Islam can ensure peace and tranquillity in the modern world by standing up against the forces of ignorance, bigotry, racial and religious hatred and against authoritarian regimes, thereby developing the creative faculties of human beings: without these conditions, progress towards science and technology cannot flourish. While stressing the responsibility of Islam for the intellectual development in human life, the Quran makes the quest of knowledge a duty of paramount importance for the individual as well as a supreme responsibility for the state. Ansari raises the question: 'Has an Islamic state any duty towards the citizens in respect of their intellectual development'? The plain answer is yes, as the Quran explains: Allah educated Adam, the progenitor of the human race. 'He imparted to Adam the knowledge of the nature of all things' (Surah 11: 31). The Quran lays down the law that divine blessings are meant to be transmitted to others: 'and do then good (to others) as Allah has done good to thee' (Surah 28: 77). Thus knowledge imparted by God is meant to be transmitted to mankind, generation after generation, and to be developed further and further by them. Ansari interprets these verses from the Quran as follows: 'This makes it incumbent on the Islamic state to undertake the development of knowledge to higher and higher levels and to organize and enforce the education of all its citizens with a view to their intellectual advancement, with all the resources at its command.'[42]

It is encouraging to add here that the Organization of Islamic Conference, OIC, at the Third Islamic Summit Conference held in Makkah, Saudi Arabia, in January 1981, decided to set up a Committee for Scientific and Technological Cooperation among its member states. There is no denying that many present-day Muslim countries are not advanced in scientific and technological spheres, but this is the legacy of European colonial rule over these Muslim countries: Islam has nothing to do with this sad state of affairs. If Muslim countries take up the issue of science and technological cooperation among themselves in accordance with the teaching of the Quran, Islam will provide the greatest incentives for the development of science and technology in the Muslim *ummah* (the world of Islam). According to Sir Muhammad Iqbal, all search for knowledge, which is stressed so much in the Quran, 'is essentially a form of prayer. The scientific observer of Nature is a kind of mystic seeker in the act of prayer.'[43] In Islam, Iqbal stresses, the 'birth' or 'awakening of inductive intellect' is a middle term between 'Islam ' and 'modern science'; he even goes as far as to bracket 'science' with 'God-consciousness'. Iqbal wrote his book in terms of contemporary developments in science and philosophy. He hoped that this would 'be helpful towards a proper understanding of the meaning of Islam as a message to humanity.[44] Iqbal also brings out the fact that one of the purposes of the Quran is 'to awaken in man consciousness of that of which Nature is regarded a symbol.' He refers to the 'general empirical attitude of the Quran which regendered in its followers a feeling of reverence for the actual and ultimately made them the founders of modern science'.[45] Iqbal's views about the emphasis on science in Islam are shared by many others who have made a proper study of the Quran.

The Quran introduced the idea of law and order in nature, ascribed natural phenomena to material causes, infused a spirit of rational thought, encouraged a first-hand study of nature by observation and experiment, produced a universal longing for scientific inquiry by encouraging *tafaqu'ah, tafakkur* and *ta'aqqul* (contemplation, research and investigation); and thus paved the way to the true understanding of nature and natural phenomena.[46]

The following verses from the Quran illustrate how Islam proves that there is everywhere in nature law and order and not chaos, that the universe is working according to a definite plan destined to progress up to a certain goal:

> And the Sun runs his course for a period determined. For Him: That is the decree of (Him) the Exalted in Might, the All-Knowing.
>
> And the moon—we have measured for her Mansions (to traverse) till she returns like the old (and withered) lower part of a datestalk.
>
> It is not permitted to the sun to catch up the Moon, nor can the Night outstrip the Day. Each (just) swings along in (its own) orbit (according to Law).[47]

The laws of nature are fixed and, the passages just quoted are related to the study of astronomy. These verses of the Quran deal with things in the physical world around us, and we can learn the deepest truth if we earnestly apply ourselves to them.[48] Sir James Jeans tells that the greatest problems of science cannot be resolved without believing in God,[49] something that the Quran stresses again and again. Islam by no means constitutes an obstacle to scientific knowledge: on the contrary, it reinforces the achievements of science in the modern age.

It is not only astronomy which is stressed in the Quran; other branches of science are also emphasized: archaeology (Surah 30: 9); mineralogy (Surah 57: 25) medicine (Surah 16: 39)—which can be studied with the knowledge of biology, anatomy, etc. Surah 2: 29 states: 'Is it He who has created for you all things that are on earth; moreover His designs comprehended the heavens, for He gave order and perfection to the seven firmaments; and of all things He has perfect knowledge.' This verse makes it clear that every thing is for man's use; he should bring into his use everything he requires; this cannot be done until the use of everything is known. This encourages and results in the development of different branches of science which deal with nature and the properties of things in their different aspects.[50]

It is clear from the various verses quoted from the Quran that Islam gives scientific knowledge the highest priority. If the Islamic *ummah* is to survive and flourish in the present age of science and technology, the guide-lines given in the Quran will hasten its progress and prosperity. The Muslims have to be true to the Quranic message and its fundamental teaching. At the cost of repetition, we may point out that modern discoveries of science have not in any way disproved the Quranic message. Its great emphasis on acquiring knowledge in order to understand the real meaning of the ways of God is the surest path for the all-round development of human intellect and faculties. Islam has certainly not become outdated because of recent developments in science and technology.

Before we conclude our discussion on the Islamic message and ideals, we would like to point out that the Holy Book of Islam, the Quran, repeatedly asks the followers of Islam to command good, forbid evil, establish prayer and pay *Zakat* (alms). The Islamic message wants Muslims 'to establish a political order on earth for the sake of creating an egalitarian and just moral and social order. Such an order, should, by definition, eliminate 'corruption on the earth' and 'reform the earth'.[51]

Now how can such an ideological world order be brought into existence? The Quran speaks of *jihad*, the holy war for achieving noble causes: most unfortunately, as Dr Fazlur Rahman points out, Western Christian propaganda has confused the significance and the meaning of the world *jihad* by popularizing the slogans: 'Islam was spread by the sword', and 'Islam is the religion of the sword'. Rahman rightly points out 'that what was spread by the sword was not the religion of Islam, but the political domain of Islam so that Islam could work to produce the order on the earth that the Quran seeks.'[52] He concedes that *jihad* was sometimes misused by late Muslim rulers whose primary aim was territorial expansion and not the ideology they were asked to establish. He further adds that the means of *jihad* can vary—in fact armed *jihad* is only one form. He concludes that 'there is no single parallel in Islamic history to the forcible conversion to Christianity of the German tribes en masse as carried out by Charlemagne . . . although, of course, locally and occasionally isolated cases of such conversions may well have taken place.[53] In India, Muslim rule lasted for more than six hundred years, yet the majority of the Indian population remained non-Muslims. Even in the areas where the Muslim emperors in India established their strongest hold very close to their seats of power, like Delhi or the United Provinces, the majority of the population continued to retain their faith, that is why the Muslims in India continued to be a minority group after six hundred years of Muslim rule. This is one of the best examples of the religious tolerance that the Quran has asked its followers to practise: In one of the concluding verses of the Quran—Surah *Kafirun*—it is clearly stated: 'I worship that which I worship . . . To you be your way, and to me mine.'

This is one of the finest principles of religious tolerance at a time of human history when religious tolerance was unheard of. This principle of 'unto you your religion and unto me my religion' falsifies the conception that 'Islam is the religion of the sword'.

Before we conclude our discussion on fundamentals of Islam as stated in the preceding, we would like to quote from two Western scholars who have embraced Islam: Annemarie Schimmel and Charles Lee Gai Eaton.

Charles Le Gai Eaton, commenting on Islam's 'Five Pillars' and a Muslim's unconditional and total submission to Allah says:

> When, in accordance with the first Pillar of his religion, the Muslim makes the confession of Faith he attaches himself to the essential and puts aside all that is—in appearance—other-than-God, and he acknowledges the truth brought by the messengers. When, in accordance with the second Pillar, he prays—whether in a mosque or on the desert sands, in a Western city or at the polar regions—he places himself at the centre of all possible worlds, for God has promised that He will be present wherever His name is mentioned, and the place where He is present is necessarily central in every dimension.
>
> When, in accordance with the third Pillar, this Muslim pays the poor-due and observes the obligation of loving-kindness towards his fellows, he acknowledges the rights of other

creatures—made in the same image as himself—and recognizes that God, who is close to him. When he fasts, in accordance with the fourth Pillar, he detaches himself from the locality in which he is temporarily housed, the better to prepare himself for his everlasting home.

And when, as a pilgrim, he stands before the Ka'ba in Mecca (after circling it seven times), the centrality already prefigured by his orientation when he prayed far off is made actual. Clothed only in two pieces of plain, unsewn cloth, he has left behind him the characteristics which identified him in this world, his race, his nationality, his status; he is no longer so-and-so from such-and-such a place, but simply a pilgrim.

Beneath his bare feet, like mother-of-pearl, is the pale marble of this amphitheatre at the centre of the world, and although he is commanded to lower his eyes when praying elsewhere, he is now permitted to raise them and look upon the Ka'ba, which is the earthly shadow of the Pole or Pivot around which circle the starry heavens. Although Paradise may still seem far distant, he has already come home.

Praise is (due only) to Allah, Lord of the Worlds.[54]

The dynamic aspect of the Quranic principles were emphasised by Charles Le Gai Eaton and by Annemarie Schimmel.

Eaton remarks:

The Muslim believes in One God, who is all-powerful and has no partner; believes in His messengers, sent to mankind for their guidance from the beginning of time; believes that the Quran is the World of God. If membership of the community of believers requires acceptance of the Quran as the revealed Word of God, then denial of any part of the Quran or of any statement made in the Book may be assumed to call belief into doubt. This is so, and yet we have here an area of ambiguity. Certain verses. particularly those relating to matters of law, are plain enough, but there are many parts of the Quran which lend themselves to a variety of interpretations; and indeed it is said that, in principle, every single verse contains layer upon layer of meaning. It is natural that there should have been wide variations in interpretation, variations which have on the whole been accepted provided they did not contradict the literal meaning.[55]

Schimmel puts it in the following words:

The Koran is the basis for the entire life, be it the regulation of religious duties or problems of art. Hence it is natural that a vast range of interpretations and commentaries should have developed in the course of the centuries; in the first generations after Muhammad most of the pious refused to interpret the Koran: they were afraid lest they be led into dangerous aberrations and speculations by introducing legendary material. But there has never been a completely uniform exegesis. Rather, the possibility of interpreting the Book in the most diverse ways seems to be a strong proof of its supernatural origin. As God's word it has to be as infinite as He Himself, and thus its different possibilities have never ceased to occupy the minds of scholars, mystics, and simple believers. Developments in modern times have challenged many religious positions, and representatives of both scholarship and piety are looking for a new understanding of the Koran. Since it is considered valid for all times as the final revelation, it must contain all the scientific discoveries of the modern age.[56]

Notes

1 See Khurshid Ahmed's Introduction to Abul A'la Mawdudi, *Towards Understanding Islam* (revised edition), Leicester, 1979.

2 Sayyid Abul A'la Mawdudi, 'Iman: Its Nature and Character', in *Toward Understanding Islam*, 14.

3 This meaning and broad interpretation of *tawhid is based on Dr Mohammad Fazlur Rahman Ansari, The Quranic Foundations and Structure of Muslim Society*, Karachi World Federation of Islamic Missions, Islamic Centre, vol. 1, chap. 4.

4 M Abdul Rauf, *Islam Creed and Worship*, Washington D.C., Islamic Centre, 1974, 2-3).

5 *Ibid.*, 148-49.

6 *Ibid.*.

7 Syed Ameer Ali, *The Spirit of Islam*, London, 1935, reprinted Pakistan, 1985, 166.

8 Abul A'la Mawdudi, *Let Us Be Muslims*, Leicester, 1985, 115.

9 *Ibid.*.

10 Annemarie Schimmel, *Islam: an Introduction*, New York 1992, 30-31).

11 Muhammad Asad, *The Message of The Quran*, Gibraltar, 1987

12 Frithjof Schuon, *Understanding Islam* (tr. D M Matheson), London, 1976, 13.

13 *Understanding Islam and The Muslims*, Washington D.C., Islamic Affairs Department, Saudi Embassy.

14 Annemarie Schimmel, *op. cit.*, 41.

15 Ansari, M Fazlur Rahman, *The Quranic Foundation and Structure of Muslim Society*, Karachi, 1973, vol. 1, 121.

16 See *Understanding Islam and The Muslims, loc. cit.*

17 Sayyid Abul A'la Mawdudi, *Let Us Be Muslims*, Leicester, 1985, 3.

18 Annemarie Schimmel, *op. cit.*, 35.

19 *Understanding Islam and The Muslims*,

20 Fazlur Rahman, 'The Message and The Messenger', in Kelly, Marjorie (ed.), *Islam, The Religious and Political Life of a World Community*, New York, 1984, 29.

[21] Fazlur Rahman, *Major Themes of the Quran,* Minneapolis, 1980.
[22] A K Brohi, *Islam in the Modern World,* Lahore, 1975, 137.
[23] Abdullah Yousef Ali, *Meaning of the Glorious Quran*, Cairo, n.d., 1593.
[24] See Universal Islamic Declaration of Human Rights, Islamic Council, 1981, 1
[25] *Ibid.*, 7-13.
[26] See *Understanding Islam and The Muslims*, 1.
[27] Yousuf Ali, *op. cit*, 206.
[28] *Ibid.*
[29] *Ibid.*, 1052
[30] Cited in *ibid.*
[31] Annemarie Schimmel, *op. cit.*
[32] See Golam W Choudhury, *The Prophet Muhammad: His Life and Eternal Message,* London, 1993
[33] A K Brohi, *Islam in the Modern World*, 2nd ed., Lahore, 1975, 141.
[34] *Ibid.*, 29.
[35] J Esposito, *Islam and Politics*, New York, 1977, 24.
[36] See Muhammad Qutb, 'Islam and the Crisis of the Modern World', in K Ahmad (ed.), *Islam: Its Meaning and Message*, Islamic Council of Europe, 1976, 243.
[37] *Ibid.*, 24-25.
[38] E W Said, *Orientalism*, New York, 1979, 287, 296.
[39] Fazlur Rahman, *op. cit.*, 44.
[40] Cited in Said, *op. cit.*, 314.
[41] Cited in Qutb, *op. cit.*, 244.
[42] Ansari, *op. cit.*, vol. 2, 362-4.
[43] Muhammad Iqbal, *The Reconstruction of Religious Thought in Islam*, London, 1934, 73.
[44] *Ibid.*, 6.
[45] *Ibid.*, 11.
[46] Khwaja Abdul Waheed, *Islam and the Origin of Modern Science*, Lahore, 1978, 8.
[47] Yousef Ali, *op. cit.*, vol. 2, 1178-79.
[48] *Ibid.*
[49] Qutb, *loc. cit.*
[50] *Islam and the Origin of Modern Science*, 3.
[51] Fazlur Rahman, *op. cit.*, 262.
[52] *Ibid.*, 63.
[53] *Ibid.*, 63-64.
[54] Charles Le Gai Eaton, *Islam and The Destiny of Man*, New York, 1985, 241-242.
[55] *Ibid.*, 4.
[56] Annemarie Schimmel, *op. cit.*, 47-49.

Chapter II
Political Order in Islam

Does Islam enjoin its followers to form any political unity? If so, does the Quran lay down any guidelines for an Islamic state? Did the Prophet of Islam leave any model for a polity? These and similar questions agitate the minds not only of Muslims but also of non-Muslim scholars and political scientists.

At the end of World War II many independent Muslim states emerged onto the map of the world, and they were busy finding out proper and adequate answers to these questions relating to the concept of an Islamic state. What should be the place of Islam in their newly independent national states which were also anxious to modernize their socio-political economic systems?

Are Islam and Modernization (not Westernization) Compatible?

We cannot answer this question unless we examine the relationship between religion and politics in Islam.

'Islam', as a Western scholar puts it, 'was not only a spiritual community, rather it also became a state empire. Islam developed as a religio-political movement in which religion was integral to state and the society. Muslim belief that Islam embraces faith and politics is rooted in its divinely revealed book, the Quran, and the example, *Sunnah*, of its founder, the Prophet Muhammad, and thus has been reflected in Islamic doctrine, history, and politics. The Islamic expression, *Allahu Akbar* (God is most great) summarizes the centrality of God and the wedding of personal religious conviction and political life in Islam.'[1]

Islam embraces within its legitimate sphere not only those acts and performances to which the followers of many other religions confine the application of the word 'worship' but also all aspects of individual, communal, national and international activity. It lays down and prescribes the underlying principles of international relationships, of the laws of war and peace, of statecraft, of social relationships and so on. According to Islam the regulation of all aspects of one's life in accordance with these principles is the continuous worship of God. As a distinguished Pakistani professor, the late Dr I H Qureshi, put it, 'to us a religion is not like a Sunday suit which can be put on when we enter a place of worship and put off when we are dealing with day-to-day life.'[2]

This fundamental aspect of the relationship between religion and politics in Islam has not yet been fully appreciated. That is perhaps the main reason why the current resurgence of Islam has been misconstrued variously as religious intolerance, a return to medievalism, and so on. Religion is no longer stressed as an essential attribute of nationality. Most modern nations flourish without insisting on uniformity of religious belief. But, at the risk of repeating a well-known dictum, it may be stated that Islam is not so much a set of dogmas and rituals as a way of life with its own distinctive social and cultural order. As Richard N Frye states: 'it [Islam] is the totality of a culture of both its social and individual aspects, it is also a way of life.'[3]

According to Islam, as 'God is one and indivisible, so is life and human personality. Each aspect of life is inseparable from the other. Religious and secular are not two autonomous categories; they represent two sides of the same coin. Each and every act becomes related to God and His guidance. Every human activity is given a transcendent dimension, it becomes sacred and meaningful and God-oriented.'[4]

The Prophet of Islam was not only a spiritual guide but also the head of a state, organized for the first time in the history of Islam in 7th century Arabia. He was the organizer of a new socio-political order with all that such a role implies. 'This type of figure, who is at once a spiritual being and a leader of men, has always been, relatively speaking, rare in the Christian West, especially in modern times. Political life has become so divorced from spiritual principles that to many people such a function appears as an impossibility, in proof of which Westerners often point out the purely spiritual life of Christ, who said, My kingdom is not of this world.'[5]

In Islam there is nothing comparable to the concept of the Western

Christian world in relation to the doctrine of 'Two Swords', the separation of politics and religion: Give unto Caesar the things that are Caesar's and unto God the things that are God's. Islam leaves no scope for the compartmentalization or separation of human life between spiritual and secular spheres and as such there has not been the conflict between religious and temporal authorities that we find in the Western Christian world in the medieval period.

Allama Syed Suleman Nadvi, an eminent Muslim scholar, examined the relationship between *din* (religion) and state in Islam in his classic work *Seerat*. Nadvi made the following relevant remarks about the relationship between state and religion in modern Western countries and in Islam:

'There are two types of states in the world: those in which state and religion are utterly separated and it has been stated, "Give unto the king what belongs to him and give unto God what is His."'

In this formula, God and king (state) have been regarded as two distinct separate entities. The commands of one are not applicable to the other. The states in Europe are all founded on this principle. And on this basis, spiritual and temporal matters have been compartmentalized. The second type of state is the one in which religion has not been separated. In this state there is no king. In it there is only one supreme dispenser and omnipotent God. In this state sovereignty belongs to God. His commands are obeyed by all. The worldly rulers and powers are to be obeyed only when their orders are in conformity with divine commands and are derived from them or at least are not repugnant to them. The Prophet of this *din*, and in the state he founded, was its first *amir*, ruler and sovereign. Obeying his orders was obeying the divine commands. God says in the Quran, 'He who obeys the Prophet, obeys God.'[6]

This distinctive aspect of the relation between religion and politics in Islam was neatly pointed out by Sir Muhammad Zafrullah Khan, Pakistan's first Foreign Minister, as follows:

> The conception that religion and politics occupy distinct spheres which should not be permitted to overlap is born of failure to grasp the full significance of religion. What is religion and what is its function? Religion is the way of life that should enable each individual to attain the highest possible development of his spiritual, moral, physical and intellectual faculties. Its function is to establish and maintain the most harmonious relationship between man and his Maker on the one hand, and between man and man in all aspects of their relationship on the other. Politics as only one aspect of their relationship between the sphere of

> religion and the sphere of politics being mutually exclusive puts too narrow a construction upon the functions of religion. To them religion signifies, at its highest, purely individual spiritual communication with the Creator, and normally only the performance of certain formal and ceremonial acts of what they call worship. This is not the Islamic conception of religion.[7]

Muhammad Asad asks if 'mixing of religion with politics is a genuine postulate of Islam or not?' His answer, based on his study of the original source of Islamic law, the Quran and *Sunnah*, is that Islamic teachings 'not only circumscribe man's relation to God but also lay down a definite scheme of social behaviour to be adopted as a result of that relation.' He adds that 'what is needed is a precise body of laws which would outline, however broadly, the sphere of human life in all its aspects—spiritual, physical, individual, social, economic and political. It follows, therefore, that the organization of an Islamic state or states is an indispensable condition of Islamic life in the true sense of the word.'[8]

Fazlur Rahman Ansari begins his discussion on the fundamental principles governing Muslim society and the Islamic state by quoting from the Quran the obligation of the Muslim community (*millat*) to look after and promote the spiritual, moral and general welfare of the individual. Collective efforts for establishing what is right and eradicating what is wrong, for the individual, and for the creation of a condition where truth, perseverance in truth and mutual compassion and well-doing prevail for the benefit of the individual, is directly affirmed and emphasized in the Quran: do what is right and forbid what is wrong. He adds, again quoting verses from the Quran, that side by side with that, the concept of collectivism is the very fibre of Islam. These Quranic injunctions, according to Ansari, 'necessitate the establishment of the Islamic state . . . the collective effort for the moral perfection and happiness of the individual cannot gain its ends truly and comprehensively unless it transforms itself into a free theo-democratic state whose functions should be to enforce the Islamic way of life in its totality and to act as a condition for the natural flowering of the ideals of Islam. Hence the establishment of the Islamic state, whenever and wherever possible, forms, according to the Holy Quran, the duty of the *millat* (the Muslim community) not only towards Islam but also toward the individual.' Ansari concludes, 'that this is an unavoidable duty, in case of ability, is borne out by the fact that the Holy Prophet established the state of Madina at the very first opportunity . . . fulfilment of Islam as a way of life is not possible without the establishment of the Islamic state.'[9]

We could cite a number of other scholarly sources who have

understood correctly the nature of relationship between state and religion in Islam and its implications for the contemporary world of Islam. However, two other illuminating aspects of Islamic political thought should be mentioned.

Islamic political thought reflects some fourteen centuries of Islamic philosophical and theoretical inquiry into the nature and role of government, its relationship to religious and temporal affairs, and its relationship to social change and social revolution. The theoretical and intellectual basis of Islamic government and society has been given only scant attention by Western scholars in examining the forces of change impacting on contemporary Islamic societies. Indeed, Islam has usually been perceived as a 'traditional' force, resisting progressive change and consequently constituting a negative influence or barrier to social and political development. This image of Islam as a static rather than dynamic system of thought has contributed to the failure to recognize the significance of Islamic solutions to the issue of social and political development.

The separation of state and religion in modern Western societies produced a clear separation between the realms of religious and temporal affairs. While spiritual and ethical issues became the domain of philosophy and theology, temporal issues became the domain of political and sociological theory. In this framework, religious and social thought developed independently, and the issues of social and political change were rendered distinct from the issues of spiritual and ethical development. However, in a religiously based socio-political system, this separation does not exist.[10]

According to an eminent scholar of Islam, the discussion in Islamic political thought on 'divine rights' means the 'right of the society' and the discussion on 'God's jurisdiction and domain' actually means, in political terms, 'the jurisdiction of the nation and its domain . . . There is no contradiction here in the fact that the domain belongs to God but the political jurisdiction and Government in Islamic society lay in the hands of the Moslem people.'[11]

With no distinct separation between the profound and the profane, political and social issues must be addressed within the framework of religious ideology; and political and social conflicts must be manifested in spiritual and ethical contention. As a socio-political religious system, Islam incorporated both temporal and spiritual affairs. The nature of the political state and the spiritual state, of political legitimacy, of ideology and doctrine, are not conceptualized and analysed distinctly, but are highly interrelated in Islamic thought. Thus, the development of Islamic thought reflected upon the dynamic of social change that catalysed it. This manifested itself in the problem of succession.[12]

Main Features of An Islamic State: Divergent Views—Modern vs. Orthodox

Now what are the main features of an Islamic state? Whilst there is broad agreement that as there is no separation between politics and religion in Islam, and that the idea of an Islamic state is quite appropriate for countries where the majority of the population is Muslim, there is a wide divergence of views among Muslims themselves about the characteristics of an Islamic state.

What are the principles laid down in the Quran relating to the constitution of the Islamic state? According to one school of thought there are only two or three clear principles relating to constitutional matters in the Quran. The first is that Muslims should obey God, His Prophet and those who from amongst themselves are put in authority over them. It means that a Muslim's first duty is to God and he should do nothing which comes into conflict with that duty. He must not obey an un-Islamic order of the government. In other words, an Islamic government can never ask its people to carry out an un-Islamic policy. Obedience to those who are in power is stressed, but rebellion is permitted in case of gross tyranny and when the authority issues an order against the dictates of Islam.

The second principle is that Muslims should cooperate in righteousness and justice, which probably means that the basis of human action should be moral and not merely political; there should be no divorce between fundamental morality and political activity. This is applicable to states and individuals alike.

The third principle is that government has to be organized on a basis which makes it possible for decisions to be the result of mutual consultation. Muslims are expected to order their affairs by mutual consultation and a majority view should prevail. This is, therefore, regarded as perfectly compatible with the democratic principle of majority rule.

However, other Muslim scholars, such as Fazlur Rahman Ansari, Muhammad Asad and *'ulama'*, like Sayyid Abul A'la Mawdudi, hold the view that the Quran provides a number of further guidelines regarding the constitution of an Islamic state. In order to analyse the system of government from the standpoint of Islam, these principles have to be studied. Ansari, in his two volumes of *The Quranic Foundations and Structure of Muslim Society*, has listed these principles by quoting the relevant verses from the Quran. We shall reproduce some of these verses from the original sources.

According to Ansari the Quranic concept of the state rests on the following sovereignty of God.

(i) Sovereignty belongs to God.
'. . . Authority and control belong to Allah only. He hath commanded that ye serve none save Him: that is the right religion, but most human beings understand not.' (Surah 12: 40)
'Is not His the command? And He is the swiftest in taking account.' (Surah 6: 62)
'To Him belongeth the kingdom of the heavens and the earth.' (Surah 43: 85)
'He does not share His command with any person whatsoever. (Surah 18: 26)
(ii) The Right to Legislate.
a) The right to legislate belongs to God.
In the Holy Quran we read:
'Lo! We [God] have revealed unto thee [O Muhammad] the Scripture with truth, that thou mayest judge between mankind by that [law] which Allah hath shown.' (Surah 57: 25)
b) Having been given the divine law it is not permitted for Muslims, when they have their own state, to adopt any law which is repugnant to it. The following verse emphasizes this fact:
'If any do fail to judge and command by [the light of] of Allah hath revealed, they are Unbelievers.' (Surah 5: 47)

It should be noted that the Quran prohibits only the violation of 'what Allah hath revealed'. But it does not lay down, either in the verses quoted above or anywhere else, that Muslims are forbidden from following any laws which God has not revealed, thus leaving it open to frame new laws for meeting the exigencies of new situations. Of course, all such laws should be in conformity with divine guidance, as the Holy Book says: 'Thus, a controlled and limited, but positive, freedom has been given to the Muslims in respect of legislation.' (Surah 5: 47)
(iii) Status of Government Authority
Human beings are vicegerents of God, hence, governmental authority can be held by them only as a delegated function and as a trust under the sovereignty of God.
We must add that God's authority is delegated to the entire people and not confined to any group such as *'ulama'* because Islam has no priesthood.
(iv) Objectives of the Islamic state
The objectives of the Islamic state are:
a) To maintain internal order and ward off external aggression.
b) To establish absolute justice for all citizens.
The Quran says:
'Allah doth command you to render back your Trusts to those to

whom they are due; and when ye judge between man and man (whether Muslims or non-Muslim), that we judge with justice: Lo! Comely is the teaching which He giveth you! Lo ! Allah is He Who heareth and seeth all things.' (Surah 4: 58)
'Oh ye who believe! Stand out firmly for justice, as witnesses to Allah, even as against yourselves, or your parents, or your kin, and whether it be [against] rich or poor: For Allah can best protect both. Follow not the lusts of your hearts, lest ye swerve, and if ye distort [justice] or decline to do justice, verily Allah is well acquainted with all that ye do.' (Surah 4: 135).
c) To do all that lies in its power and to employ all means and media, including *tabligh* (conveying of messages), for the establishment of 'all that is right (*al-ma'suf*) and elimination of all that is wrong (*al-munkar*).'
d) To organize institutions for spiritual and social welfare. With respect to this point and to (c) above, the Quran says:
'[Muslims are] those who, if we bestow on them [authority] in the land, establish regular prayer [pursue spiritual welfare] and give regular charity [pursue economic welfare], enjoin [all] that which is right and forbid [all] that which is wrong [pursue moral and political welfare]. And unto Allah is the end of [all] affairs.' (Surah 22: 41)
'If one commandeth a deed of economic well-doing or justice or *islah* [i.e. the establishment of peace, happiness and order] among human beings: to him who does this, seeking the good pleasure of Allah, We shall soon give a reward of the highest value.' (Surah 4: 114)

Moreover, from the social and economic point of view, the function of the Islamic state is to transform the Muslim community into a community of middle-roaders—of middle-class standard—with elimination of the evils of poverty on one hand, and the evils of riches on the other. Islam steers the middle course between capitalism and communism and bears witness to the evil of their extremism.
(v) Democratic Rights of the People
People are to be free and in possession of democratic rights. People in the Islamic state are to be free from subjection to any human being, because their government is the government of law and they are subjects of God alone.
'The authority and control belong to Allah only. He hath commanded that ye serve none save Him. That is the right religion but most human beings understand not.' (Surah 12: 40)
Then the Quran lays down the following principle in respect

of the collective life of Muslims.
'. . . Who [conduct] their affairs [or government] by mutual consultation . . .' (Surah 42: 38)

It is evident that the administration of the state must be on the basis of mutual consultation which is impossible and unthinkable without the citizens enjoying freedom and full democratic rights.

Moreover, it is the essential condition and consequence of the establishment of absolute justice enjoined vehemently by the Quran that the people should be in possession of freedom and equally of opportunity—in other words, full democratic rights.

How should the ruler in an Islamic state conduct his business?
He should rule the state in consultation with the people. Thus, there should be a parliament. According to the Quran, the Prophet was commanded by God, in spite of his unique position as God's messenger, to administer the state in consultation with the people, who were his followers.

The command reads:

> . . . And consult with them upon the conduct of affairs. (Surah 3: 59)

The Prophet, in his capacity as the ruler of the first Islamic state, regularly practised the cardinal principle of mutual consultation in his dealings with public affairs. He conducted governmental matters by following the principle of mutual consultation. Decisions relating to public matters were made after due consultation with his people, thus laying the foundation of the government of the people, by the people and for the people, much earlier than this principle was established in the West. His rule was not authoritarian nor arbitrary. It was based on the consent and approval of the people provided the public approval was in accordance with the fundamental principles of the law of God. The Prophet was a benevolent and responsible ruler. He also used to encourage his appointees—the provincial governors and tax collectors—to be benign and just in their dealings with the public. The Prophet was an ideal ruler and in no way was he dictatorial or despotic.

Thus, as successor to the Prophet, the head of the Islamic state cannot assume the position of an autocrat or a dictator, and cannot disturb the democratic rights of the people.

The people's right to differ
The citizens of the Islamic state have the right to differ with the head

of the state; and when such a situation arises, the dispute is to be referred to the Quran and the Prophetic guidance (*Sunnah*) for arbitration. The right to differ is directly contained in the right to give opinion, while the principle for settlement of differences is given in the following verse:

> If ye differ in anything among yourselves, refer it to Allah and His Messenger, if ye do believe in Allah and the Law Day: That is the best, and most suitable for final determination. (Surah 4: 59)

Supremacy of the Law

The above indicates that the head of the Islamic state is not above the law, his function being not to administer the state arbitrarily and at will, but positively, on the basis of truth and justice as given in the divine law, as the following verse establishes:

> . . . So judge between mankind with truth, and follow not caprice of the heart, lest it cause thee to err from the path of Allah [i.e. do not subordinate the welfare of the people to thy personal inclinations and interests, because that would lead thee away from absolute obedience to the Divine Law and upholding it as supreme]. (Surah 4: 59)

Separation of the Executive and Judiciary

If as we have noted, the head of the Islamic state is subordinate to the law given by God and His Messenger, the principle of the supremacy of law is established. Now, the only way to ensure the supremacy of law is keeping the judiciary independent of the executive, and total avoidance by the head of state of tampering with the functioning of the judiciary.

Duties of the Executive and Judiciary

Ensuring the spiritual welfare of the people

The Quran proclaims 'extortion to Truth' as one the essential conditions of human success (Surah 103: 3).

Hence, it is the duty of the Islamic state, holder of God's authority and successor to the Prophet and representative of the people, to uphold, propagate and ensure the functioning of truth, and consequently the spiritual values which from the basic content of truth in the lives of Muslims.

The Quran says:

> [Muslims are] those who, if we establish them [in authority and power] in the land, establish regular prayer and give regular charity, enjoin the right and forbid the wrong: With Allah rest the end [and decision] of [all] affairs. (Surah 22: 41)

Ensuring the moral welfare of the People
Surah 22: 41 lays down 'enjoining what is right and forbidding what is wrong' as one of the functions of the Islamic state. Viewing this function in the perspective of morals, the fact stands out as self-evident that it is the duty of the Islamic state:

a) to organize and institute the moral education of the people, and to do all that is necessary in that respect.
b) to take all positive steps, including the enactment and enforcement of laws, for ensuring the proper practice of Islamic morals with a view to preserve and promote moral welfare.
c) to adopt all measures necessary, including the enactment and enforcement of laws to combat all tendencies, acts and forces that are detrimental to the cause of moral welfare, and to punish offenders.

Duties relating to the intellectual development of the people
When we study the attitude of the Quran to the intellectual development of human beings, we find that:

a) it classifies humanity distinctly into two groups—the possessors of knowledge and the ignorant—and emphasizes clearly the superiority of the former:
   'Are the possessors of knowledge equal with those who possess not knowledge? It is the possessors of understanding that are mindful.' (Surah 39: 9)
b) but it goes further because, while emphasizing most vehemently the importance of intellectual development in human life, it makes the quest for knowledge a duty of paramount importance for the individual.

To the question—has the Islamic state any duty towards the citizens in respect of their intellectual development?—the plain answer is yes, as the following observations bear out:

According to the Quran, God educated Adam, the progenitor of the human race:

> And he imparted to Adam the knowledge of the nature of all things. (Surah 2: 31)

Then the Quran lays down the law that divine blessings are meant to be transmitted to others:

> . . . and do thou good [to others] as Allah has been good to thee. (Surah 28: 77)

The knowledge imparted by God to Adam was meant to be transmitted to mankind, generation after generation, and to be developed further and further by them.

Now, who can organize this difficult and great pursuit better than the possessor of the powers and authority of God?

Thus it is the duty of the Islamic state to organize universal education for the intellectual development of its citizens. The Quran has taught the prayer:

> O my Lord! advance me in knowledge. (Surah 20: 114)

This shows that it is God who advances human beings in knowledge. He does so, however, through human beings, of which the institution of prophethood is the proof. All the prophets, from Adam to Muhammad, were the vicegerents of God par excellence and, as such, the teachers of mankind. Every state is also the vicegerent of God, the Islamic state supremely so, because besides its status as 'state', it is also the inheritor of the blessings conferred on mankind by God through His Messengers. This vicegerency makes in incumbent on the Islamic state to undertake the development of knowledge to higher and higher levels, and to organize and enforce the education of all its citizens with a view to their intellectual advancement, with all the resources at its command.

The Quran refers to the establishment of justice and a balanced life among human beings as the objective of divine guidance and, consequently, as the objective of the Islamic state:

> We sent aforetime Our Messengers with clear signs and sent down with them the Book and the Balance [of Right and Wrong], that men may stand forth in justice . . . (Surah 57: 25)

This objective cannot, however, be achieved without a universal, compulsory dissemination among people of knowledge of the Islamic way of life. The Islamic way of life is, in its turn, built upon divine guidance, which is the highest knowledge, and as such necessitates the acquisition of all knowledge for its proper understanding.

Thus, free, compulsory and universal education, based on divine guidance, with the promotion of the Islamic way of life as its objective and the widest in scope, stands out as one of the foremost duties of the Islamic state.

The Quran commands Muslims to build up their power to the utmost and in all respects (Surah 8: 60). The objective is only achievable, among other things, through 'universal and basic religious and general education of the people: the highest theological, philosophical, scientific and technological education of those who possess the proper aptitude must be imparted.'

Thereby a community of intellectuals is built up which should endeavour ceaselessly to attain the highest level in every field of knowledge. All this education should, of course, be inspired by the ideal of truth and justice, whereby alone the mission of Islam is fulfilled. The crux of the above discussion is that, in respect of intellectual development, it is the duty of the Islamic state:

(i) to organize, establish and enforce free compulsory basic universal education.
(ii) to devise ways and means whereby all branches of knowledge are cultivated at the highest level.
(iii) to harness all intellectual endeavour in the cause of the advancement of truth and justice.[13]

What picture of an Islamic state emerges from the Islamic principles as laid down in the Quran? First, that the sovereignty belongs to God and God alone. But does it mean a revival of the old theory of the 'Divine right of kings'? The answer is clearly negative because the sovereignty of God is not delegated to any individual or any group like the *'ulama'* (the religious teachers). The sovereignty is to be exercised by the people and no one else. The representative of the people, chosen through election, will exercise sovereignty as the agent of God. The sovereignty of God in Islam does not imply any idea of theocracy as it is understood in Western political thought. Islam does not recognize any priesthood which alone can exercise authority or interpret the injunctions of God. It is the people and their elected representatives, their elected head of state, who will exercise powers as given by God. So, there is no conflict between the Islamic concept of the sovereignty of God and the idea of popular sovereignty which is the fundamental ingredient of democracy.

Two other essential features of a democracy, the rule of law and the equality of all citizens, are also stressed in the Quranic concept of an Islamic state; similarly the fundamental right of citizens, including the right to resist an arbitrary ruler who may be unjust or becomes a tyrant, is fully recognized. Even the highest authority in an Islamic state is not above the law. Independence of the judiciary and separation of powers between the executive and judiciary are clearly laid down. Equal emphasis is given to social justice and for a fair and equitable economic order—these are widely regarded as essential ingredients for a modern democratic state; there is no scope for any dictatorship in Islam.

Is there any scope for a legislature in an Islamic state? Some fundamentalists argue that since the *shari'ah* (Islamic law) contains provisions governing the whole field of human activity, there is no scope in an Islamic state for a legislature to make any laws. But we find injunctions in the Quran and the *shari'ah* that give general principles and leave large scope for legislation on matters where there are no specific provisions in the *shari'ah*. The Pakistani intelligentsia, like I H Qureshi, raise the question, should we accept the *shari'ah* as it stands today without any reinterpretation or reorientation? He answers, 'it has been recognized in all Muslim countries that in many respects the mutable part of the *shari'ah* requires considerable overhauling and the immutable parts (i.e. the Quran and the *Hadith*) need a new interpretation.' Who will do this work of 'overhauling' and the 'new interpretation' of Islamic laws? Not the *'ulama'*.

It is obvious that the only place where discussion can take place in connection with the reinterpretation and reorientation of the *shari'ah* is the legislature, because as the supreme representative of the people, the legislature alone can speak for them and accept on their behalf what seems rational and proper out of a mass of argument and commentary putting forward different points of view.[14]

This dynamic concept of the *shari'ah* as expressed by Qureshi was also supported by the leading Muslim jurists and philosophers in India before partition. Sir Mohammad Iqbal, who is regarded as the originator of the idea of a separate state of Pakistan, in his book, *The Reconstruction of Religious Thought in Islam*, stressed the dynamic nature of Islamic law; he pointed out that the assimilative spirit of Islam is more manifest in the sphere of law that in anything else. While commenting on the Quran as the source of Islamic law, he observed that the Quran is, however, not a legal code. Its main purpose is to awaken in man the higher consciousness of his relationship with God and the universe. No doubt the Quran does lay down a few general principles and laws of a legal nature. However, it is perfectly clear that from leaving no scope for human thought and legislative activity, the intense breadth of these principles virtually acts as an awakener of human thought.[15]

The Extremist 'Ulama''s *Concept of an Islamic State*

The concept of an Islamic state, as we have given in the preceding pages based on Quranic principles, interpreted in broad and dynamic ways is, however, not accepted by some sections of the *'ulama'* (religious teachers) who seem to give rather rigid and inflexible interpretations of Quranic principles.

Let us now examine the *'ulama'* concept of an Islamic state. The present author undertook extensive research to examine the *'ulama'* conception of an Islamic state. In Pakistan in the 1940s and 1950s there were great debates about the concept of an Islamic state. We have gathered some valuable data and materials for the assessment of the *'ulama''s* views.

There were extensive discussions on the subject in Pakistan. It was revived during the presidency of former Pakistan president Zia-ul-Haq in the 1980s, who also examined and did research on the subject. The *'ulama'* also took part in this reinterpreting of the Islamic state: they produced several reports on the subject.

What does the 'Islamic state' signifies to the *'ulama'*. It is not, however, possible to present a unanimous interpretation of an Islamic constitution: the *'ulama'* themselves are divided on it; there had been hundreds of cheap and ready-made suggestions about the concept of an Islamic state. The author primarily tried to ascertain the views of the *'ulama'* from the following important and reliable sources:

(i) The transactions of the *Board of Talimat-i-Islamiah*. This Board of the *'ulama'* was appointed by the Constituent Assembly of Pakistan to advise it on matters relating to Islamic principles.
(ii) 'Fundamental Principles of an Islamic State' as laid down at a conference of *'ulama'* of the various schools of thought who met in Karachi in January 1951. The report was published by Jama'at-i-Islami, Karachi (Pakistan).
(iii) *Report of the Court of Inquiry (1953) for Punjab Disturbances.* This Committee, which was set up under Justice Munir who later became the Chief Justice of the Federal Court of Pakistan, to enquire into the religious movement of the Ahmadis, examined in detail the views of the *'ulama'* on the future constitution.

The *'ulama'* would like to adopt the institutions of the early caliphate; they want to reproduce a society which no longer exists and a polity which was suited to the early days of Islam, as if all that was done at that time was the final interpretation of Islam and as if it were not possible for the human intellect to deviate from it in any detail.

In constructing an Islamic constitution, the *'ulama'* feel, Pakistan's task is to look back to the past history of Islam and reproduce once again the actual state of affairs that obtained in the 7th century. They fail to distinguish between the principle and the method of expression of the principle. They are not content with the principles of Islam alone but wish to adopt in a constitution of a Muslim country every action and institution which was set up in the 7th century. That the form of government in a Muslim country, if that form is to comply with the principles of Islam, will not be democratic is conceded by the *'ulama'*.

According to the *'ulama'* since Islam is a perfect religion containing laws governing the whole field of human activity, there is in it no sanction for what may, in the modern sense, be called legislation. Maulana Abul Hasanat, President, Jami'at-ul-Ulema-i-Pakistan, on being questioned by the Court of Inquiry on this subject said, 'Our law is complete and merely requires interpretation by those who are experts in it. According to my belief no question can arise, the law relating to which cannot be discovered from the Quran or the *Hadith*.' The same view was expressed by Sayyad Ata Ullah Shah Bukhari. Legislation in its modern sense, according to some *'ulama'*, is unknown to the Islamic system. The religio-political system, which is called *Din i-Islam*, is a complete system which contains in itself the mechanism for discovering and applying law to any situation that may arise. During the Islamic republic of the 7th century there was no legislation in its modern sense and for every situation or emergency that arose law could be interpreted and applied by the judges or those in authority.[16]

However, it must be pointed out that some of the *'ulama'* recognized the need for legislation in a Islamic state. Maulana Abul A'la Mawdudi, the President of the Jama'at-i-Islami, an extremist religious and political party, was of the opinion that legislation in the true sense is possible in an Islamic state on matters which are not covered by the Quran or the *Sunnah*. He explained this point by a reference to the institution of a body of persons whom the Prophet, and after him the caliphate, consulted on all matters relating to affairs of state; also this view was endorsed by the Board of Talimat-i-Islamiah of the Constituent Assembly of Pakistan.

On the question of the position of non-Muslims in the Islamic state, the *'ulama'* hold views which are fundamentally at variance with those of the Muslim modern intelligentsia and reformists. According to some *'ulama'* the position of non-Muslims in the Islamic state should be that *dhimmis* (by *dhimmis* is meant an allied and protected people, non-Muslim by religion, living within *Dar al-Islam*), they would not be full citizens because they would not have the same rights as Muslims.

Maulana Abul Hasanat on being questioned on the subject by the Court of Inquiry stated, 'their [non-Muslims] position will be that of Dhimmis. They will have no voice in the making of laws, no right to administer the law and no right to hold public offices.'[17] This view was endorsed by a number of leading *'ulama'* who were questioned by the Court of Inquiry. Maulana Abdul Hamid Badayuni expressed the view that non-Muslims should not be taken into the army or the judiciary or be appointed as ministers or to other posts involving the reposing of confidence. The same view was expressed by Maulana Shabbir Ahmed Osmani in the Pakistan Constituent Assembly in the course of the debate on the Islamic state. The *'ulama'* point out that during the Islamic republic of early days, the head of the state, the *khalifah*, was the source of all channels of legitimate government. He and he alone was competent to rule, although he could delegate his powers to deputies and collect around him a body of men of outstanding piety and learning called *Majlis i-Shurah* or *Ahl al-Hall wa-'l-'Aqd*. The power which was vested in the *khalifah* could not be delegated to non-Muslims. Mawardi, however, holds that it is only the unlimited sovereign authority which cannot be delegated; limited authority can be delegated.[18]

In addition to the exclusion of the non-Muslims, the Board of Talimat-i-Islamiah raised objection to giving the right of franchise to women, Muslims or non-Muslim. According to the Board:

> The idea of placing the burden of extra-domestic activities upon the shoulders of women at the expense of or in addition to the very important assignments which they are required to carry out in their own sphere of activity is repugnant to Islam and is not permissible except in times of extraordinary crisis and then too with many a limitation: participation of women in elections militates against many a requirement of Islam.[19]

The other features of the Islamic state as demanded by the *'ulama'* are that there should be a board of the *'ulama'* which should have powers to declare any law *ultra vires* if it is repugnant to the Quran and the *Sunnah*; the law of the land shall be based on the Quran and the *Sunnah*; the state should be based not on geographical, racial, linguistic or any other materialistic concepts, but on the principles and objectives of the Islamic scheme of life; it should be incumbent upon the state to uphold the right (*ma'ruf*) and suppress the wrong (*munkar*) as postulated in the Quran and the *Sunnah*, to take all measures for the revival and exultation of the tenets of Islam and to revive Islamic education; to strengthen the bonds of unity and brotherhood among all the Muslims of the world; the head of the state must be a male Muslim and the responsibility of the administration of the state should primarily be vested in the head of the state, although he might delegate any part of his powers to any individuals or body; no interpretation of the government which might be in conflict with the provisions of the Quran or the *Sunnah* should be valid. Maulana Mawdudi further wants all the existing laws of an Islamic state to be brought into conformity with the Islamic *shari'ah*, moral training in accordance with the Islamic principles and standards of conduct should be made compulsory for all services, central, provincial, military and civil, and all that is against Islamic teaching and Islamic ethics should be eliminated.[20]

An analysis of the *'ulama'* picture of the Islamic state proves that they fail to see the inherent impossibility, not to say meaninglessness, of reproducing in one age the activities or constructions of another. Manifestly, a modern Muslim country like Malaysia or Pakistan, in fact, any contemporary Muslim country, cannot adopt institutions or activities which were suitable for 7th century Arabia. The *'ulama'* give too narrow an interpretation of Islamic principles. They look upon Islamic law as a dead, unprogressive, and static collection of injunctions and prohibitions. They fail to comprehend that Islam cannot be content merely with precedents and traditions but needs a new interpretation at every stage of its development. In order to apply Islamic principles in modern society, it must be given a dynamic interpretation. Islam does not discard precedents and traditions but it lays emphasis upon the progressive unfolding of the creative instincts of mankind. The difficulty with the *'ulama'* is that they consider the interpretation of the principles of Islam their closed preserve, and while interpreting they cannot make the proper distinction between a principle and its method of expression. The *khalifah*, for instance, was elected but the mode of election was altogether different from modern elections. The principle of election was there but the method was different: some *'ulama'* would describe an election as un-Islamic if it does not agree with the particular method which was suitable in 7th century Arabia; they are not satisfied unless every particular and detail which existed in the early days of Islam has been adopted. They have betrayed their inability to distinguish between the essence and the form. It is weak and dependent souls who cannot go beyond the form of things; the *'ulama'* in Pakistan as in other Muslim countries have considered any digression from the beaten path as taboo. They seem to believe there is only one form of state deserving the adjective 'Islamic', namely the form manifested under the first four Caliphs and that, therefore, any deviation from that model would detract from the Islamic character of the state. This idea is, however, entirely erroneous. If one examines the political laws and ordinances forthcoming from the Quran and the *Sunnah*, one finds that in reality there is no specific form of Islamic state. The *shari'ah* does not prescribe any definite pattern to which a state should conform nor does it elaborate in detail a constitutional theory, but on the contrary it allows great latitude in governmental methods and administrative procedure. The result is that in every Muslim country there has developed a wide gulf between the orthodox *'ulama'* and the intelligentsia. This has done great harm to Islam.

The picture of an Islamic state conceived by the *'ulama'* is not acceptable to a modern Muslim country. The intelligentsia are elaborating a new 20th century and authoritative interpretation of Islam, and when they wish to see a Muslim country become Islamic, their picture of an Islamic state is altogether different from that of the *'ulama'*, and it is not greatly dissimilar from that of a modern democratic state. As it was put by Khwaja Nazimuddin, Prime Minister of Pakistan in the 1950s:

> The principles enunciated by Islam had to be interpreted in the terms of democratic constitutional practice of the twentieth century . . . so that we could bring about a synthesis not only of the fundamental teachings of our faith but the requirements of the twentieth century and best elements in our own tradition and history.[21]

The notion of an Islamic state in the modern Muslim state has not led to any major suggestion of giving privilege or exclusive power to the *'ulama'*. An Islamic state is not one which is framed by or run by Islamic theologians. It is the people or people's elected legislature which is committed to the task of working out an interpretation of the Islamic state and not the *'ulama'*; since Islam has no priesthood, it cannot argue. Muslim scholars of the contemporary period emphatically refuse to identify the 'Islamic state' with theocracy. We have noted that some *'ulama'* believe that since Islam is a perfect religion containing laws governing the whole field of human activity, there is no scope in an Islamic state for what may, in the modern sense, be called a legislature. Quite contrary is the view held by the Muslim intelligentsia. Professor I H Qureshi (formerly Education Minister of Pakistan) raises the question, 'should we accept Shari'ah (Islamic law) as it is today without any reinterpretation or reorientation?' He answers, 'It has been recognized in all Muslim countries that in many respects the mutable part of the *shari'ah* requires considerable overhauling and the immutable parts (i.e., the Quran and the *Hadith*) need a new interpretation.' Who will do this work of 'overhauling' and 'new interpretation' of Islamic laws? Not the *'ulama'*.

It is obvious that the only place where discussion can take place in connection with the reinterpretation and reorientation of the *shari'ah* is the legislature, because as the supreme representatives of the people, the legislature alone can speak for them and accept on their behalf what seems rational and proper out of a mass of argument and commentary putting forward different points of view.

The early Muslim jurists, taking the Quran as its groundwork, evolved a number of legal systems. The *'ulama'* speak finally for the popular schools of Muslim law. But this attitude of the *'ulama'* is not correct. Since things have changed and the world of Islam is today confronted with and affected by new forces set free by the development of human thought in all directions, this attitude should be discarded and the claim of the present generation of Muslim liberals to reinterpret the fundamental legal principles in the light of their own experience and the altered condition of modern life is perfectly justified. Sir Ameer Ali, in *The Spirit of Islam*, discusses this problem in his chapter on 'The Political Spirit of Islam'. He says that Islam gave to the people a code which, however archaic in its simplicity, is capable of the greatest development in accordance with the progress of material civilization. It conferred on the state a flexible constitution, based on a just appreciation of human rights and human duty. It limited taxation; it made men equal in the eye of the law; it consecrated the principles of self-government. It established a control over the sovereign power by rendering the executive authority subordinate to the law—a law based upon religious sanctions and moral obligations.[22] What is clear from these utterances is that the Muslim intelligentsia can never accept the *Shari'a*h as something static and fixed once and for all. Wilfred Smith rightly says that Muslim intelligentsia see the *shari'ah* not as a static system but as a dynamic development, a process of which the historical stages in the past are available for study and guidance, but of which the proper present and future developments are matters of creative extrapolation. This interpretation would accent continuity and revision.[23]

So according to this interpretation of Islamic laws, there is definite scope for a legislature in an Islamic state. The legal sovereign should be the Muslim law, but its definition should be in the hands of a legislature, representing the people, which would decide how to apply the principles of Islam to the needs of the community in varying circumstances. The political sovereign should be the people who would elect and dismiss their legislature and government.

For the Muslim intelligentsia the concept of an Islamic state also signifies a dynamic morality; to them an Islamic state means that the Islamic principles, particularly those of equality, brotherhood and social justice should be applied to guide it. They believe that the ideals preached by Islam are democratic and progressive. Their view is that the basis of the state must be the ideals of Islam, but unlike the *'ulama'*, they refuse to include in their conception of Islam such practices as might have been adopted at some stage in its history to meet temporary or local needs.

The problem before the modern Muslim countries, therefore, is to determine how far it is possible to define the principles which should actuate an Islamic polity and how far it is possible to discard precedents without injuring the principles. It is pointed out that the Quran has not laid down any definite form of government or defined any institution. What is found in the Quran is a code of principles which are to be applied and interpreted in accordance with the varying needs of the people. The foundations of the polity were established in the Quran and in the teaching of the Prophet; the edifice is to be built in accordance with the needs of the successive generations by the creative spirit of the Muslim people guided by the teachings of Islam.

Now one may raise the question that if the Quranic concept of the Islamic state and a modern democratic state are basically the same, why do Muslims insist on what may be termed as Islamic democracy rather than simply democracy. In order to appreciate this fact we have to go deeper and explain the *raison d'ětre* of the Muslims for an Islamic state or Islamic democracy. Muslims draw their faith from Islam, which, at the cost of repetition, is not just a mode of worship but provides for the Muslim a whole code of life. When Muslims want to establish a society which is fair, free and just to everybody, irrespective of race, colour, language, sex and religion, and caste, with equality in all spheres of life-political, economic and social, they sincerely believe that the Quranic principles relating to an Islamic state are the best and the only guide for them to establish such a good society. This is the main justification for insisting upon Islamic democracy rather than just democracy as it is understood in a modern secular state. We shall conclude our discussion on the Islamic state by referring again to Wilfred Smith's comments on this desire of Muslims for 'Islamic democracy'. He seems to have appreciated the significance and true meaning of the phrase 'Islamic democracy'. Smith points out, 'Islamic democracy gains its significance from the fact that the democracy has both a political and an ethical element. It cannot exist without the concurrence of both a governmental form and a popular ideal. The ethical aspect is a no less important ingredient. A democrat must believe not only in the democratic structure of the state; he must also believe in the fundamental significance and value of the other persons in his society. For the West, this faith, the ethical element, comes from two main sources: the Greek tradition and the Judaeo-Christian. In the case of Muslims, that ethical element is Islam. Moreover, for a Westerner on certain matters, judgements of value, even though their content be Christian, would be cast in a form derived from the Graeco-Roman tradition. Westerners—to some extent Muslims educated in Western ways—are accustomed, for example, to considering political questions by means of concepts, categories and modes of thought stemming from the Greek root of Western civilization. For a Muslim his whole civilizational heritage is, if not religious, set in Islamic forms. Herein lies the true significance of the phrase "Islamic democracy".'

Smith continues that this is the 'Muslims' way of saying that they should build for themselves a good society—not merely an independent or a strong or a wealthy or a modern society. All these things it should be perhaps, but it should also be a good society.' He concludes that 'a Muslim's apprehension of goodness is coloured by his environment, the pressures and complexities and limitations of his particular time and place, and by his own capacity, his moral acumen and the sensitivity of his spirit. It is coloured also, and more uniquely, by the fact that he is a Muslim.'[24]

Islam and the Religious Minorities

Islam stands for the equality of all races and colours: all are alike in its great brotherhood; all can aspire to any position or vocation. Islam also inculcates respect and toleration for other religious; this spirit was embodied in the charter which was granted to the Jews by the Prophet Muhammad after his arrival in al-Madinah and in the notable message sent to the Christians of Najran and neighbouring territories after Islam had fully established itself in the Arabian peninsula. The latter document pledged the security of the lives, religion and property of the Christians: 'There should be no interference with [the practice of] their faith or observances, nor any change in their rights or privileges.' There have been occasional lapses in the observance of these principles; but the principles themselves have never been modified. As Professor Arnold has pointed out: 'The theory of the Muslim faith enjoins toleration and freedom of religious life for all those followers of other faiths who pay tribute in return for protection, and though the pages of Muhammadan history are stained with the blood of many cruel persecutions, on the whole, unbelievers have enjoyed under Muhammadan rule a measure of toleration the like of which is not to be found in Europe until quite modern times . . . the very existence of so many Christian sects and communities in countries that have been for centuries under Muhammadan rule is an abiding testimony to the toleration they have from time to time endured at the hands of bigots and fanatics who have been excited by some special and local circumstances rather than inspired by a settled principle of intolerance.'[25]

The critics of the Islamic state, on the other hand, maintain that whatever may be the theory of tolerance in Islam, history contradicts it. Even in the best days of the Islamic state, non-Muslims suffered in spite of the Prophet's assurance. In support of the thesis that non-Muslim subjects of Islamic states labour under severe disabilities, reference is made to the narrow views of canonists and lawyers of Islam. In an Islamic state, the critics point out, the best status that the non-Muslim can have is that of *dhimmis* (people living in alliance with and under the protection of Islam in a Muslim land). It is argued that *dhimmis* have protection for their lives, families and property, but they have a definitely inferior status. They are not full-fledged citizens but enjoy the status of protected wards. They are to be accorded toleration and protection, but are outside the full community of the state. They must pay a special tax in return for protection. They are allowed to retain their own religious organizations, personal status, places or worship and religious trust.

It may be added here that before the partition of India, some distinguished Hindu scholars admired the broad and liberal principles of Islam and believed that a state based on these principles of Islam need not be out of tune with democracy. Radhu Kamal Mukherjee, an eminent Indian sociologist and ardent member of the extremist Hindu Sabha, writes in his *Democracies of the East*:

> The communal-democratic system of politics, founded upon the basis of theocracy in the Islamic Commonwealth, is one of the most remarkable phenomena of political evolution, not less significant than the development of the Athenian democracy and the Roman Republic . . . The democratic spirit of the Islamic Law corresponded with the Demotic idea of a republican state and with a large measure of freedom and independence that were still reserved for local bodies, tribal councils, and communal assemblies. The history of the Caliphate proves that election by the people or nomination by them was regarded as the only valid title to sovereignty. Sacredness was attached to the oath of allegiance and homage to the sovereign-elect.

During the Caliphate of Omar, all business was conducted on rightly ordered constitutional lines. The laws of the Republic and rights of the citizens, Muslims and non-Muslims, were proclaimed by the messengers in the provinces and towns by Abu Baker and Omar and in these perhaps the most significant feature was the concept of law ruling through the utterances of justice and the noteworthy separation between judicial and executive authority.

He examined in detail the administrative system of the early *khalifahs* and reached the conclusion:

> All testify to the remarkable development of the democratic spirit of the Islamic administration . . . In Muslim India (i.e. Pakistan) the development towards modern constitutionalism was made easier by building on the original and essential democracy of the time-honoured Majlis and Punchayat; the renewal of the Mussalman Commonwealth on this basis will be a new experiment in communalistic policy which will be more satisfying than the importation of western democratic institutions and methods.[26]

Wilfred Smith has analysed the problem of non-Muslim minorities under an Islamic constitution. He says:

> It is fundamental to remember that the rights accorded to any minority or other non-powerful group in any state depend on the ideal of those in power . . . A state may be democratic in form but unless it is democratic also in ideal, unless the majority of its citizens are actively loyal to the transcendent principles of democracy, recognizing the ideal validity of every man's status as a man, then the arithmetic minority has, through the democratic form, no rights at all . . . If Muslims do in fact treat non-Muslims unjustly then a democratic framework (without the Graeco-Roman and religious tradition of democracy to vitalize it) would merely give them as a majority the constitutional authority for doing so without let or hindrance.[27]

The Source of Islamic Law

There are four basic sources of the Islamic law, *shari'ah*. The first is the Quran. The revealed Book of Islam, the Quran, was delivered to the Prophet Muhammad by God. The legal rules set forth in the Quran are regarded by Muslims as absolutely binding. But the

Quran gives only guiding principles and states few definite rules. So a large section of the Islamic law, *shari'ah*, is not derived directly from the Quran. Sir Muhammad Iqbal, the great poet-philosopher of Muslim India commented in *The Reconstruction of Religious Thought in Islam* on the Quran as the primary source of Islamic law, but he also points out that the Quran is, however, not a legal code. Its main purpose is to awaken in man the higher consciousness of his relation with Allah and with the universe. As he explains, no doubt the Quran does lay down a few general principles and laws of a legal nature: but it is perfectly clear, he adds, that far from leaving no scope for human thought and legislative activity, the extensive breadth of these Quranic principles acts as an awakener of human thought.[28]

The Muslim jurists in the early phase of Islamic history evolved a number of legal systems based on the broad principles and teachings of the Quran. During the last seven or eight centuries, Muslim jurists have not made any such new legal system. The Quranic injunctions have remained dormant. It is high time that the Muslim intelligentsia take the initiative to develop the Islamic legal system in accordance with Quranic principles in the context of the 'extraordinary development of human thought in all its directions.'[29] The distinguished Muslim jurist of Muslim India, Syed Ameer Ali, in his book *The Spirit of Islam*, expresses similar views. He writes that Islam gave to the people a code which, however archaic in its simplicity, was capable of the greatest development in accordance with the progress of material civilization. It conferred on the state a flexible constitution, based on a just appreciation of human rights and duty. It limited taxation; it made men equal in the eyes of the law; it consecrated the principles of self-government. It established a control over the sovereign power by rendering the Islamic executive authority subordinate to the law—a law based upon religious sanctions and moral obligations.[30]

What is clear from these sources is that the *shari'ah* is not something static and fixed once and for all. Wilfred Smith rightly says that the *shari'ah* is not a static system but a dynamic development; a process in which the historical stages of the past are available for study and guidance, but in which present and future developments are matters of creative extrapolation. This interpretation accentuates continuity and revision.[31] So, according to this interpretation of Islamic law, there is definite scope for legislature in an Islamic republic. The legal sovereign should be the Muslim law, but its definition should be in the hands of the legislature, representing the people, which decides how to apply the principles of Islam to the needs of the community in varying circumstances. The political sovereign should be the people who elect and dismiss their legislature and government.

The second important source of the Islamic law is the *Sunnah*. The *Sunnah* is the practices and sayings of the Prophet Muhammad. A proper study of the Prophet's tradition, if used as an indicator of the spirit in which the Prophet himself interpreted his revelation, is of great help in understanding the value of the legal principles enunciated in the Quran.[32] The Prophet, in his noble actions and deeds, was the greatest embodiment of the true spirit of the Islamic message as laid down in the Quran. The *Sunnah* is, therefore, the second important source of Islamic law. There are various interpretations of what the Prophet said and did, so there are different collections of *Sunnah* with different, if not conflicting, contents. The Sunnis and Shi'ahs, who have divergent views about the rightful successors to the Prophet's leadership of the Islamic *ummah* (community) have conflicting collections of the Prophet's practices. However, notwithstanding such divergent views about the *Sunnah*, it is regarded by the overwhelming majority of Muslims as legally binding.[33]

The third source of Islamic law is *ijma'*, which Iqbal terms as the 'most important notion' in Islam. It is accepted by Muslims, in particular by Sunni Muslims, that if there is a consensus among Muslim jurists of a particular generation on a point of view, this view should be accepted. But the great debate continues in contemporary Muslim countries as to whether the consensus arrived at by the early jurists should be final or whether the Muslim jurists of every generation should work out a consensus. In the modern age, when things are changing so fast in the context of science and technology, should not the Muslims try to interpret the Quranic teachings? Who should try to evolve *ijma'* or consensus in a modern democratic Muslim country? The only place where it can be done is in the elected legislature of a Muslim country. Islam does not recognize any particular group or priesthood who should have a monopoly on interpreting the will of God. In Islam, every believer has the right to interpret the Quranic injunctions. As we have already pointed out, the Muslim intelligentsia regard the *shari'ah*, the Islamic legal system, as dynamic and capable of meeting the requirements of a modern complex Muslim society. Professor I H Qureshi, as already noted, asks whether we should accept the *Shari'ah* as it stands today. He answers that it has been recognized in all Muslim countries that in many respects the mutable part of *shari'ah* requires considerable overhauling and the immutable parts (i.e., the Quran and the *Sunnah*) need a new interpretation. Who will do this work of overhauling and reinterpreting Islamic law? Qureshi feels, like many other modern Muslim scholars, that this task cannot be done by the *'ulama'* (the religious teachers) alone. According to modern Muslim

scholars the only place where discussion can take place in connection with the reinterpretation and reorientation of the Islamic legal system, without violating the clear and unambiguous injunctions of the Quran, is the legislature, because as the supreme representative of the people who according to the Quran are the vicegerent of God and, as such, entitled to exercise their knowledge to understand the meaning of the will of God, the legislature of a modern Muslim state alone can speak for them and accept on their behalf what seems rational and proper from a mass of argument and commentary putting forward different points of view.[34] Iqbal expresses the same view that only in a popularly elected legislature can *ijma'* be worked out. He writes: 'In this way alone can we stir into activity the dormant spirit of life in our legal system and give it an evolutionary outlook.'[35]
Ijtihad or *qiyas*: Muslim jurists have tried to expand the legal principles as laid down in the Quran and *Sunnah* so as to regulate all aspects of human activity, using criteria that are definitely Islamic. Muslim scholars used analogical reasoning, known as *qiyas*, to achieve this end (*ijtihad*). *It was argued that 'a freer use of human reasoning was necessary for developing an understanding of the ultimate principles and purposes of the shari'ah'*[36] The use of *qiyas* is being widely discussed as Muslims seek to find answers to broad social, economic and political questions 'for which more innovative and flexible interpretive techniques seem to be required.'[37] There is no dearth of such innovative techniques in Islam. The Muslim, Iqbal rightly claims, 'is in possession of the ultimate ideas on the basis of revelation, which, speaking from the inmost depths of life, internalizes its own apparent externality. With him the spiritual basis of life is a matter of conviction for which even the least enlightened man among us can easily lay down his life; and in view of the basic idea of Islam that there can be no further revelation binding on man, we ought to be spiritually one of the most enlightened peoples on earth.'[38]

Notes

1 John L Esposito, *Islam and Politics*, New York, 1987, 1.
2 I H Qureshi's speech in the Pakistan (First) Constituent Assembly in 1949, cited in G W Choudhury, *Constitutional Development in Pakistan* (2nd ed.), London, 1969, 120.
3 See *Current History*, Philadelphia, June 1956.
4 Khurshid Ahmad, *Towards Understanding Islam*, Leicester, 1979, 10.
5 Sayyed Hossain Nasr, *Ideals and Realities of Islam*, London, 1971, 69.
6 Cited by Pakistani President Zia-ul-Haq in his speech to the Pakistan National Assembly on 17 October 1985, see *Pakistan Times*, 18 October 1985.
7 Sir Muhammad Zafrulla Khan's speech in the Pakistan (First) Constituent Assembly, see *CA Assembly Debates*, vol. 5, no. 5, 66-67.

[8] Muhammad Asad, *The Principles of State and Government in Islam*, new ed. Gibraltar, 1980, 2-4.
[9] Muhammad, Fazlur Rahman Ansari, *The Quranic Foundation and Structure of Muslim Society*, vol. II, Karachi, 1973, 342-4.
[10] Tareq Y Ismail and Jacqueline Ismail, *Government and Politics in Islam*, London, 1985, 3.
[11] Muhammad Umarah, *al-Islam wa Sultan al-Dunya*, cited in Ismail, *Government and Politics in Islam*.
[12] *Government and Politics in Islam*, 46-47.
[13] This part of our discussion on the Quranic concept of an Islamic state is based on Fazlur Rahman Ansari's work *The Quranic Foundation and Structure of Muslim Society*, vol. II, Karachi, 1973, 7, whose value we gratefully acknowledge.
[14] I H Qureshi, 'The Conception of Sovereignty and Executive Goverment in Islam' in Choudhury, *Constitutional Development in Pakistan*, 71.
[15] See *ibid.*, 72.
[16] See *Constitutional Development in Pakistan*, 66-67.
[17] *Ibid.*
[18] Cited in I H Qureshi, *Administration of the Sultanate of Delhi*, London, 1944, 79-80.
[19] Pakistan, *Board of Talimat-i-Islamiah*, unpublished report to Pakistan (First) Constituent Assembly, 2.
[20] *Fundamental Principles of an Islamic State*, prepared by various groups of *'ulama'* in Pakistan, Karachi, 10-12.
[21] *Pakistan (First) Constituent Assembly Debates*, vol. 2, no. 2, 57-58.
[22] *The Spirit of Islam*, London, 1935, 277.
[23] W C Smith, *Pakistan as an Islamic State*, Lahore, 1951, 23-25.
[24] *Ibid.*
[25] T M Arnold, *Preaching of Islam*, London, 1913, 420.
[26] R K Mukherjee, *Democracies of the East*, London, 1923, 174-6.
[27] Smith, *op. cit.*, 41-3.
[28] Sir Mohammad Iqbal, *The Reconstruction of Religious Thought in Islam*, London, 1934, 131-3.
[29] *Ibid.*
[30] Syed Ameer Ali, *op. cit.*, 277.
[31] Smith, *op. cit.*, 25.
[32] Iqbal, *op. cit.*, 137.
[33] See Ann Elizabeth Mayer, 'Islamic Law' in Marjorie Kelly (ed.), *Islam: The Religious and Political Life of a World Community*, New York, 1984, 230.
[34] I H Qureshi, *The Concept of Sovereignty and Executive Goverment in Islam*, Proceedings of the All-Pakistan Political Conference, Karachi, 1952.
[35] Iqbal, *op. cit.*, 138.
[36] Iqbal, *op. cit.*, 142.
[37] *Ibid.*
[38] *Ibid.*

Chapter III
The Beginning of the Islamic Political Community

As we have already pointed out there is no separation between politics and religion in Islamic political philosophy; the word 'religion' signifies a much wider connotation and meaning in Islam. Unlike in the West, the word 'religion' in Islam is not confined only to a mode of worship in Islam. According to Islam, religion epitomises consistent, persistent and wider relationship between man and his creator. The *mu'min* (believer) Muslim begins most of his daily routine life with the words 'in the name of Allah, the Merciful'. In Islam 'God' is all pervasive, all mighty. There is no sphere of life which is outside the scope of the jurisdiction of 'God' in Islam. Therefore, it is quite natural that political life, which constitutes an important aspect of human life, would be within the scope of religion as it is understood in Islam.

An all-powerful, all-embracing authority of God might lead one to compare Islam with modern totalitarianism but that will not be a fair interpretation, because modern totalitarianism is meant for the power of an individual, a dictator or a group of individuals, or a ruling oligarchy. However, the all-comprehensive authority of God in Islam is exercised for the welfare and good not of any particular person or group of persons. It is meant as authority binding on the followers of Islam to do justice and exercise fair play to everybody. The power of God is not to be exercised by any individual or privileged group, so the comprehensive holding of the power of God in Islam should not be confused with any dictatorial power.

Moreover, it may be argued, the sovereignty of God ensures that on the other hand, that civil authority must not be subservient to the advantage of one, or of a few, for it is established for the good of all; and if those who are in authority should rule unjustly, or of they should err through arrogance or pride, if their measures should be injurious to the people—then let them know that hereafter an account must be rendered to God. In such a conformation of the state, there is nothing that may be incompatible or out of tune with the spirit and tradition of democracy or of rule by the people. When there is emphasis on the moral aspect of civil and political authority, it may help to ensure that laws aim at the common good and are determined by truth and justice, and that authority is restrained from deviating from what is just and overstepping the limits of power.

As a perceptive Western scholar, Wilfred C Smith, has pointed out, like other religions or any philosophy, Islam has been expressed in many forms—intellectual, mystical, but more than some others, social. In fact, Islam is characterized among the religions by the particular emphasis which it has from the beginning given to the social order. The Prophet Muhammad not only preached ethics, he organized a state. Indeed, Islamic history is calculated to begin not on the year when the Prophet was born (after the fashion of the Christian era), nor when he began to receive Divine Revelations, but when the Muslim community came to power in a state of its own. The year AH (*anno hegirae*) marks the establishment of Islam as a religio-political sovereignty in al-Madinah. That state was organized in accordance with God's revelation; it prospered and expanded and Islam as a process in human history was launched on its career. That career has continued until today, with many human ups and downs, many variations of fortunes and of forms, many vicissitudes, both of achievement and of aspiration, but never very far from being central has been its concern with itself as an organized community. There are many illustrations of this fact; one is the supreme importance in Islam of law. Islam has been a social gospel from the beginning. Major sectarian differences in Islam have had to do with divergences not primarily over dogma but over questions as to how the community should be organized. While the Protestants seceded from the Catholic Church on points of doctrine, the Shi'ah seceded from the majority community on a dispute regarding political leadership. Islam is by tradition and in its core a practical religion, a religion of ethics, including social ethics, and of organized, legalized ethics.[1]

This union between religion and politics was first implemented and practised by the Prophet of Islam, Muhammad, who may rightly be credited to have given the 'first written constitution in the world'.[2] When the Prophet Muhammad came to al-Madinah the followers of

Islam from Makkah also followed him. This small community of the Muslims at al-Madinah faced serious challenges and problems both internal and external. However, Muhammad through his wisdom and far-sightedness solved these problems in a magnificent way. Those Muslims who came from Makkah were known as *muhajirun* (immigrants) they were uprooted from their homes and hearth. They voluntarily gave up all their worldly belongings for the sake of their faith. The Muslims of al-Madinah who gracefully welcomed Muhammad and his followers were known as *ansar* (Medinite 'helpers'). They were also a large number of non-Muslims, in particular the Jews, living in al-Madinah. The Muslim community was not sure about the attitude of the Jews towards Islam and its Prophet. Muhammad, therefore, met the Jewish leaders and persuaded them to form a community with the Muslims. There were also pagans living in al-Madinah.

Constitution of al-Madinah—The First Islamic State

As a result of Muhammad's successful negotiations with various segments of the society in al-Madinah, he prepared a document which is known as 'The Constitution of al-Madinah'. The document concluded between *muhajirun* and *ansar* on the one side and Jews on the other was drafted by Muhammad. It not only brought union between the immigrants and the inhabitants of al-Madinah, but it also brought the Jews under one political entity. Muhammad Husayan Haykal in his biography on the Prophet made the following comments about this political background: 'it established the freedom of faith and opinion, the inviolability of the city, human life, and property, and the forbidding of crime. It certainly constitutes a breakthrough in the political and civil life of the world of that time. For that age was one in which exploitation, tyranny, and corruption were well established. Though the Jews of Banu Qurayzah, Banu al-Nadir, and Banu Qaynuqa did not sign this covenant at its conclusion, they did enter later on into like pacts with the Prophet. Thus al-Madinah and all the territories surrounding it became inviolate to their peoples who were now bound to rise to their defence and protection together. These peoples were now bound to guarantee one another in the implementation of the covenant, in the establishment of the rights arising therefrom, and in the provision of freedom it has called for.'[3]

The Constitution of al-Madinah can be rightly termed as a

remarkable document and a great milestone in the human struggle to lead a free life in a free society. It established a single community consisting of Muslims as well as non-Muslims who enjoyed equal political, religious, cultural freedoms without any discrimination. It was a time when concept of human rights or the rule of law were unknown. Muhammad set a unique example of religious toleration, freedom, justice and fair play to all members of a community irrespective of their race, colour and religion. There were 47 articles in the constitution of al-Madinah. Montgomery Watt wrote that Muhammad was given extensive powers and roles under the Constitution of al-Madinah but the Prophet conducted himself with marked humility. He created a polity which banned all privileges; the only criteria of his political order was service and sacrifices.[4]

Under the Constitution of al-Madinah the Muslims and the Jews were granted equality of status and were gathered together as one nation and, we may say, that it recognized a compositie state which does not discriminate between the followers of different religions. According to an interpreter of the Constitution of al-Madinah there are features of the document which support the contention that 'Islam accepts a composite state of Muslims and non-Muslims ensuring equality of status, treatment and liberty of both groups. For instance, it states that the Jews who attached thus to our commonwealth shall be protected from all insults and vexations; they shall have an equal right with our own people to our assistance and good offices. It further provided that Jews would practise their religion as freely as the Muslim.'[5]

When the largest Islamic state in the contemporary world namely—Pakistan was established in 1947—its founder, Muhammad Ali Jinnah, declared: 'You may belong to any religion or caste or creed—that is nothing to do with the business of the state. There is no discrimination, no distinction between one community and another, no distinction between one caste or creed or another. We are starting with the fundamental principle that we are all citizens and equal citizens of one state.'[6]

Jinnah's comments led many people to interpret that he was not a believer in the concept of an Islamic state, that he forsook his theory of the 'two nation theory' with which he fought for Pakistan and that he now advocated a secular State. Again this is an unfair interpretation of Jinnah's speech. What Jinnah said in the Pakistan constituent assembly was reflected in the constitution of al-Madinah as founded by the Prophet of Islam. Islam strictly forbids religious intolerance and fanaticism. Islam is tolerant to other religions. When some Muslims, whether a king or a despot or a group of people, destroy the place of worship of any other religious group, such as a temple or church, in the name of Islam, they do positive disservice to the ideals and principles of Islam. 'Islam prevailed because it was the best social and political order the times could offer. It prevailed because everywhere it found politically apathetic peoples, robbed, oppressed, bullied, uneducated and unorganized and it found selfish and unsound governments out of touch with people. . . It was the broadest, freshest and cleanest political idea that had yet come into actual activity in the world and it offered better terms than any other to the masses of mankind.'[7]

Reverting to our analysis of the Constitution of al-Madinah, we find that Muslims were given some special obligation: they were to cherish fellow Muslims who were indebted and not kill a believer because of his action with non-believers.

It has to be pointed out the Constitution of al-Madinah was a simple document set up on the strong moral base of Islam. Some of the common paraphernalia that one finds in a modern constitution was lacking in it. For instance, there was no provision for an organized secretariat, no regular police force, no established court of justice, there was only a voluntary army. Muhammad repeatedly impressed upon the people, both Muslims and non-Muslims, that they were to maintain law and order by themselves and that they must guard the security of the state.[8]

While discussing the features of an Islamic state we pointed out the principle of mutual consultation or *shurah* as one of the fundamental requirements of an Islamic state. The Prophet practised the principle of mutual consultation on every crucial problem; before taking any important decision he would consult with his companions as well as with various groups of society.[9] This was no doubt a democratic principle at a stage of human history when the idea of a ruler exercising public affairs through mutual consultation was an unknown phenomenon. As Ameer Ali in his classic work, *The Spirit of Islam*, tells us: ' . . . Muhammad a mastermind, not only of his age, as Munir calls him, but of all ages. No wild dreamer he, bent upon pulling down the existing fabrics of society, but a statesman of unrivalled powers, who in an age of utter and hopeless disintegration, with such materials and such polity as God put ready to his hands, set himself to the task of reconstructing a state, a commonwealth, a society upon the basis of universal humanity.'[10]

Not only was religious protection given to the Jews, a similar guarantee was given to the Christians of Najran and the neighbouring territories after Islam fully established itself in the Arabian peninsula. Christians were given the security of their lives, religion and property. He declared: 'There should be no interference with the practice of their faith or their observance nor any change in their rights or privileges.'[11]

Ameer Ali's concluding remarks on the Prophet's Constitution of al-Madinah were:

> Islam gave to the people a code which, however archaic in its simplicity, was capable of the greatest development in accordance with the progress of material civilization. It conferred on the state a flexible constitution, based on a just appreciation of human rights and human duty. It limited taxation, it made men equal in the eye of the law, it consecrated the principles of self-government. It established a control over the sovereign power by rendering the executive authority subordinate to the law—a law based upon religious sanction and moral obligations.[12]

The First Four Khalifahs *(Caliphs),* al-Khulafa' al-Rashidun

The Prophet Muhammad's death in 632 created a big vacuum in the infant community of Islam. According to the Quran, Muhammad was the seal of prophethood, he was the last prophet (Surah 33: 40); his successors, *khalifahs*, inherited the office of leading the community in matters such as prayer, war, and adjudicating disputes among the followers of Islam in the context of Quranic principles. Muhammad did not designate any successor because in Islam there is no principle of hereditary succession; the rulers in an Islamic state must be selected by the people in whom the sovereignty of God is vested. It is, therefore, no wonder that the Prophet himself or his immediate four successors, the 'Rightly Guided Caliphs', did not choose any of their successors; when the head of the state in an Islamic state dies or leaves office, the succession will have to be decided by the Islamic principle of *shurah*, mutual consultation, which in modern times must mean through the universal electorate, as Islam does not recognize any privileged group. There is no priesthood in Islam, there are no special agents of God recognized, the right to rule is not necessarily associated with any special form of government nor any particular group. Nobody can claim the automatic right to govern because the sovereignty of God is to be exercised by the people as a whole and not for the interest of one person or one group.

The short period of the 'Rightly Guided Caliphs' (632-661) may be regarded as the golden era in the history of the growth of the Islamic community. Though there was fighting, tension even, during this golden era, the first four successors of the Prophet Muhammad were the embodiment of all virtues. They tried to lead the emerging Islamic community on the right path as taught in the Quran and as practised by Muhammad. It provided an idealistic period to which Muslims have looked back for inspiration and guidance, a time, to be remembered and emulated.

The spiritual guidance of Muhammad and his practical life had inculcated a sense of devotion to the right causes, a sense of self-sacrifice and service to humanity. The first four caliphs tried to follow Prophet Muhammad's practices as the head of the state to the best of their abilities but, of course, the highest guiding factor was the Quran itself.

Abu Bakr, the Prophet's father-in-law and the first adult male who converted to Islam became the first caliph. Abu Bakr applied himself in organizing and strengthening Islamic rule in Arabia. There was a series of trivial revolts. Factionalism which was controlled by the Prophet himself began to raise its head and Abu Bakr was successful in crushing the trivial revolts and consolidating Muslim rule over the entire Arabian peninsula, thus preserving the unity and solidarity of the Islamic community. Abu Bakr's rule was very short, 632-634. But even during this short period he set a unique example of fair and just rule.

Abu Bakr's successor, 'Umar, was a great military leader, he assumed the title of 'Commander of the Faithful'. He successfully sent Muslim troops to both east and west. Damascus was conquered in 635, Egypt in 639-645 and most of Persia between 640-644. 'Umar was assassinated in 644.

'Uthman Ibn 'Affan became the third caliph (644-656). Tribal conflicts and rivalries characterized 'Uthman's reign. In 656, 'Uthman was assassinated by a group of mutineers from Egypt. 'Uthman made the final rescension of the Quran. He was killed while reading the Quran. His murder began the era of fightings and tension within the Islamic community which greatly hampered its political development.

'Uthman was succeeded by 'Ali who was the cousin and son-in-law of Prophet (the husband of the Prophet's only surviving child, Fatimah). 'Ali was successful in inspiring loyalty and commitment, but within a short period the caliphate was plunged into civil war. 'Ali's authority was challenged by two opposition movements: by a coalition headed by the Prophet Muhammad's widow, 'A'ishah, and by the forces of Mu'awiyah, governor of Syria, and a relative of 'Uthman. 'Ali was successful in crushing the first movement led by 'A'ishah but Mu'awiyah was more serious and threatening. He had organized a strong army in Syria; yet 'Ali was near victory when he made a truce with Mu'awiyah, but Mu'awiyah broke the truce and in the subsequent fighting 'Ali was killed and Mu'awiyah became the successor. Thus ended the period of the Four Rightly Guided Caliphs.

Despite the turmoil during the early caliphal years, Muslims regard, as stated above, the period of Muhammad and the first generation of companions or elders as normative for a variety of reasons. First, God sent down His final and complete revelation in the Quran and the last of his Prophets, Muhammad. Second, the Islamic community-state was created and bonded by a common religious identity and purpose. Third, the sources of Islamic law, the Quran and the example of the Prophet, originated at this time. Fourth, this period of the early companions serves as the reference point for all Islamic revivals and reforms, both traditionalist and modernist. Fifth, the success and power that resulted from the near-miraculous victories and geographic expansion of Islam, constitute, in the eyes of believers, historical validation of the message of Islam.[13]

With Mu'awiyah began the Umayyad dynasty in 661 and it lasted for a century. The Umayyad rulers moved to Damascus which became the capital of the Muslim world, while al-Madinah became the centre of the religion but without political power. Now the Islamic world extended from the western borders of China to southern France, not only did the Islamic conquest continue during this period through North Africa to Spain and France in the west and to Sind (of present-day Pakistan), central Asia and Transoxiana in the east but the basic social and legal institutions of the newly founded Islamic world were established.

When Mu'awiyah's son Yazid took power in 680, 'Ali's younger son Husayn, then in his fifties, made a bid to capture power; after all, he was the grandson of the Prophet. His elder brother Hasan had died earlier—many suspected that he was poisoned, although he had given up his claim to the caliphate. Husayn, his companions and members of the family were killed in the battle of Karbala in southern Iraq on 10 Muharram, the first month of the Islamic year.

On 10 Muharram also began the effective division of the Islamic community into two sects, namely the Sunni and Shi'ah.

Fundamental differences between Sunni and Shi'ah Muslims

The fundamental difference between Sunni and Shi'ah Muslim is the Shi'ah doctrine of the Imamate. Sunni *khalifahs* was selected or elected successors of the Prophet. They succeeded to political and military leadership, but not to Muhammad's religious authority. By contrast, for the Shi'ah the leadership of the Muslim religious community is vested in the *imam* (leader) who, though not a Prophet, is divinely inspired, sinless and an infallible religious political leader of the community; he must be a direct descendant of the Prophet Muhammad and 'Ali, the first *imam*. He has to be both political leader and religious guide, the final authority for interpreting God's will as formulated in Islamic law. Whereas after the death of Muhammad, Sunni Islam bestowed religious authority for interpreting Islam on the consensus (*ijma'*), or collective judgement, of the community, the Shi'ah believe in continuous divine guidance through their divinely inspired guide, the *imam*.

Sunni and Shi'ah Muslims also developed differences of doctrine concerning the meaning of history; for Sunni historians the early Islamic success and power were signs of God's guidance and reward to a faithful community, as well as the validation of Muslim belief and claims. For the Shi'ah, history was the theatre for the struggle of an oppressed and suppressed minority community to restore God's rule on earth over the entire community under the Imam.[14] The lives of suffering of the *imam*, like that of Husayn, were seen as embodying the oppression and suppression experienced by a persecuted minority community; the realization of a just social order under the *imam* was to remain an earnest expectation for centuries as the Islamic community remained under the Sunni *khalifahs*.

Commenting on differences between Sunnis and Shi'ahs, Ameer Ali in his *The Spirit of Islam*, points out:

> The Shiahs hold that the spiritual heritage bequeathed by Muhammad developed on Ali and his descendants. They naturally repudiate the authority of the *Jama'at* (the people) to elect a spiritual head who should supersede the rightful claims of the Prophet's family. According to the Shiahs, therefore, the Imamate descends by divine appointment in the apostolic line. The Imam, besides being a descendant of the Prophet, must possess certain qualities—he must be a *Ma'sum* or sinless, bear the purest and most unsullied character, and must be distinguished above all other men for truth and purity. It is not proper, not could it be the intention of the Almighty, they argue, that a man whose character is not unimpeachable should have the direction of the human conscience. Human choice is fallible, as is proved by the history of mankind; and the people have often accepted the worst men for their leaders. God could never have left the religious needs of man to his unaided faculty. If an

> Imam be needed, he must be one whom the conscience must accept. Accordingly they declare that if the choice of an Imam be left to the community, it would be subversive of all morality; and consequently the spiritual guidance of mankind has been entrusted to divinely-appointed persons.

According to the Sunnis, the imamate is not restricted to the family of Muhammad. The *imam* need not be just, virtuous, or irreproachable (*ma'sum*) in his life, nor need he be the most excellent or eminent being of his time; so long as he is free, adult, sane, and possessed of the capacity to attend to the ordinary affairs of state, he is qualified for election. Another doctrine in which they agree with the Church of Rome was full of momentous consequences to Islam. They hold that neither the vices nor the tyranny of the *imam* would justify his deposition: nor can the perversity or evil conduct of the *imam* or those who preside at the public divine service invalidate the prayers of the faithful. They also hold that the imamate is indivisible, and that it is not lawful to have two *imams* at one and the same time. As Christianity could yield obedience to but one pope, so the Muslim world could yield obedience to but one lawful caliph.[15]

There were also divisions and subdivisions within both Sunni and Shi'ah. The Sunnis are divided into several sub-sects, each differing from the other on various points of dogma and doctrine. These minor sectarian differences have often given rise to great bitterness and persecutions. In the main, however, they are agreed on the fundamental bases of their doctrines and laws, deriving them from four unvarying sources, viz.: (1) the Quran; (2) the *Hadith* or *Sunnah* (traditions and practices handed down from the Prophet); (3) the *ijma' al-ummah* (concordance among the followers); and (4) the *qiyas* (analogy leading to private judgement). The four most important persuasions or sects among the Sunnis are designated Hanafi, Shafi'i, Maliki and Hanbali, after their respective founders.

Isma'ilis

Another small group is known as Isma'ilis. The Isma'ili community today is known as a prosperous merchant community led by the Aga Khan; sometimes we tend to forget their early revolutionary origin. The early Isma'ilis were a revolutionary missionary movement; they attacked and assassinated Sunni political and religious leaders at one *hajj*. They extended, however, from Egypt to Sind in present-day Pakistan. For Isma'ilis, as for the Shi'ah, the Quran had two meanings, the literal and esoteric; this secret knowledge was given to the Imam and through a process of initiation to his representatives and missionaries. The followers of the *imam*, as distinguished from the majority of Muslims, constituted a religious élite who possessed the true guidance necessary for salvation and the mission to spread and propagate, by force if necessary, the message and rule of the *imam*. Often functioning as a secret organization to avoid the 'Abbasid police, Isma'ilis also used *taqiyyah*, a common Shi'ah practice that permits concealment of one's belief for self-protection or survival as a persecuted minority.

A descendant of Hasan al-Sabah, Hasan 'Ali Shah, received the honorary title Aga Khan through marriage to the daughter of the Shah. He fled to India in 1844 after an abortive revolt in Persia. Then he settled in Bombay; the Isma'ilis are led by an *imam* known as the Aga Khan whose personal fortune is immense. They have also successfully settled in East Africa, South Asia, Britain and Canada. The present Aga Khan, Prince Karim, was educated at Harvard University. As the *imam* he has been able to meet the challenges of modern times. He also supervises extensive overseas commercial and industrial investments of the Ismailis and the many educational, medical and social institutions of the Aga Khan Foundation.[16]

Reverting to our discussion of the history of Islamic political community, we now turn to 'Abbasid caliphate. The 'Abbasids ruled for more than 500 years. They shifted the capital to Baghdad which soon developed into a great centre of learning and culture, as well as the administrative and political heart of a vast Islamic world. Gradually their power waned and they remained only symbolic rulers bestowing legitimacy upon various sultans and princes who, in practice, wielded the real military power. The early centuries of 'Abbasid rule were noted for an unparalleled splendour and economic prosperity which was immortalized in the Arabian Nights (*Thousand and One Nights*) with its legendary *khalifah*, Harun al-Rashid, who ruled from 786 to 809.[17]

In a departure from the past, 'Abbasids' successes were not only by military conquest but also through trade, commerce, industry and agriculture. The enormous wealth and resources of the *khalifahs* enabled them to become great patrons of art and culture and this created a significant and lasting legacy of the 'Abbasid era in Islamic history. The development of Islamic law, the *shari'ah*, constitutes their greatest contribution to Islam. Since their predecessors, the Umayyad caliphs, failed to implement an effective legal system, 'Abbasid *khalifahs* gave a substantial impetus to legal development. The early law school, which had began during late Umayyad period (around 720), developed further under the patronage of the 'Abbasid *khalifahs* and the *'ulama'*. Although Islam has no priesthood, the '*ulama*' had become more or less a group of a distinct social class with the task of interpreting the religious laws. Their prestige and authority, however, rested in their knowledge and learning of Islamic sources, namely the Quran, *Hadith* and *Sunnah*.

The 'Abbasid caliphs were also patrons of culture and art. They also made remarkable contributions to the growth of Islamic philosophy. Islamic philosophy was the product of the successful 'transplant from Greek to Islamic soil where it flourished from the 9th to 12th centuries. Muslim philosophers acquainted themselves with Greek political philosophers like Plato, Aristotle and others.'

'The result was Islamic philosophy was indebted to Hellenism but with its own Islamic character. Its contribution was of equal importance to the West. Islamic philosophy became the primary vehicle for the transmission of men like al-Farabi, who had come to be known as the second teacher or master, the first being Aristotle, and Ibn Sina (Avicenna) noted as the great commentator on Aristotle.' Thus one finds many great medieval political philosophers, such as St Thomas Aquinas and others, acknowledged their intellectual debt to their Muslim predecessors.[18]

The reputed Western scholar Annemarie Schimmel elaborates the Islamic contributions to Western philosophy:

> One characteristic trait of early Islamic philosophy is the belief that there is fundamentally no difference between Plato and Aristotle: this viewpoint is clearly expressed in the writings of Aristotle's first great commentator, the Central Asian al-Farabi (d. 950 in Aleppo). He, as well as his successors, claimed the unity of philosophy and Islamic revelation, and taught that God created the world by His thinking. Ibn Sina, physician and philosopher (famed in the West as Avicenna) (d. 1037), continued the ideas of his predecessors: God is the *prima causa*, and everything that might possibly exist has its essential pre-existence in God's knowledge.

Ibn Rushd, known in the West as Averroes, further elaborated the doctrine of the fundamental agreement between philosophy and revelation. Philosophy has to explain the truth of the prophets' messages in a more sophisticated form, and human kind has to be instructed in one way or another according to their capacity of understanding.

Avicenna's work on medicine was used in Europe for many centuries. Numerous concepts in science reveal an Arabo-Islamic heritage—the names of stars, and mathematical terms like 'algebra' and 'algorithm', as well as Arabic numerals which, like zero, originated in India and were brought to the West by the Muslims. Without these mathematical tools, modern mathematics could not have developed. Optics and geometry are also part of the Islamic heritage. In medieval Islamic society natural sciences and medicine occupied an important place. The scientific achievements of medieval Muslims are especially remarkable; they not only translated, reworked, and enlarged the Greek sources at their disposal, but by doing so they essentially formed the bases for modern exact sciences.[19]

Among later Muslim philosophical thinkers, Ibn Khaldun (d. 1406) deserves pride of place; he has been styled the 'first sociologist', not only in Islam but in all history. His fundamental concept is that of *'asabiyyah*, the *ésprit de corps*, common activity, or group spirit. The *'asabiyyah* is a tremendously important socio-psychological factor which, combined with religious zeal, can lead a people to victory over others. Ibn Khaldun shows how states grow, reach their zenith after some three generations, and then spread out too far weakening and waning, while at their borders new, young states emerge, which wax and wane in the same rhythm. This process repeated itself time and again in Islamic history.[20]

Ibn Khaldun's contributions of linking Islamic heritage to the West is widely acknowledged. As Akbar S Ahmad tells:

> Ibn Khaldun's *Kitab al-'Ibar*, world history, ranks high in the esteem of scholars. For Arnold Toynbee 'it is undoubtedly the greatest work of its kind that has ever yet been created by any mind in any time or place'. In it the author deploys his knowledge of history, philosophy, logic, dreams, tribal ways, mathematics, and climate from the Arab world and beyond. Arab narrative and interpretive history culminated in the work of Ibn Khaldun. He was a jurist, historian, scholar, traveller and statesman, and for us today, the father of sociology, to which he gave the name *'Ilm al-imran*, the science of society. Some of the central formulae of the modern age are reflected in Ibn Khaldun's theories: Karl Marx's stages of human history which provide the dynamics for the dialectics of conflict between groups; Max Weber's typology of leadership; Vilfredc Pareto's circulation of elites; Ernest Gellner's pendulum swing theory of Islam, oscillating from an urban, formal, literate tradition to a rural, informal and mystical one.[21]

The 'Abbasid caliphate was finally abolished when Hulagu the Mongol captured Baghdad, destroying much of the city including its invaluable libraries, books, etc.

Islamic History in Asia After the Mongols: Post Caliphal Period (1500-1920)

The Mongols devastated the eastern lands of Islam and ruled from the Sinai desert to India for a century, but they were later succeeded by Timur and his descendants who made Samarqand their capital, now in the modern Central Asian republic of the demised Soviet Union. The Timurids ruled from 1369 to about 1500.

The post-caliphal period was both a dynamic and an expansionist period of Islamic history. 'The central and unifying caliphate system was replaced by a number of Muslim sultanates which governed an area that eventually extended from North Africa to South-east Asia as Islam progressively renovated East, West and Central Africa, Central and South-east Asia, and Eastern Europe.'[22]

By the sixteenth century, three major Muslim empires were established in the midst of the sultanates: the Ottoman empire in the Middle East and Eastern Europe, the Shi'ite Safavid empire in Persia, and the Mughal empire in India. Harnessing gunpowder technology, these 'gunpowder empires', whose central governments were supported by a blend of religious ideology and military strength, dominated the heartlands of the Islamic world: North Africa, the Middle East and South Asia. With the dynamic expansion of Islam during the period of these three Muslim empires, history continued to witness the vitality, success and divine guidance of God's commonwealth.

The great success and glory of the Islamic empires during the sixteenth and seventeenth centuries were really spectacular. The problems of dealing with the great diversity of peoples and cultures that had been brought under the control of the Muslim empires were, however, complex and created a chain of strains and stresses within the Muslim world. The three Muslim empires had to adjust to regional and local conditions and traditions; but, overall, Islamic tradition continued to govern the world of Islam. Religious toleration towards non-Muslim subjects of the three Muslim empires was a remarkable feature of the Islamic spirit of equality and justice to all. This religious tolerance remained one of the strong points of the foundation of the Muslim empires. The great expansion of Islam during the 16th and 17th centuries did not challenge the old cultures within the fold of the three large Muslim empires. As Marshall Hodgson, wrote: 'it was a florescence within established lines of tradition, rather perfecting than launching them . . . perhaps we may say that this florescence was not of origination but rather of culmination in a culture already long mature.'[23]

In the course of time, internal stresses and external challenges brought the downfall of the three Muslim empires. Of the three, the Ottoman empire was perhaps the most firmly established. The Ottoman sultans could, in a broad sense, assert leadership in Islamic terms as caliphs—not in the universal sense of the 'Abbasid caliphate, but as upright and just sovereigns who respected the *shari'ah*. Ottoman intellectuals, following earlier Islamic scholars that any law-abiding Muslim ruler could be termed a caliph, argued that Ottoman emperors should be known as the greatest caliphs because they did more than any others to expand the rule of Islam and because they paid proper homage to the *shari'ah* and its guardians, the *'ulama'*.[24]

The fall of the Ottoman empire accelerated in the nineteenth century and it was caused by both internal and external forces. Attempts at reform to revitalize the empire were not adequate, separatist movements gradually diminished the effective control of the central authority. More important, interventions by the European powers greatly curtailed the sovereignty of the Ottoman empire. The European intrusions took the form of imposed settlements, such as the resolution of the Greek insurrection of the 1820s; Muhammad Ali's conquest of Syria in the 1830s; the Civil War in Lebanon in 1860; and the Balkan crisis in the 1870s. The Ottoman empire became the 'sick man of Europe'. Subsequently the Europeans engaged in outright partition of the Empire. Britain had already established dominance over the Arab sheikhdoms in the Gulf and Saudi Arabia. France conquered Algeria in 1830 and extended its control over North Africa, including Tunisia in 1881 and Morocco in 1912. Italy occupied Libya in 1911. The Fertile Crescent provinces which were part of the Ottoman empire were reorganized and placed under mandatory British administration under the auspices of the League of Nations after the First World War. Turkey proper was defeated in the First World War and much of its empire was parcelled out to France, Italy, Great Britain, the Armenians and the Kurds, though this was resisted by the Turks under Ataturk's leadership. By 1918, then, the entire Middle East, with the exception of the Yemen and central Arabia, had been partitioned into zones of foreign occupation or influence. Iran and Afghanistan, the two independent Muslim countries of south-west Asia, were brought under the indirect foreign influence of Britain and Russia.

The collapse of the Safavid and Mughal empires was due to internal dissensions and crises rather than direct foreign intervention. The Europeans came into the picture when the two empires were already in the process of disintegration.

The Mughal empire in India was confronted by deteriorating relations between Muslims and Hindus (who constituted the majority of the population) and a weakening of the central authority over the provincial governments. Power-struggles over the succession to the throne were another important factor. Aurangzib (1658-1707) was the last effective Mughal emperor and the post-Aurangzib era was marked by various regional tensions and conflicts between Muslim and non-Muslim local lords or princes. The Hindus in the south, who had been subdued by Aurangzib, rose up against the imperial authority in Delhi and pushed their way north.

Another great setback to Mughal power was the invasion by Nadir Shah from Iran in 1739 which made the empire vulnerable to successive invasions by Afghans. More disastrous was the fact that by the second half of the eighteenth century, French and British colonialists started penetrating along the south-east coast, and in Bengal European activity became an element in the disintegration of the Mughal Empire. Controlling only a small territory around Agra and Delhi, 'the Mughal dynasty was among many on the Indian chessboard.'[25] The Mughals lasted, on paper, until 1857 when the British finally consolidated their empire after crushing an Indian uprising known as the Sepoy Mutiny.

The Safavid empire in Iran was also in the process of withering away. By 1736, the Safavids were ousted. The emperor was not in control even in his capital, Isfahan.

The 'Dark Period'—Domination of the Muslim World by European Colonial Rulers

The fall of the Muslim empires was followed by the European colonial empire, created with the help of their industrial, technological and military powers. Now began a 'dark period' for the world of Islam, which continued until the end of the Second World War and the subsequent destruction of the European colonial empires, which began in 1947 when the then largest Muslim state, Pakistan, was created out of the British empire in India. Muslim subjugation to European powers in the two preceding centuries was a terrible shock to Islamic tradition and heritage. 'It has never been easy for Muslims to submit to the rule of a non-Muslim or to countenance the loss of lands where Islam had once prevailed. The era of European imperialism evokes bitter memories for Muslims.'[26] The fact was that the Muslims were subjugated to the same Christian European powers with whom they had fought holy wars during the era of the Crusades. The Muslim duty to wage *jihad* (holy war) to expand the lands under Islam was often misconstrued as the forcible conversion of Christians. 'By the same token, Muslims had learned about the "church militant" through the crusades, which led, at times, to the despoiling of mosques, the theft of art objects and manuscripts, the forced conversion of some Muslims and the massacre of others. Memories such as these aroused a deep and often bitter antagonism between the two religions.'[27] With this bitter historical background, it was a tragedy beyond measure for the world of Islam to accept the domination and rule of Christian colonial powers. Thus began a new era in the history of Islam: an era of seeking liberation and emancipation from alien political and social orders imposed on them by superior military might. The depth of the pathos of the Muslims was quite often not properly or adequately understood in the West. For example, Professor Bernard Lewis, a noted orientalist, wrote: 'To the modern Western mind it is not conceivable that men would fight and die in such great numbers over mere differences of religion, there have to be some other "genuine" reasons underneath the religious veil.'[28] Similar misconceptions about the protests of the Islamic world against an alien political subjugation, about their cultural and spiritual heritage, and about their cherished ways of life, are found in works such as John Laffin's *Dagger of Islam*, G H Jansen's *Militant Islam*, and in other works on Islam.

Islamic Reaction to European Colonialism

Muslim thinkers and intellectuals began to examine the factors for the eclipse of Muslim rule and their subjugation to Western European powers. What led to the decay of the dynamic elements in Islam? Why had the vigour and glory of Islam's early days withered away? 'The fundamental malaise of modern Islam', as Wilfred Cantwell Smith tells, 'is a sense that something has gone wrong with Islamic history. The fundamental problem of modern Muslims is how to rehabilitate their history; to set it going again in full vigour, so that Islamic society may once again flourish as a divinely guided society should and must.'[29]

We shall give a resumé of the reforms suggested by the Muslim thinkers during the 'dark period' of colonial rule and of the Muslim nationalist movements for liberation from foreign rule.

Politically, the Muslim renaissance has expressed itself in movements to throw off outside domination and attain national independence. A serious effort to stem the internal decay of the community was launched in India by Shah Waliullah of Delhi in the late 18th century and carried on by his descendants and disciples through the early decades of the 19th. However, the struggle against the Europeans achieved serious proportions in the last quarter of the 19th century. The earliest hero of the rebirth was an energetic Muslim of disputed origin named Jamal al-Din, sometimes called al-Afghani, who travelled throughout the Islamic world urging Muslims to reject foreign hegemony and seize their own destiny afresh through revolutionary means.

In the period between the two World Wars, pressures mounted throughout the Muslim world for the end of foreign domination. The Arab countries, where nationalism had stirred in the 19th century, obtained their independence from Ottoman rule as a consequence of the First World War, only to fall under European mandates.

The Rise of the Muslim Reformist Movement

Serious efforts to stem the internal decay of the Muslim community were launched by a group of reformists. Let us now refer to some of these great reformers who started this process of rethinking and rediscovering the true spirit and meaning of Islam.

'Europe,' as a perceptive Muslim scholar points out, 'England, France, Germany, Japan, Portugal, Italy, insatiably swallowed Muslim lands; Russia displayed a similar appetite for the Muslim Central Asian states, one by one, kingdoms and states, large and small, fell. The Europeans were able to subjugate what had been established as a complex civilization. Colonial rule paralysed Muslim societies, congealed thought and froze their history. European notions of race and class entered and became part of Muslim society. Worse, the colonial period destroyed Muslim confidence creating in them an image of child-like helplessness.'[30]

One of the earliest reformists was Sayyid Jamal al-Din al-Afghani (1838-1897). He was 'a philosopher, writer, orator, journalist and political activist; he travelled widely from India and Afghanistan to Istanbul, Cairo, Paris, London, stirring in Muslims the consciousness of their potential strength in the face of colonialism. He is the father of modern Muslim nationalism, proponent of Pan-Islam and the main aspiration for the reform movement in Islam. He expresses almost all the attitudes and the themes that are commonplace in Muslim apologetics from 1900 to the present.' Afghani said 'let me repeat for you, reader, one more time, that unlike other religions, Islam is concerned not only with the life to come, Islam is more: it is concerned with its believers' interests in the world here below and with allowing them to realize success in this life as well as peace in the next life. It seeks "good fortune in two words", in its teaching it decrees equally among different peoples and nations.'[31]

He lamented: 'the times have been so cruel and life so hard and confusing that some Muslims have lost patience and assert with difficulty that Islamic principles are their oppressors and they gave up using religious principles of justice in their actions. They resort even to the protection of a foreign power but are filled with regret at the things that result on that course of action.'[32] He then stated that the divisions which have affected Muslim states originate only from the failure of the rulers who deviate from the road followed by their early ancestors.

Afghani, in his various speeches and writings, pinpointed the Muslims' lack of progress in science and technology. He attributed the success of European colonial powers to their achievements in science. He strongly argued that the Muslims acquire modern scientific knowledge without which the Muslims would not be able to get rid of European subjugation. His call was for 'reopening the door of .i.*ijtihad* (independent opinion) ;so as to put an end of stagnation in Islam.[33]

> The Europeans have now put their hands on every part of the world. The English have reached Afghanistan. The French have seized Tunisia. In reality these usurpations, aggression and conquests have not come from the French or the English, rather it is science that everywhere manifests its greatness and power. Ignorance has no alternative to prostrating itself humbly before science and acknowledging its submission.'[34]

To Afghani 'philosophy and science should no longer be concerned with celestial souls and bodies, the Platonic Idea, the four elements of water, earth, air and fire, the incorruptibility of the souls, passive and active categories. Rather their subject-matter would henceforth have to include questions such as causes of the inferiority and backwardness of the community, the proper remedy for such a distressing condition and the best available means to be used in bringing about reform.'[35]

Afghani travelled through the Islamic world, urging Muslims to reject foreign domination through revolutionary means. His aim was to rediscover the inherent strength of Islam and its proper spirit and meaning in changing modern circumstances.

Shaykh Muhammad 'Abduh (1849-1905) and Others

'Abduh received a traditional religious education but was

transformed by his contact with Jamal-al-Din al-Afghani. Exiled by the British, he spent time in Beirut and Tripoli, then in Paris, where for a period he edited a weekly paper with Afghani. He returned to hold high religious posts, including that of Mufti of Egypt. His desire to reform Islam and put it in harmony with modern times by a return to primitive purity pushed him to theological reflection and writing which made him the founder of modernist school in Islam.[36] Religiously, the Muslim awakening was characterized by a conviction of Islam's relevance to the changed circumstances of modern life. Far from abandoning their ancient religious heritage, the Muslims have seen its reaffirmation as the key to their future strength and success. The principal pupil of Jamal al-Din al-Afghani, the Egyptian savant, Muhammad 'Abduh, for example, advocated a modernizing reform of traditional religious education and put forward an interpretation of Islam by which he hoped to open the door to progress and new life. He attacked the principle of *taqlid* (the four traditional schools of Muslim Law), and the pettifogging of medievalist lawyers. 'Abduh held that Islamic teaching is, above all, rational in its essence, that Islam approves, indeed urges, the exercise of the intellectual faculty so that religion and science can never be in conflict. He wished to see Islam reborn of its own strength by a return to its original character. His work was also motivated by the need to defend Islam against both implied and explicit criticisms of the West.

The religious revival of Islam is also notable for its dynamism. Modernist thinkers believe Islam, when truly understood, to be an imperative to determined action. The concept of reform in Islam during the period of its struggle against European colonialism was developed by thinkers in the Salafiyya movement. After the death of 'Abduh, Rashid Rida became the 'mouthpiece of 'Abduh'. Rida, however, maintained his own distinctive position. 'Islamic reform', John Esposito points out, 'was the *sine qua non* for the revitalization of the Muslim community and restoration of its lost political power and prosperity.'[37] Rida attributed the decline in Islam to stagnation and the blind following of the medieval schools of Islamic jurisprudence. Like Iqbal, Rida was in favour of the reform and reconstruction of Islamic law through the process of *ijtihad*—the use of analogical reasoning in legislation: Muslim thinkers must resort to speculative reason in interpreting Islamic law. Islam, according to these reformers, is not static, but a dynamic force capable of meeting the needs of changing circumstances. Rida stated: 'creed and ritual were completed in detail so as to permit neither additions nor subtractions . . . but as for the rules of *Muamalat* (social laws), beyond decreeing the elements of virtue and establishing penalties for certain crimes, the Lawgiver, Allah, delegated the affair in its detailed applications to the leading *'ulama'* and rulers, who according to law, must possess knowledge and moral probity, to decide by consulting one another what is more beneficial for the community according to the circumstances of the time.'[38] The Islamic reformists, such as Rida in the Middle East and Iqbal in India, were firm believers in the need for the development of a modern Islamic legal system. According to these reformists there are two parts in *shari'ah*, the immutable and the mutable parts. The former consists of clear and unambiguous Quranic injunctions which cannot be changed; but the Quran gives only broad guidelines and general principles. Where the Quran is silent, it is for the Muslim thinkers and intellectuals to resort to *ijtihad*, individual judgment, to bring about desirable changes in accordance with needs and changing circumstances. Without this dynamic element, Islam would not be able to meet the challenges from the West, nor would the Islamic forces enable Muslims to carry out their struggle for national liberation against Western colonial rule.

Parallel Islamic reform and nationalist movements took place in the Maghrib in the late 19th and early 20th centuries. The Salafiyyah movement spread to the Maghrib. Political parties like the Istiqlal party in Morocco, the Dester and Neo-Dester parties in Tunisia and the National Liberation Front in Algeria were examples of such manifestations. 'Islam was integral to the development of nationalist ideologies: Egyptian, Arab, and Iranian nationalism, as well as Tunisian, Algerian, Moroccan and Pakistani nationalism.'[39] It is, however, obvious that not all political activities in the world of Islam in the 19th and early 20th centuries were exclusively Islamic in character. Most of the prominent leaders of the Muslim nationalist movements belonged to an upper middle-class elite and many of them were educated in the West—in England, France or the United States. They were influenced by Western concepts of modern nationalism in the modern period. Their orientation was therefore partially secular, but they found in Islam an effective and useful force for the unification of tribal or regional and linguistic groups into well-knit national identities. So even the Western-educated section of the Muslim nationalist movements did not relinquish their religious identity, the common Islamic heritage. The development of modern Muslim nationalism was therefore a product of Islamic tradition (reformed by thinkers like 'Abduh and Rashid Rida in the Middle East and Iqbal in the Indian subcontinent), as well as secularism. 'Islam served', as a Western scholar points out, 'as a unifying rallying cry, providing an identity and allegiance, ideology and symbols, leadership and mosque-based communication centers.'[40]

The 'dark period' of Islamic history finally ended after the Second World War when the European colonial powers were so exhausted and confronted with so many internal problems of economic reconstruction that they could not longer face the challenge of the nationalist movements in the Islamic world, as well as in other parts of Asia and Africa. The process of the liquidation of the colonial empires of the Western powers began, in some cases, in a voluntary manner (as in British India), but in many cases after bitter fighting (as in Algeria, Morocco, Tunisia, Indonesia, Malaya, and in many other Afro-Asian countries). But once the process began, in the 1950s and 1960s, one country after another began to gain independence. Today the world of Islam consists of about sixty countries.

From the mid-20th century, the fortunes of the Muslims began to improve: Iran and Turkey became unfettered in the 1920s, Syria and Jordan in 1945 and 1946; Pakistan in 1947 and Indonesia in 1949, forming at the time the two largest Muslim countries with a combined population of over 200 million. Then in the 1950s and 1960s the African Muslim countries started gaining independence, so that by the mid-1960s the Muslims of the Central Asian Republics of the USSR and of the Indian union (post-1947) remained the most sizeable groups under non-Muslim rule. The 'dark period' of colonial rule was over. 'Independence brought a surge of confidence to Muslim societies, as they were now relieved of the weakness of the declining years of alien rule.'[41] Islamic political revitalization is still in the process.

Reformist Movement in South Asia

Let us now turn to the South Asian sub-continent, namely British India. As the Mughal empire began to crumble under British economic and military penetration, as well as to the rise of internal revolts, Sayyid Ahmad Shahid (1786-1831) and Isma'ili Shahid (1779-1831) took up the task of purification of Islam and proclaimed *jihad* in its true and real meaning against foreign domination, as well as to achieve a free and fair society. Their movement, however, derived inspiration from the puritan teaching of Shah Waliullah (1703-62), and his son 'Abd al-'Aziz (died in 1824). Shah Waliullah was a great personality and has a great place in the Islamic reformist movement in the early stage of European colonial imperialism. They had argued in their various speeches and writings the urgent need of reviving Islam and eliminating the harmful effect of foreign rule on Islam. They were successful in establishing a short-lived state in the tribal region of north-west frontier of the British empire and parts of Afghanistan, but this state began to crumble soon after its foundation; finally it was destroyed in 1831. Shah Waliullah and his son were the pioneers of the Islamic reformist movement in the Indian sub-continent.

Shah Waliullah tried to give what was termed as the true meaning of the Quran. The Quran, according to him, was 'obfuscated by and hidden under numerous, commentaries and super-commentaries—philosophical, philological and mystical interpretations that have been composed through the ages.'[42]

Glowing tributes have been paid by many scholars to Shah Waliullah's contributions to the reformist movement in India. A Western author tells about Shah Waliullah's role: 'Shah Wali Allah lived during a critical period for Indian Muslims. The power of the Mughal empire was in decline. A Muslim minority community faced not only the disintegration of its political rule, challenged by Hindu and Sikh uprisings, but also the internal disunity of conflicting factions: Sunni and Shi'i, *Hadith* and legal scholars, *'ulama'* and sufis. Educated in Mecca and a contemporary of Muhammad ibn 'Abd al-Wahhab, Wali Allah was also a member of the revivalist-oriented Naqshbandi order. He followed in the footsteps of the great revivalist of seventeenth-century India, Shaykh Ahmad Sirhindi. Like Shaykh Ahmad, he asserted the need for Muslims to purge their lives of un-Islamic practices and to reform popular Sufi practices, which he believed were responsible for much of the religious syncretism that threatened the identity, moral fibre, and survival of Indian Islam in its multiconfessional setting. As with other revivalists, the purification and renewal of Islam were contingent on a return to the pristine *shari'ah*, grounded in its two infallible sources, the Quran and *Sunnah*.'[43]

It may be added here that 'Islam, from its earliest days, possessed a tradition of revival and reform. Muslims had been quick to respond to what they regarded as the compromising of faith and practice: Kharijite secession, Shi'i revolts, the development of Islamic law, and Sufism. In succeeding centuries, a rich revivalist tradition expressed itself in a variety of concepts and beliefs in the lives and teachings of individual reformers, and in the activities of a host of movements.' 'The concepts of renewal (*tajdid*) and reform (*islah*) are fundamental components of Islam's world view, rooted in the Quran and *Sunnah* of the Prophet. Both concepts involve a call for a return to the fundamentals of Islam (the Quran and *Sunnah*). *Islah* is a Quranic term (7: 10; 11: 117, 28: 19) used to describe the reform preached and undertaken by the prophets when they warned their sinful communities and called on them to return to God's path by realigning their lives, as individuals and as community, within the norms of the *shari'ah*. This Quranic mandate, epitomized in the lives and preaching of the prophets, especially that of Muhammad, coupled with God's command to enjoin good and prohibit evil (3: 104,110), provides the time-honoured rationale for Islamic reformism, however diverse its manifestations in history.'[44]

Sir Sayyid Ahmad Khan

When Indian Muslims were passing through a very dark period of persecution and prosecution by British authorities, after the mutiny of 1857 which is now called as 'the first independence war', there emerged a Muslim leader of great vision and personality. He was Sir Sayyid Ahmad Khan (1817-1898). His role was greatly misunderstood by his contemporary Muslims in India. He advised the Muslims to become cooperative rather than confront British authority. This he did out of his assessment of the realities prevailing at that time. The orthodox leaders, *'ulama'* asked the Muslims not to learn English or to have anything to do with modern science and scientific education. Sir Sayyid Ahmad could foresee the danger of such a path. Already the Indian Muslims were backward in many respects as a result of British policy at that time. The Muslims, according to Sayyid Ahmad, were not in a position to continue a confrontational attitude towards the British authorities. So, like many other Muslim reformists, Sayyid Ahmad advised the Muslims, to learn English and modern sciences. He established the Mohammedan Anglo-Oriental College at Aligarh in 1874 which became the Muslim Aligarh University.

Sir Sayyid Ahmad's policy was interpreted as timid and pro-British, but history has proved that his policy was not merely out of his alleged loyalty to British authority. It was sincere advice and guidance to the Muslims of India at that stage of political development. Subsequently, Aligarh University played a vital role in the Muslim rationalist movement in the Indian sub-continent. In fact, during the movement for a separate state of Muslims (Pakistan), Aligarh University turned out to be the main proponent and produced hundreds of young Muslims who played significant roles in the creation of Pakistan under the leadership of Muhammad Ali Jinnah. Aligarh University was a great source of inspiration. Without Sayyid Ahmad's advice, Muslims would have remained in a state of backwardness for a long time.

Sir Muhammad Iqbal (1877-1938)

Sir Muhammad Iqbal was the most dynamic and foreceful political figure in the Indian Muslim nationalist movement till the rise of Muhammad Ali Jinnah. It was Iqbal, who in his presidential address at the Muslim League meeting in 1930, first gave expression to the idea of a separate state for the Muslim of India. He was, however, basically a poet-philosopher. He acquired a Western education in Germany. In his classic work, *The Reconstruction of Religious Thought in Islam*, Iqbal made strong arguments in favour of redefining Islam. He was a great believer in using *ijtihad* or *qiyas*; like Muhammad 'Abduh and his follower Rashid Rida, Iqbal was a great believer in overhauling the classical four schools of Islamic law. He was in favour, as 'Abduh and Rashid Rida were, of the dynamic interpretation of Islamic laws. Iqbal believed in individual judgment in reinterpreting the existing four schools of Islamic law. Iqbal was a fascinating personality among the Muslim reformers.

The Quran gives basic principles and guidance without deviating from the fundamentals of the Quran; the Muslim must give proper and dynamic interpretation of Islamic laws. The Quran is a great awakener of the human faculty of knowledge. God has created human beings with knowledge and they must exercise knowledge in order to make Islam a working force in accordance with changing circumstances and time. 'The Koran', as Schimmel rightly says, 'is the basis for the entire life, be it the regulation of religious duties or problems of art . . . The possibilities of interpreting the Book (The Koran) in the most diverse ways seems to be a strong proof of its supernatural origin. As God's word, it has to be as infinite as He Himself and thus its different possibilities have never ceased to occupy the minds of scholars, mystics and simple believers'[45]

The Muslim reformers whom we have discussed in the preceding pages did great services to the subsequent Muslim nationalist movements for liberation against colonial rule.

Islam's Role as a Nation-Building Force

There are always many factors in the creation of any nation state, viz. political, economic, cultural, sociological etc. Religion is also an important factor particularly in the Afro-Asian world. So, Islam played a significant role in liberation of the Muslim world from European domination. We do not claim that Islam was the only factor or even the most important factor in the creation of contemporary Muslim states; with the exception of a few cases such as Pakistan and Saudi Arabia, religion had no vital role in the national movement. In most of the cases a national movement was carried forward by a Western-educated urban élite. Western political philosophers, like

John Locke, J S Mill and others, had a great impact on the minds of urban Muslim leaders while they were engaged in fighting against foreign domination.

However, in order to get wide support from the Muslim masses they had to rely on Islam. Islam provided them an excellent tool in rousing enthusiasm and support from the Muslim rural population.

As we have pointed out, Islamic movements like the Salafiyya, Wahabbi, and Mahdi movements, were of great significance in the liberation movement of modern Muslim states. As John Esposito puts it 'revival and reform have been dominant themes in Islam since the eighteenth century, as Muslims responded to internal and external forces that challenged their faith and social order. Islam was used effectively in the formation of Islamic socio-political reform organizations and Islamic modernist movements . . . which demonstrated the power of an appeal to Islam in providing a rationale for community decline and initiating religio-political movements bent on social and moral reform.'[46]

Notes

1 W C Smith, *Pakistan As An Islamic State*, Lahore, 1951, 5-6.
2 For text of the 'Constitution of Medina', see W Montgomery Watt, *Muhammad at Madina*, London, 1956, 221-28.
3 Muhammad Husayn Haykal, *The Life of Mohammad*, 1976, 183.
4 See *Muhammad at Madina*, 228.
5 Rafiq Zakaria, *The Struggle within Islam, the Conflict Between Religion and Politics*, New York, 1989, 29.
6 See Quadi Azam M A Jinnah's speech in Pakistan (First) Constituent Assembly on 11 August, 1947, cited in G W Choudhury, *Constitutional Development in Pakistan* (2nd Edition), London, 1970, 120.
7 H G Wells, *Outlines of History*, London, 1956, 613-614.
8 Rafiq Zakaria, *op. cit.*, 31.
9 See Choudhury, G W, *The Prophet Muhammad: His Life and Eternal Message*, London, 1993, chapter 3.
10 *Spirit of Islam*, 58.
11 G W Chowdhury, *op. cit.*, 121.
12 *Spirit of Islam*, 277.
13 John L Esposito, *Islam: The Straight Path*, New York, 1992, 40.
14 *Op. cit.*, 45-46.
15 *Spirit of Islam*, 318-319.
16 *Islam: The Straight Path*, 47-48.
17 *Op. çit.*, 53.
18 *Op. cit.*, 54-55.
19 Annemarie Schimmel, *Islam: An Introduction*, New York, 1992, 87-89.
20 *Op. cit.*, 88.
21 Akbar S Ahmad, *Discovering Islam: Making Sense of Muslim History and Society*, London, 1989, 101.
22 John L Esposito, *Islam and Politics*, New York, 1987, 24.

[23] G S Hodgson Marshall, *The Venture of Islam*, Chicago, 1974, vol. 3, 14-15, cited in John Obert Voll, *Islam: Continuity and Change in Modern World*, vol.1, Boulder, 1982, 8.
[24] See I Metin Kunt, 'The Later Muslim Empire' in Marjorie, Kelly (ed.), *Islam: The Religious and Political Life of a World Community*, New York, 1984, 127.
[25] *Ibid.*
[26] Arthur Goldsmith Jr., 'Colonial Period', in Marjorie Kelly, *op. cit.*, 137.
[27] *Ibid.*
[28] Bernard Lewis, 'The Return of Islam' in *Middle East Review*, No. 12, 1979.
[29] Wilfred Cantwell Smith, *Islam in Modern History*, Princeton, 1957, 41.
[30] Akbar S Ahmad, *op. cit.*, 117.
[31] John J Donohue and John L Esposito, *Islam In Transition: Muslim Perspectives*, New York, 1982, 16 and 23.
[32] *Ibid.*
[33] *Islam: The Straight Path*, 128.
[34] See Youssef M Choneirj, *Islamic Fundamentalism*, Basten, 1990, 37.
[35] *Ibid.*
[36] *Islam In Transition: Muslim Perspectives, op. cit.*, 24.
[37] John Esposito, *Islam and Politics,* 61.
[38] Malcolm H Kerr, *Islamic Reform: The Political and Legal Theories of Muhammad Abduh and Rashid Rida*, Berkeley, 1966, 60.
[39] John Esposito, *Islam and Politics*, 58.
[40] *Ibid.*
[41] See Francis Ralinsen, *The Atlas of The Islamic World Since 1500,* New York, 1982, 158-9.
[42] Annemarie Schimmel, *op. cit.*, 128.
[43] *Islam: Straight Path*, 122.
[44] *Op. cit.*, 115.
[45] Annemarie Schimmel, 47.
[46] *Islam: The Straight Path,* 154-55.

Chapter IV
Islam in Modern Nation States

We have discussed how Islam, along with other factors, played a significant role during the liberation struggle against European colonial domination. Islam furnished in many cases those unifying forces which make different groups, tribes, ethnic factions gather and mould together into a nation. One after another, countries with a majority Muslim population began to emerge, sometimes in peaceful and smoother ways, sometimes after a bitter struggle with the colonial powers. These Muslim countries wanted simultaneously to make their homelands modernized, economically, scientifically and technologically developed, as well as to preserve and to foster their cultural and spiritual heritage in their socio-economic and political order.

Great debates started over the role and place of Islam in the newly-independent countries. Can a nation become modernized, as distinguished from westernized, and yet preserve Islamic values and its true spirit? This is a major issue occupying the minds of Muslim scholars, political leaders, students, journalists—in fact, all segments of Muslim society over the entire Islamic world or *ummah*.

The contemporary Muslim nation states may be classified into several categories, broadly speaking:

(i) There are some Muslim states like Afghanistan, Iran, Pakistan, Saudi Arabia, and Sudan which designate themselves Islamic states.
(ii) There is, however, the vast majority of Muslim countries which do not claim to be Islamic states; there are references to

Islam sometimes in a form such as 'state religion', or in some other way. These countries are governed mainly by Western legal codes but in personal matters such as marriage, inheritance etc., Islamic law or *shari'ah* is used. The *shari'ah*, however, is not the same in all Muslim countries. Like the term 'Islamic State', *shari'ah* has also wide and different connotations and interpretations. It is our honest contention that Islam and its ideology, if they are interpreted and applied in their true perspective as laid down in the Quran and as the Prophet of Islam, Muhammad, and his immediate four successors, 'the Rightly Guided Caliphs' had practised, Islam is perfectly compatible with a modern Muslim nation's aspirations for progress towards modernization, science and technological advancement.

As a reputed and Western-born Muslim author points out, 'the Koran is the entire basis for life, be it the regulation of religious duties or problems of art. Hence, it is natural that a vast range of interpretations and commentaries should have developed in the course of centuries . . . possibilities of interpreting the Book in the most diverse way seems to be a strong proof of its supernatural origin. As God's Word, it has to be as infinite as He Himself and thus its different possibilities have never ceased to occupy the minds of scholars, mystics and simple believers'.[1]

A conflict is going on between what we may term the traditional and the reformist groups. Whether Islam will survive the modern challenges of science and technology will depend, to a great extent, on how Islamic law, *shari'ah*, is to be treated. The role of Islam in modern Muslim nation states will be largely determined by the way the followers of Islam treat the *shari'ah*. Is it a body of static and dead injunctions, or a dynamic force capable of meeting the needs of changing times and circumstances? We can not address adequately the role of Islam in the contemporary world without resolving the fundamental issues of interpreting properly the *shari'ah*. The role of Islam in a modern complex society is a big issue and it will contribute to generating substantial debates and discussions.

(iii) There are very few Muslim countries which would prefer to have a 'Secular State' on the pattern of the Western concept of the separation of politics and religion (in the narrow concept of religion as a 'mode of worship' and not in the broader concept of Islam, which regards religion as a code of the entire human life). Turkey under Kemal Ataturk made an attempt to have a

> 'secular' constitution under the Republic of Turkey, and more recently Bangladesh after its break-away from Pakistan in 1971 made a short-lived and futile attempt to 'import' from India the concept of a secular constitution. The Bangladeshi one met its natural death in no time—now Islam is the 'State Religion' of Bangladesh and secularism has been formally given its natural burial.

In Turkey, Kemal's concept at westernization is facing new and bigger strains and stresses and perhaps the day is not far off when its secularism will also meet the same fate as in Bangladesh.

Secularism is a Western concept. It cannot be introduced in a traditional Muslim country unless there are fundamental changes in the way of life, behaviour patterns, in thinking 'on life' and 'of life' among the people. Even in India, secularism is in great trouble as a result of the rise of Hindu fundamentalist factions very recently. Seventy years of suppression, oppression and persecution and prosecution of the Muslims of the Central Asian Republics of the demised Soviet empire could not eliminate Islam and the inherent strength of Islam in the minds of 40 million followers in the demised Soviet Union is still alive. It is, we believe, a futile attempt to import secularism in the world of Islam.

Are contemporary Muslim countries Islamic?

When political scientists or scholars of comparative governments discuss the definition and connotation of a democratic state, they apply certain criteria, such as free and fair elections at periodical intervals, to be contested by more than one party, the existence of an independent judiciary, which is given the task of enforcing the fundamental rights of the citizen equally before the eyes of the law or the rule of law.

Similarly, one should apply certain criteria in judging the nature and contents of an Islamic state. Now what are the criteria for deciding whether a country's constitution is Islamic? We have stated that the Quran does not provide a blueprint for any particular constitution or any form of government. However, it provides certain basic principles for organizing a political system. The Prophet Muhammad, who is rightly described as 'Quran in practice', formulated a constitution—The Constitution of al-Madinah—which may be regarded as the model of an Islamic political order. Similarly, the actual functioning of the constitution of al-Madinah under the 'Four Rightly Guided Caliphs' may also be used as a guide to determine the character of an Islamic state.

The first principles of the Islamic constitution is the acceptance of the sovereignty of God in unqualified terms. However, the sovereignty of God does not mean that there is any individual or individuals or special group or groups who alone is or are to exercise God's authority. In the true spirit of Islam, sovereignty of God and modern democratic theory of popular sovereignty are perfectly complementary. So an Islamic state must be ruled ultimately by the people as a whole as the representatives of God. Secondly, Islam gives great stress to the rule of law. In an Islamic state nobody, even the highest authority, the ruler, (male or female) is not above the rule of law; there is no scope for arbitrary rule in a polity which claims to be based on Islam. *Shurah* (mutual consultation) in public affairs is again and again stressed in the Quran and the Prophet of Islam, as the head of the first Islamic state, would decide public affairs after mutual consultation. It means that in an Islamic state, the decision-making process must be based on a universally-elected legislative body. No hereditary succession is permissible in any Islamic state, nor any form of personal rule or dictatorship. An Islamic state should also be a welfare state ensuring neither the concentration of wealth in the hands of a few men, as in capitalism, nor state socialism. *Zakat* (as a social security tax) is an important ingredient of an Islamic state.

Judged by these criteria we are constrained to say that none of the existing Muslim countries fulfil the criteria of a true Islamic state. Some of them such as Saudi Arabia in the Middle East, Pakistan in south Asia, Iran and Afghanistan in south west Asia, or Malaysia in south-east Asia, may be described as aspiring to be Islamic states. There is always a gap between theory and practice. Modern democratic states did not attain their present stages of political development in a day or in a decade. When Magna Carta, the bill of rights, was signed in England, when the American or French Declarations of Independence were proclaimed to the world, none of these countries could be described as truly democratic. But the process had started. Similarly, the contemporary Muslim countries, which emerged after centuries of colonial domination and consequent exploitation and neglect, need lengthy periods of peace and stability before they attain the status of truly Islamic states.

There is no denying that contemporary Muslim states are far from the ideals and principles of a true Islamic state. Free choice of the ruling authority of the people is rare. Ruling authorities in the majority of Muslim countries are not chosen by the people; there are kings, dictators, or so-called Islamic socialist states; abuse of political and economic power by the ruling authority, and neglect of public welfare are some of the sad phenomena of contemporary Muslim countries. However, that is not the fault of Islamic ideology and principles; on the contrary Islam and its ideology are the only hopes for the salvation, unity, welfare, modernization, economic and scientific development for the world of Islam. Islam taught its followers certain broad and universal principles fourteen centuries ago but they are as applicable today as they were in 7th century Arabia. Those principles must be given a proper and dynamic interpretation as sought by the great reformists of Islam whose work and vision of Islam we have already discussed in the preceding chapter.

We shall now examine the role of Islam in the modern nation states of the Muslim world. We shall begin with two opposite cases: Saudi Arabia, which claims to be a fully fledged Islamic state, and Turkey, which under Kemal Ataturk opted for a secular state in a predominantly Muslim society, but where secularism is already being challenged and modified.

Saudi Arabia

Saudi Arabia is the most spectacular example of an Islamic state in the contemporary world of Islam. John Esposito, in *Islam and Politics*, writes that the origins of contemporary Saudi Arabia in central Arabia in the 18th century 'reflect both the tribal and Islamic sources of its legitimacy.' Muhammad ibn Saud, founder of the Saudi dynasty, was the ruler of a town, Dir'iyyah, and he belonged to the 'Anaza tribe which enjoyed *sharif* or noble status. The foundation of present-day Saudi Arabia was the result of a mutually advantageous alliance between Saud and a great reformer of Islamic traditions in the 18th century, Muhammad ibn 'Abd al-Wahhab. 'Abd al-Wahhab was a strong believer in the original purity of Islam. He revolted against laxity and corruption among local Muslim rulers and preached a return to the central doctrine of Islam—the unity of God or *tawhid*, whose meaning and significance have been discussed. His teachings are known as *muwahhid* or, popularly, as Wahhabism. In 1744 'the religious leader 'Abd al-Wahhab and the prince [Saud] wedded spiritual vision and temporal ambition, producing a successful religio-political movement that occupied Makkah and Medina in 1802 and united the disparate tribes of Arabia in what seemed to its followers a recreation of Islam's seventh century beginnings under the Prophet Muhammad'. As the new state included the holiest places in Islam, Makkah and al-Madinah, it occupied a unique status in the Islamic *ummah*.[2]

The new state, however, aroused opposition from Muslim tribes and the Ottoman sultan considered it a serious threat to his control of the pilgrimage to Makkah, an aspect of the Sultan's leadership of the Islamic *ummah*. He sent Muhammad 'Ali of Egypt to destroy the new kingdom of the Saudi dynasty. In 1819 'Ali razed Dir'iyyah, the capital of the Saudis. The prominent members of the Saudi family took shelter in Kuwait. By the beginning of the 20th century, 'Abd al-'Aziz ibn 'Abd al-Rahman led a successful campaign to recover the region. By 1932, the state of Saudi Arabia had re-emerged in the world of Islam. Today the state occupies the central position in the Islamic *ummah*, both as the custodian of the holiest sites of Islam and for its consistent and persistent support of the aspirations and hopes of the people of its fellow Muslim countries.

King 'Abd al-'Aziz, after consolidating his position, began to make his country stronger and to make its impact felt in the international Islamic community. He annexed the province of the Hijaz, which had a different population and culture, to his kingdom; the annual *hajj* (pilgrimage) and external trade also gave the Hijaz a more cosmopolitan and heterogeneous character than other parts of the kingdom. He organized a powerful militia, *Ikwan* (brethren). The *Ikwan*, groups of Bedouin, were strongly committed to Wahhabi ideals. King 'Abd al-'Aziz was, however, soon confronted with a revolt by the *Ikwan*. The king had to take some pragmatic steps to deal with his new obligations and role in the Islamic community. He also had to deal with the British in the Gulf and his new northern border after the annexation of the Hijaz. Some of his lieutenants became unhappy with the king's compromising attitude toward non-Muslim powers and his toleration of some practices which the *Ikwan* considered repugnant to their concept of Islamic tradition. The *Ikwani* leaders revolted against the king, but 'Abd al-'Aziz crushed the rebellion; true to the spirit of Islamic generosity, he forgave the leaders. These earliest symptoms of tensions in Saudi Arabia between traditional values and the pragmatic measures that the Saudi government had to take to deal with the outside world, including the non-Muslim Western powers, had subsided.

King 'Abd al-'Aziz did not deviate from the basic principles of Wahhabi Islam, which continue to form the ideological foundation of the kingdom of Saudi Arabia. An able-statesman, King 'Abd al-'Aziz maintained the delicate balance between traditionalism and modernism, and during his reign (1902-53) the country enjoyed political stability and socio-religious peace.

In its early days following World War I, the new state gained prestige throughout the Islamic world because it was one of the few areas that retained political independence and did not become part of any Western colonial empire. Secondly, and more important, when in Turkey Kemal Ataturk abolished the caliphate and established a secular state, disregarding Islamic values and tradition, Saudi Arabia firmly committed itself to Islam and its basic principles. This earned special respect and regard for the state of Saudi Arabia in the world of Islam in addition to its role as the custodian of the holiest places in Islam.

Islam in Contemporary Saudi Arabia

From its very inception, Saudi Arabia has declared Islam its *raison d'ětre*. Saudi Arabia is often described in the West as the most theocratic of states. However, the world theocracy does not have the same meaning and connotation in Islam as it did in the medieval European Christian world. In Islam, there is, for instance, no priesthood; nor is there any divine right of the king. The ruler in an Islamic state is as subject to the rule of law as provided in the *shari'ah* as any other citizen of the state.

The constitution of Saudi Arabia is not based on Islamic principles or Islamic ideology alone. Saudi Arabia has no constitution as such. The Quran itself is the constitution of the country and the *shari'ah* is the basic law of the land. Saudi Arabia has a monarchy: in Islam, sovereignty belongs to God and the people exercise sovereign power as the vicegerents of God. No particular person or group can claim the sovereignty of God; it is the people or their chosen representative who must exercise sovereignty, which in the final analysis is vested in God. The Saudis have sought to justify their system of monarchy on the grounds that it is not automatically hereditary. Whenever a king dies or is removed, a consultative council or *Shurah*, as provided in the Quran, chooses the next king. The king, like any other citizen is subject to the rule of law: to the *shari'ah*. There is no scope for an unconstitutional or arbitrary government in Islam. The Saudis rationalize their political order by stressing the fact that it is modelled on the pattern set up in al-Madinah by the Prophet Muhammad in the 7th century. They cite the case of the removal of king Saud ibn 'Abd al-'Aziz in 1964 when he was alleged to be deviating from the *shari'ah*. In 1964 the council (*Majlis al-Shurah*) consisting of senior princes, *'ulama'* and government officials investigated the conduct of the king and decided to remove him. The council then selected the new king, Prince Faisal. This process of removing an undesirable ruler and appointing a new one by a consultative body is cited as an example of Islamic legal principles of 'public interest'. On an earlier occasion, the Saudi adherence to the *shari'ah* in their political system was illustrated in 1944 when king 'Abd al-'Aziz was charged by the *Ikwan* leader, Abu Bahz, of bringing foreigners, mostly American technicians, to manage the oil fields, which according to the *Ikwan* was un-Islamic. 'Abd al-'Aziz allowed himself to be tried before the *shari'ah* courts which administer Islamic law in Saudi Arabia. The king left his throne to appear personally before the *shari'ah* court, where he said: 'I am now not the king but only a Muslim, like you [Abu Bahz], a servant of the Prophet, 'Abd al-'Aziz, appealing for judgement to the *'ulama'*, the judges of the Islamic law which binds us both equally.' Showing a thorough knowledge of the Prophet's life and traditions, the king cited several well-attested cases when the Prophet employed non-Muslims individually and in groups. 'Am I right or wrong?' The judges replied unanimously that he was right. 'Am I breaking the *shari'ah*, therefore, when I follow the footsteps of the Prophet and employ foreign experts to work for me?' The judges returned a verdict of not guilty.[3]

In a sense, as a perceptive Muslim scholar Akbar S Ahmed, has pointed out, 'Saudi Arabia is attempting the key question of our time: how Islamic must a Muslim government be? The answer was solved neatly in eighteenth-century Arabia. Religion and government fused when Sheikh Mohammad Wahhab gave his daughter to Mohammad Ibn Saud, a petty chief in Darryah near Riyadh, the capital of the Najd. An alliance which would stand the test of time was formed. Division of labour was demarcated between the two, the sheikh would provide religious direction and Saud exercise political authority.' King Faisal wanted to live up to the idea of Islam; for instance, he bought about four thousand slaves in Saudi Arabia giving each one thousand pounds sterling and gave them their freedom. There is a story that when Henry Kissinger warned King Faisal that the Saudi oil wells might be captured and blown up, Faisal's reply was 'We will go back to living in the desert and off our date-trees.' According to Akbar, 'there is little doubt that he meant it.' Akbar adds, 'Saudi Arabia is the rare true welfare state providing the entire range of human needs from education tc medicine for its citizens.' He continues, 'Islam permeates Saudi Arabia: Islam as theology, as food, as clothes. And now with the Saudis, Islam as politics'.[4] Saudi Arabia, observed al-Farsy, a Saudi American-educated scholar, is 'the only nation to use a sacred scripture, namely the Quran, as a constitution.'[5]

Thanks to its enormous wealth from oil, Saudi Arabia is facing its new challenges and problems. Under King Faisal Saudi Arabia has entered into what may be termed 'pragmatic fundamentalism'. In 1962 Faisal, then prime minister, announced a ten-point programme which was a synthesis of traditionalism and modernism. The Saudi system provides an example of Islam as a dynamic force and shows that its ideology, properly interpreted and applied, can meet the needs and requirements of a modern developing society. Islam cannot in any way hamper the growth and development of a modern state.

Islam has been a prominent factor in Saudi Arabia's foreign policy. Unlike some other Arab countries, particularly Egypt under Nasser, which stressed regionalism in the form of pan-Arabism, the Saudi government has stressed pan-Islamism, thus enhancing its status and image in the world of Islam, particularly among non-Arab Muslim countries like Pakistan, Bangladesh, Malaysia and the African Muslim states. The Saudi government's initiatives and generous help, both moral and financial, in organizing institutions like the Muslim World League (*Rabitat al-'Alam al-Islam*), which is engaged in social and philanthropic activities in many Muslim countries, is greatly appreciated throughout the Muslim world. Similarly, Saudi Arabia is the greatest source of strength for the Organization of the Islamic Conference (OIC), which is the first pan-Islamic political organization consisting of both Arab and non-Arab Muslim countries. The headquarters of the OIC is in Jeddah, Saudi Arabia. The present author had the opportunity of closely observing the activities of the OIC; the creation of the OIC, with active help from Saudi Arabia, has been a great milestone in Muslims' aspirations for an international political grouping consisting of both Arab and non-Arab countries. The Saudi government has also given considerable help and encouragement to Islamic movements. The formation of the Gulf Cooperation Council has given Saudi Arabia great scope to play an increasingly important role in strategically important areas in the Gulf regions. In recent years the Saudi government has raised its strong protest against Israel's occupation of Jerusalem and applied itself vigorously to its liberation by making it a world-wide Muslim issue. That the Saudi government is an exponent of pan-Islamism is also shown by the fact that when al-Aqsa mosque, which (after those of Makkah and al-Madinah) is the third holiest place in Islam was burned in 1967, it summoned an Islamic summit conference, which was attended by a majority of Muslim countries. Similarly, in 1988, when Israel threatened to destroy the missiles which Saudi Arabia had acquired from China, the Saudi government tried to get the support of the entire Muslim world. Many Muslim countries, Arab as well as non-Arab, showed their solidarity with the Saudi government in its attempts to check Israeli expansion. By stressing Islam as a factor in foreign policy, Saudi Arabia has established its credentials as one of the greatest exponents of the Islamic *ummah*. This policy began under King Faisal and has been continued by his successors, King Khalid and King Fahd.

We shall conclude our discussion on the role of Islam in modern Saudi Arabia by quoting Prince Faisal in 1963, one year before he became king: 'What does a man aspire to? He wants 'good'. It is there in the Islamic *shari'ah*. He wants security. It is there. Man wants freedom. It is there. He wants remedy. It is there. He wants propagation of science. It is there. Everything is there, inscribed in the Islamic Shari'ah.'[6]

Modern Turkey

We will now examine the relationship between state and religion in modern Turkey, which is almost opposite to that of Saudi Arabia. When the Ottoman empire was liquidated after World War I, Mustafa Kemal, subsequently known as Kemal Ataturk, founded a new state known as the Turkish Republic. Of the total population of the new state 97.3 percent were Muslims, many of whom, particularly those living in rural areas, were pious and religious followers of Islam and its tradition. Yet Kemal rejected the Islamic tradition in his new Republic. He introduced secularism in Turkey without realizing that Western secularism cannot be imported merely by a constitutional or legal declaration into a traditional society unless there are changes in attitudes, behaviour, patterns and ways of life. The Islamic tradition had developed very deep roots among Turkish Muslims during a period extending over several centuries.

Kemal seemed to have failed to recognize the historical, cultural and spiritual heritage of the Turkish people when he amended the constitution of his country by deleting the provision that 'the religion of the Turkish Republic is Islam'. He abolished the sultanate and the caliphate in 1922. Then in his zeal to make the country 'Europeanized' he introduced a number of reforms which were not based on any Islamic tradition.

Before we comment on Kemal's alleged 'anti-Islamic' reforms, we have to take into consideration the circumstances when he introduced those reforms. According to Hegel's dialectic method of historical changes, thesis is followed by anti-thesis, then emerges a synthesis. In a sense, Kemal's alleged antipathy towards Islamic tradition has to be explained by Hegel's dialectic method: the Ottoman empire was humiliated, defeated and was in the process of totally withering away after World War I; Kemal put the blame for this threat which was not only on the Ottoman empire but also what is today the Republic of Turkey, on Islam. He put up a gallant resistance to save his homeland, Turkey; that is why he is called *Ghazi* (the Great Fighter and Winner). Kemal is respected not only in modern Turkey but in many Muslim countries like Bangladesh and Pakistan.

As Kemal held the weak and inefficient sultanate of the Ottoman empire responsible for the misfortune that befell his homeland, his reaction was, no doubt, one of indifference to Islam. As he was a passionate lover of his country and a genuine nationalist, he seemed to have come to the conclusion that the old system had to be replaced by a modern one—he found such modern systems only in Europe at that stage of history in the 1920s.

As the old system was based on Islam—not the true one but the distorted version of Islam of the *'ulama'*—it was in these unfortunate circumstances Kamal began to organize his new state on those principles which he thought were the only solution for modern Turkey. We are not condoning some of his anti-Islamic reforms, but we must give the benefit of the doubt to this great personality of the contemporary Muslim world. His reforms included the following.

The Ministry of Religious Affairs and Pious Endowments was abolished, the educational system was changed, making it 'secular', eliminating traditional Islamic education. The *shari'ah*, the Islamic law, was replaced by a Swiss- and Italian-based legal system. By enfranchising women Kemal thought that he had made a great departure from Islamic principles. But in Islam, women can and do enjoy full political rights; for example, in the Islamic Republic of Pakistan, a woman was the prime minister of the country; and a woman candidate for presidential election in 1964 was supported by all opposition parties including the so-called fundamentalist party—Jamaat-i-Islami.

Today there are two Muslim women prime ministers—one in Bangladesh and other in Turkey itself. Islam, as we have elaborated, is not against giving women political roles. Kemal not only introduced 'reforms' abolishing Islam as interpreted by the *'ulama'* of the Ottoman era in constitutional, legal and educational systems, he introduced Western dress and even went to the extent of making measures such as wearing Western-style hats a constitutional provision! All these measures—legal, constitutional and purely trivial—were clear evidence of Kemal's apparent prejudice against Islam. He failed to recognize that a nation need not give up its past and its heritage in order to make progress. Some contemporary Muslim countries (e.g., Bangladesh, Pakistan Malaysia and Saudi Arabia) have made progress in development and modernization without abandoning their past cultural and spiritual heritage. There are non-Muslim countries with ancient civilizations, such as China, India and Japan, which have made vast progress and development without sacrificing their traditions or heritage.

A modern Turkey, thanks to the military genius of a *ghazi* known as Mustafa Kemal Ataturk, who is rightly recalled as 'the Father of the Nation', emerged in 1920. Ataturk, however, considered the decline and fall of Ottoman Empire mainly due to the influence of a narrowly interpreted Islam. The causes of the decline of the Ottoman Empire were mainly external—the European intervention mentioned above. However, Ataturk rejected the past and what Akbar S. Ahmed stated: 'Ataturk consciously, furiously rejecting the past, succumbed to the European obsession. From the profound to the trivial, Kemal europeanized Turkey's culture, social and religious life: the Santa Sophia mosque was converted to a museum, the fez was banned and replaced by European hats. Sufi and Dervish orders were suppressed. Islamic law was superseded by European legal code and Latin, no Arabic letters were used for the Turkish script. In order to communicate his message, emphatic sometimes crude symbolism was used. A new Turkey, europeanized, purged of its past, was to be born. Affiliation with the past almost became a crime: a women covering her head or a man cultivating a beard, both suggesting Islam, risked termination in government services'.[7]

However, Ataturk is still a great hero in Turkey. His picture is everywhere in government offices, in restaurants, even in private houses, and the anniversary of his death on 10 November is observed with great honour and solemnity. Ataturk is deeply and profoundly respected by the Turks although in recent years his complete europeanization of the country has been challenged; and Islam has raised its head in certain ways.

Some of Ataturk's reforms were beneficial and liberal. In Turkey there was a system called *Imam nikahẹ* which is a marriage, not attested by the municipality but solely by the *imam*. It was practised in pre-modern days in rural areas when a man wanted to take a second or third wife, but Ataturk abolished it when he introduced the Swiss legal code in 1925.

Similarly the veneration of *pirs* or saints is an unacceptable aspect of Islamic tradition, particularly among the people of rural areas. But Ataturk rightly abolished *pirism* in 1925. He prohibited all sufi activities in Turkey as he wanted to stop the bad influence of the *pirs* on the religious people of Turkey.

Kemal's secular republic survived without any major challenges as long as he maintained a one-party dictatorship under which any opposition to his policies or actions was not allowed. As soon as a multi-party system was introduced in the mid-1940s and new political parties emerged, 'sensitivity to the power of Islam in the lives of most Turks' was revived. By the 1950s many of Kemal's secular 'reforms' were changed in favour of Islamic ones; religious education was reintroduced, the faculty of divinity was re-established at the University of Ankara; new mosques were built and old ones repaired; the number of Turkish people going to Makkah to perform *hajj* (pilgrimage) increased so much that by 1962 the Turkish delegation was the third largest.

The New trends in 'Secular' Turkey

At the beginning of the 1940s Zia Gokazp started talking about the westernization, turkification and islamization of Turkey. The break with the Islamic past began to be challenged.

After twenty-five of years of strictly legal 'secular' education the government re-introduced religious classes in schools and in 1949 *Illahiyat Fakultesi*, a Theological faculty was set up in Turkey where Turkish teachers and scholars, *imams*, were taught not only in classical Islamic sciences but also modern fields such as sociology; the psychology of religion was also studied. In the course of four decades a number of such non-secular trends started in Turkey. Particularly since the 1950s women need not cover their head and they now do. This trend towards islamization in Turkey is significant.

The people of Turkey, like the people in other parts of the Islamic *ummah*, are deeply pious. The Democratic Party, which defeated Kemal's Republican Party in the 1950s election, formed an alliance with a religious party known as the Followers of Light, which favoured the revival of an Islamic state in Turkey; other rightists, such as the Party of Union (1966) and the National Order Party (1970), also emerged. The National Order Party was banned by the military junta for its alleged 'anti-secular' religious activities. But the party re-emerged in 1972 with a new name, the National Salvation Party. During the 1973 election, the NSP made remarkable headway: it was not simply the largest majority group, but it was a crucial bargaining party, whose support was needed by any other party. It helped to form the coalition government in 1974. Its leader, Erbarkan, openly expressed his preference for the Islamic type of state as it existed in Pakistan. Once the NSP had become legitimized and a secure part of the establishment, its 'malignant' view of secularism was expressed: 'The political structure of the new Turkey contradicts the political principles of Islam. Islam entails the unification of political and religious powers under the domination of religion. In this respect, secularism and secular system are against Islam, *shari'ah* and religion. Especially, its application in Turkey is designed to assure irreligiosity.'[8]

The survival of Kemal's secularism in Turkey is due mainly to pressure from the Turkish army, in which there are still elements in favour of secularism, largely because they are afraid of a free ballot in which the majority of the Turkish people would probably opt for a democratic Islamic state such as that of Pakistan. The army, which has staged three coups over the last thirty years, regards itself as the guardian of Turkey's secularism and Turks have no doubt that it would step in once again if the country chose Islamic rule.[9] It is the fear of military rule which protects 'secularism' in a predominantly Muslim society. The recent demand by the female students of Turkish universities to be allowed to wear traditional Islamic head scarves in the university campuses—a challenge to the law—demonstrates the inherent strength of Islamic forces even among young urban women. A commentator writes: 'More is at stake than mere clothing. The scarves symbolize an Islamic revival that has been under way for several years and shows no sign of abating'.[10] The great experiments in creating Islamic states in neighbouring Iran and Pakistan, and the emerging one in a free Afghanistan, are likely to have an impact on the reassertion of Islam in Turkey. The sooner this happens the better it will be for Turkey, which is at present torn by ethnic and religious conflicts. Islam can provide the necessary unifying force.

Most Recent Developments in Turkey: Democratization, Modernization and Synthesis of Islam and Turkish Nationalism

There have been some encouraging developments in Turkey in recent years. Little more than a decade ago, Turkey was under military rule. 'Today it has not only a democratic secular government that sees itself as a model for the Islamic World'[11] (*The Times*, 28 June, 1993). President Turgut Ozal who was a towering figure and who was moving his country towards democracy, modernization in a simple way towards the Islamic world, died suddenly in April 1993. Suleyman Demirel, the former prime minister moved to the presidency after the sudden death of Ozal. 'Thus the two toughest and most charismatic leaders have suddenly gone from the daily political scene'.[12]

Turkey now has the country's first woman prime minister—Mrs Tansu Celler—the third Muslim women prime minister, the first one was in Pakistan (1988-90) and the second one in Bangladesh (1990 to the present). Tansu Celler is described as persuasive; she is Western-educated, an economist and former professor. She is reported to have been friendly with Margaret Thatcher, the first British woman prime minister. She is already dubbed as Turkey's Iron Lady. 'Though a secular woman, she claims to cherish Turkey's Islamic heritage and in the balloting she showed surprising strength among delegates from conservative rural areas.'[13]

Turkey is strategically positioned between the West and the Islamic World. With the ending of the East-West cold war, the world, according to some interpreters, may be heading towards a new conflict between the West and the Islamic world. This will be a most sad and tragic development. Turkey under a dynamic, young Muslim woman leader may be able to play a vital role in promoting co-existence between the West and the Islamic World. If Tansu Celler succeeds, she will go down in world history as a great figure. For Turkey, she is already designated as the *abla* (sister) of Turkey while Kemal Ataturk, of whom Celler is a great admirer, shall always remain 'Father' of the modern Turkish Republic. Some of Kemal's reforms, introduced in the special circumstances facing Turkey immediately after its emergence as a modern state in the 1920s, may be modified, adjusted, and re-defined and thus Turkey, we sincerely hope, will move towards democracy, modernization and broad Islamic principles; a synthesis of these are quite complementary and not contradictory. Turkey has already been playing an important role in the affairs of the world of Islam, as illustrated by its role in the Bosnian crisis, and in the emerging group in the Belt of the Crescent, ECO. Turkey is an important member of the OIC, (Organization of the Islamic Conference). While still remaining a member of NATO, Turkey is in a good position to contribute to the lessening of tension between the West and the Islamic World.

It is hoped, Tansu Celler will steer the country out of its financial crisis and high inflation, and keep democracy flourishing within the Islamic heritage and end the damaging eight-year conflict with the Kurdish rebels.

Islam in Other Muslim States of the Middle East

Egypt

Egypt has become an important state in the Muslim world. In the 1950s, Egyptian nationalism was led by a group of the urban elite who were influenced by the West, but they had to retain Islam in order to gain the support of the Muslim masses. During the two decades after independence, radical Arab regimes—Egypt, Syria, Iraq and Algeria among others—emerged in the Middle East. Of these new, so called 'progressive' and 'socialist' regimes, Egypt under Nasser became most prominent. What was 'Nasserism?' How far was it successful? Was there any place for Islam in Nasserism?

Nasserism revolved around the leadership of one individual—Gamal 'Abd al- Nasir (1918-70). Muhammad Haykal, who was close to Nasser, defined Nasserism as 'the direction of liberation, social transformation, the people's control of their own resources and democracy of the people's working forces'.[14] Though Nasser was reported to be a practising Muslim, his philosophy was based on region rather than religion. Nasser was a strong exponent of pan-Arabism, rather than pan-Islamism. He could not, however, exclude Islam altogether. In the 1956 constitution, Nasser described Egypt as a 'sovereign independent Arab state, part of the Arab nation'. However, the Egyptian charter of 1962, which Nasser added, declared Islam as the 'state religion of Egypt'. Initially, Nasserism was based on secularism but subsequently Nasser had to make some references to Islam to meet internal and external challenges to his authority. Nasser's ambition was not confined to Egypt: his dream was for a pan-Arab world under his leadership. Nasser's pan-Arabism was basically secular and socialist. His attitude towards Islam as a factor in either internal or external politics was negative. According to the Muslim Brotherhood, which Nasser ruthlessly suppressed, 'the faction which works for the separation of Egypt from Islam is really a shameless, pernicious and perverse group of puppets and slaves of Europe.'[15] The Brotherhood believes that neither Western capitalism nor modern communism based on Marxist-Leninism can solve the problems confronting the Muslim world. Only by resorting to the true spirit of Islam can the challenges and problems of Muslim countries be resolved. The Muslim Brotherhood, like Jamaat-i-Islam in South Asia, are often maligned as 'fundamentalist' or 'militant' religious groups. This description is unfair and unrealistic. What both these movements want is the restoration of the true principles of Islam in modern Muslim states, although their rigid and inflexible conceptions of Islamic law cannot meet the challenge and problems of the modern age. They sincerely believe that a return to Islam is the only path for the salvation of the Muslim world and the only defence against the threats from westernism and capitalism. Nasser, did not tolerate the Brotherhood.

An analysis of Nasser's external policies also shows that his pan-Arabism was not merely indifferent but positively opposed to Islam. To establish his credentials as a world leader, Nasser joined Pandit J Nehru of India and Marshal Tito of Yugoslavia to strengthen the non-aligned movement. He was opposed to pan-Islamic ideas sponsored by Saudi Arabia and Pakistan, and was hostile to Pakistan. During the 1956 Suez crisis, Pakistan (including present-day Bangladesh) supported Egypt against Anglo-French-Israeli military intervention, Yet after the Suez crisis Nasser said: 'Suez is as dear to Egypt as Kashmir is to India.' Nasser knew that Kashmiri Muslims had been agitating against the Indian occupation of the predominantly Muslim state of Kashmir and that, given free choice, they would have joined the Islamic state of Pakistan. Nasser's comparison of Suez with Kashmir was an affront to the sentiments of the Muslims of South Asia. Similarly, after the 1965 Indo-Pakistan War, when the Arab leaders met in 1966 at the Arab League summit, Nasser threatened to walk out of the meeting if the Arab countries condemned the Indian aggression against Pakistan on 6 September 1965, an aggression which was condemned by a vast number of countries, both Muslim and non-Muslim, including Britain. No international organization comprising both Arab and non-Arab Muslim countries could be created while Nasser controlled Egypt. (The Organization of the Islamic Conference—OIC—did not come into existence until after Nasser's demise.)

Nasser's 'Arab socialism' could not solve Egypt's socio-economic problems. The biggest blow to Nasser's prestige in the Arab world was the 1967 Arab-Israel War when Egypt, Syria and Jordan were totally defeated by Israel and Israel occupied Egyptian territories. Nasser's pro-Soviet links could not save his nation from total humiliation.

Nasser died in 1970 and was succeeded by Anwar Sadat. Anwar Sadat, was not opposed to the Islamic *ummah*. In 1970 the Islamic summit which met in Rabat, Morocco, and which consisted of both Arab and non-Arab Muslim countries, gave birth to the OIC. Anwar Sadat was more tolerant towards the Brotherhood and he recognized Islam as a factor in the nation-building force in the Middle East. There was no doubt about Anwar Sadat's personal devotion to Islam. After the 1973 Arab-Israel War he said: 'After October 6 (1973) a great change was ushered (into the armed forces) . . . there will be no question that the slogan 'freedom, socialism and unity is still valid . . . it will remain part of our basic principles. However, the slogan '*Allah Akbar*' has become our *cri de guerre*, reflecting the change in the spiritual make-up of our troops. We have the official religion of Islam. It is in our constitution. We should return to the main principles of our heritage'.[16] This was a great change from Nasser's secularism and non-Islamic Arab nationalism.

The relationship between President Sadat and the Muslim Brotherhood was better than that between the Brotherhood and Nasser. However, when Sadat made a bilateral treaty with Israel, giving Israel diplomatic recognition, there was a hue and cry over the entire Muslim world. The treaty was signed at Camp David under the direct sponsorship of the US president, Jimmy Carter. Egypt was expelled from both the Arab League and the OIC for giving recognition to Israel, and Sadat himself was assassinated by a group of young militant Egyptians on 6 October 1981.

Thus ended an important era for modern Egypt. 'Some people began wondering what had happened to twenty-five years of revolution in Egypt. Islam had indeed turned out to be a much stronger force in domestic policies than many would have admitted two decades before; national essence, local tradition, and the religious commitment of the populace indeed survived ideological cosmetics thrust upon them.'[17]

The current president of Egypt, Hosni Mubarak, has neither the charisma of Nasser nor the courage and conviction of Anwar Sadat. He is moderate both in his ideology and in his public affairs.

In external affairs, Mubarak is continuing to pursue closer relationships with the United States and thereby to get large US economic aid, including some military aid. Egypt is the second largest recipient of US aid—the first being Israel.

In spite of huge foreign aid, mainly US, Egypt's economy continues to remain bleak and disappointing. There is wide-spread popular discontent against the Hosni Mubarak regime. The Muslim groups with whom Sadat had cultivated friendly relations, but who also killed Sadat for his treaty with and recognition of Israel, are the most vocal against the present Egyptian government.

Mubarak, in the name of suppressing the so-called 'fundamentalists' has resorted to the most brutal methods against Muslim groups, some of whom might be extremist and might also have employed violent methods. How the one-party dictatorial regime of Hosni Mubarak is dealing with the so-called fundamentalists cannot be condoned. There is the common execution of members of so-called 'fundamentalist groups'. Violation of human rights is frequent and widespread. Egyptian prisons are full of the political opponents of the Hosni Mubarak regime. There is little rule of law or regard for fundamental rights.

There is presidential election under the present constitution of Egypt. But the so-called 'election' is similar to those of the communist and other authoritarian states—it is a one-party election which is the negation of one of the fundamental ingredients of a free society.

So whatever, the present political order provides in theory, the Hosni Mubarak regime is neither democratic nor truly Islamic, as Islam does not approve any oppressive system.

Islamic Socialism

There are a number of contemporary Muslim states which prefer to describe their social order using the term Islamic Socialism. Countries like Iraq, Syria, Egypt, Libya, and at certain stages Algeria, and Pakistan under Z A Bhutto (1972 -77), used the term Islamic or Arab Socialism. Let us try, to find out what 'socialism' means in Islam. Khalifa 'Abd al-Halim sought 'to situate Islamic socialism between a *laissez-faire* capitalism and totalitarian Marxism'. He added, 'Socialism is generally considered to be a remedy for removing the inequality of opportunities created by an unjust accumulation and unfair distribution of wealth. When reformists with a zeal for social justice see that society has been split up into the over-nourished and the under-nourished, with superfluous wealth extravagantly squandered on the one hand and abject poverty and insecurity on the other, their first cry is for equality'.[18]

Then he listed the factors which created hinderences for the establishment of a fair and equitable society, such as any form of hereditary monarchy and landlordism, which is a privileged class. He also stressed the benefits of *Zakat*, one of the 'Five Pillars of Islam' and also charity which the Quran encourages and the Prophet of Islam, Muhammad, practised in his personal and public life. The Quran stressed the need for helping the poor by saying, 'And in their wealth is the right of him who asks and him who is needy' (Surah 51: 19). He concludes: 'It is a principle laid down in the Quran that economic life should be so organized that wealth does not circulate only among the rich:

> Whatever Allah has restored to His Apostle from the people of the town, it is for Allah and for the Apostle and for the near of the kin and the orphans and needy and the wayfarer, so that it may not be a thing taken by turns among the rich of you only (59:7).'[19]

He further adds, 'National wealth is like blood in an organism; it should not create a plethora in one part and atrophy in another part. Islam desired to mould the economic life of society in such a manner that antagonistic class-divisions of millionaires and paupers should not come into existence. The Prophet did not approve of the private dispensation of charity, and he envisaged a state of affairs in which a person would walk through the land with charity to offer but would find none to receive it. All his efforts were directed towards the creation of a classless society, at first with the gradual emancipation of slaves and the elimination of pauperism. All surpluses should come to the state in prescribed proportions and be administered by the state, so that no individual should feel any shame in being obliged to receive charity at private hands. He considered it as the duty of the state that if it possessed enough resources, no citizen should be deprived of the fundamental needs of life.'[20]

If a society is shaped in accordance with the injunctions of the Quran as practised by the Prophet of Islam, there is no need for what is termed socialism. In fact, the Quran's concept of a social order and the spirit of socialism, not totalitarian communism, can be accommodated in a modern Muslim state.

A K Brohi speaking about the Islamic social order points out: 'To the age-old question: What is the state to do for the individual where the individual is not able to provide for himself those bare necessities of life which he is to have if he is to survive? Islam has its own answer to return. It is the responsibility of the state to provide conditions upon which not only the mind and character of its citizens must develop but also the conditions upon which its citizens are to win by their own efforts all that is necessary to full civic efficiency. It is for the state to feed, house or clothe them. It is for the state to take care that the economic conditions are such that the normal man, who is not defective in mind or body or will can, by useful labour, feed, house, and clothe himself and his family. The 'right to work' and 'the right to a living wage' are just as valid as the rights of persons or property—that is to say, they are integral conditions of a good social order. This was the concept of social order upon which the 'liberalism' of nineteenth-century European politics was based. Man's pre-occupation with the task of founding a just society is as old as the hills. This was long before Socialism—or, as a matter of fact, long before any 'ism' was born. What could you say of the economic and political system of Abu Bakr, or 'Umar or 'Uthman or of 'Ali? Were they socialists? The instruments of production were not owned by the state of their day, nor had they the type of control which a socialist state claims to have on the means of distribution of wealth. And yet they were, I suppose, consistently with conditions that obtained in their times, practising the Gospel of Islam by founding society on justice.'[21]

Another reputed Muslim scholar, Shaykh Mahmud Shaltut of al-Azhar University, examines the relationship between Islam and socialism by saying:

> Islam has traced the straight path of the ideal society; it is a party of solidarity by which the nation lives and which ensures the strength of society. With this end in view, Islam has abolished from the minds of owners (of property) and capitalists such vices as meanness and the taste for squandering luxury. It has employed all means to encourage men to give generously and to be afraid of appearing miserly and of neglecting the right of the people and of society, to such a point that it has raised liberality to the rank of faith.
>
> 'The true servants of the Merciful are those who walk humbly on the earth and say 'Peace!' to the ignorant who accost them; . . . who are neither extravagant nor niggardly but keep the golden mean; who invoke no other God besides Allah . . . '(25: 64-66).[22]

He concludes,

> Briefly summarized, such is the doctrine of Islam regarding the relations among men from the point of view of the solidarity of members of society. It contains in detail all the solid foundations necessary to make our nation a magnificent stronghold, a heaven of happiness for those who shelter there.
>
> The doctrine also contains a clear statement of what the socialism of Islam is, for adoption by those who wish to adopt it. Can man find a more perfect, more complete, more useful, and more profound socialism than that decreed by Islam? It is founded on the basis of faith and belief, and all that is decreed on that basis participates in the perpetuation of life and doctrine.[23]

Syria and Iraq

Let us now discuss the two so-called Arab Socialist Countries. One ideology that has emerged in more than one Arab country in the Middle East is a socialist movement broadly defined as 'Arab Socialism' and epitomized in the socialist Ba'th party, which is in power in both Syria and Iraq, though with differences in each country.

The Ba'th began to emerge in Syria in the 1950s. Between 1958 and 1961 Syrian Ba'thists decided to form a union with Nasser's Egypt. The experiment did not, however, last long; by 1961 Syria again became a separate state. In parallel military coups in 1963, the army and the Ba'th party gained control in both Syria and Iraq. The Ba'th party captured power in Baghdad and remained in power for a short period. Following a series of coups and counter-coups a new, more radical Ba'th party gained power in Syria in 1966 and in Iraq in 1968. The new Parties, known as Neo-Ba'th, announced programmes of a state controlled economy and land reform. The Neo-Ba'th continued the basic themes of the original party: 'emphasis on Arab unity and nationalism, the seed for a social and economic transformation in Arab society and opposition to foreign control of either state or ideology.'[24]

Turning to the attitude to Islam in Ba'th party ideology, we find that it neither rejected Islam nor gave any special role to Islam in the state as did Saudi Arabia and Pakistan. 'For Ba'th thinkers Islam is a part of the Arab consciousness and the early experience of Islam (seventh century) is seen as the first great Arab revolution and its teaching of equality and brotherhood as a foundation for a true socialist society'.[25] According to a Ba'th thinker, Alfaq, 'the Ba'th party, while secular in orientation, embodies a renaissance of the Arab spirit similar to that embodied in Islam.'[26]

There were further changes of government in both Syria and Iraq, not through the ballot but through the bullet. Finally Hafiz al-Asad become president of Syria in 1970 and Saddam Hussain gained power in Iraq in 1968. Both leaders rule through a dictatorial process rather than with the Islamic principles of equality, toleration and the rule of law. As we have emphasised, in Islam there is no scope for any dictatorial system. Both countries claim to follow the original Ba'th ideology and both accuse each other of violating the original Ba'th ideology. Syria has moved closer both to the revolutionary Islamic regime in Iran and to Moscow, while Iraq, engaged in a costly war with Iran, was aligned more with Saudi Arabia and the Gulf states for their support of Baghdad during the Iran-Iraq War (1980-87). Baghdad had signed a treaty of friendship and cooperation with Moscow, but in the later stages of the Iran-Iraq War moved closer to the Western powers, including the United States.

The Ba'thist regimes in Syria and Iraq pay lip-service to Islam but neither of them can be described as an 'Islamic state' as Islam does not permit the type of authoritarian order that prevails in these countries; neither can Syria or Iraq be described as 'secular' from the ideological standpoint. In both countries Islam is considered an important factor in both domestic and foreign affairs, though their first priority is narrow personal ambition, projecting them as serving national interests.

Iraq: A Great Miscalculation

The seven-year Iran-Iraq war was one of the saddest and most tragic incidents for the Islamic *ummah*. It was very costly for both the countries. Towards the end of this ruinous war, Iraq received help from both the then superpowers. The Iraqi president, Saddam Hussain, had friendly relations with Moscow because of the so-called 'Socialist' system; he also had support from oil-rich Muslim countries like Saudi Arabia and the Gulf States. Only Syria and the PLO were on the side of Iran.

Ultimately, Iraq was able to extract a ceasefire from Iran which was exhausted, both financially and militarily. It was not a clear victory for either side; it ended in a draw.

As soon as the Iran-Iraq war was over, Saddam vigorously set about a huge military build-up. He organized a one million-strong army equipped with all kinds of sophisticated weapons, with advanced types of tanks, armoured vehicles, etc. He had also developed an impressive air force with destructive capabilities, including missiles.

Saddam felt over-confident of his military strength. With this sense of self-assertion, he made the fatal mistake of invading and annexing Kuwait. This was an alarming development for the post Cold War world order. President George Bush organized a grand alliance under the auspices of the United Nations to force Saddam to withdraw from his aggression in Kuwait. Thus the Gulf-war of 1991 started; in no time the US in alliance with so many other countries and with UN approval defeated Iraq, compelling Saddam to vacate Kuwait.

For President Bush, it was a grand achievement; his popularity rating in his own country shot up dramatically in a pre-election year. Bush could not, however, win the presidential election in November 1992 because of his poor performance in domestic affairs. The American voters, wanted to put an end of 12-year Republican regime at the White House. They opted for a younger and dynamic Democrat, Bill Clinton.

The defeat of George Bush was widely celebrated in Iraq in an unrealistic way. Bush became stupidly furious and his last action as the US President was to 'punish' Saddam. Just one week before his departure from the White House, he ordered a military operation against Iraq on the pretext of 'protecting' the Kurds of Iraq while he was silent over the genocide in Bosnia.

President Bill Clinton, in the initial stages, seemed to incline towards depersonalizing tension with Iraq by dropping the demand for Saddam's removal as a precondition for lifting UN sanctions against Iraq. But soon Clinton faced growing discontent in his country for his poor domestic performance; he could not deliver the many assurances he gave to the American people during the 1992 presidential election. His popularity rating was going down. Under the circumstances, he resorted to a highly unacceptable technique. He ordered the bombing of Baghdad on the grounds that Saddam was involved in a plot to kill George Bush when he went to Kuwait for a 'royal welcome' by the Amir of Kuwait. There was no substantial evidence of Saddam being directly involved in the plot against Bush; even so, Clinton's brutal action of bombing Baghdad in July 1993, which killed a number of innocent civilians, was a most unfortunate instance of 'gun-boat diplomacy' in a unipolar world order.

It also backfired. Saddam who was condemned widely for his invasion of Kuwait in August 1990 became an object of sympathy, as many countries—Muslim, both Arab and non-Arab, and even Iraq's bitter foe, Iran—condemned the US action.

Saddam, in spite of his defeat in the 1991 Gulf war, is still in power. No coup or popular uprising has occurred as yet. In the difficult time since the Gulf War, Saddam often tries to whip up Islamic sentiment;

he even talks about *jihad* or holy war. But the Saddam regime is not an Islamic one. It is dictatorial and brutal.

Islam in the Arab West: the Maghrib

Tunisia

In Tunisia, the Destour party took the leading part in the earlier phases of the nationalist movement: they defined Tunisian nationalism in terms of Islamic and Arabic traditions. In the final stages of liberation the young militants led by Habib Bourguiba took control of the freedom movement, forming the Neo-Destour party in 1934. After a long and bitter struggle, Tunisia became independent in 1956, Bourguiba declaring himself president for life. He ruled the country until he was overthrown in a military coup on 7 November 1987.

What was the role of Islam in the Tunisian nationalist movement? According to John Obert Voll: 'The key feature of Islam in Tunisia during the pre-independence period was not that there was a modernist interpretation that emerged but rather that Islam provided the symbols and vocabulary for a mobilization of the people in opposition to foreign rule.'[27]

The present president, Gen. Zine el-Abidine Ben Ali, was appointed in November 1987 after a bloodless coup to replace Habib Bourguiba, who was declared 'mentally and physically unfit' for office.

The president, who had come to power in 1987, was 'elected' in April 1989 as the sole candidate with over 99 percent of the vote!

The year 1991 was dominated by the effects of the Gulf War and by the government's campaign against the Islamic opposition movement, Nahda.

Fresh moves by the government against Nahda started in February 1992. As the movement tried to capitalize on the anti-Western feelings and economic difficulties caused by the Gulf War, violent incidents took place. The government's claim of coup plots by Nahda fundamentalists were met with some scepticism. The harshness of the government's response, and particularly the execution of three members of Nahda in October 1991 was criticized and there were allegations of the use of torture and of deaths in government custody. The government's concern with 'fundamentalism' led to closer relations with Egypt but also to strains with Sudan, which the government alleged was encouraging Tunisian fundamentalists. The Nahda leader, Ghannouchi, advocated the formation of a united front of opposition groups, possibly to include the former Prime

Minister Mohammed Mzali (who left office in 1986). Ghannouchi was reported to have applied for political asylum in the United Kingdom.

The over-all situation in Tunisia, like many other Muslim Middle-Eastern countries, is sad and disappointing.

Morocco

In Morocco there was also a close alliance between Islamic forces and modern nationalist forces in the struggle for independence, firstly against the Spanish rule of northern Morocco and subsequently against the French. In northern Morocco the great tribal leader, 'Abd al Karim al Khattabi, organized a religiously oriented movement and after his death his son Muhammad succeeded in driving the Spanish out. By 1922 he had established an Islamic republic in northern Morocco, whose declared policy was combining the basic teachings of Islam with the scientific and industrial achievements of the West. In 1926 the new Islamic republic was defeated by the French, but continued to preach its goal of creating a state that would combine Islamic values with modernization, a pattern that was to emerge again when Morocco became independent in 1956. 'In Morocco, the two major vehicles expressing nationalist aspirations were a religiously-oriented national party, Istiqlal, and a monarchy whose prestige in society rested firmly on Islamic grounds. Islam provided at least some of the institutional structure for an independent Morocco.'[28]

The Political System

Under its constitution, as most recently amended in 1972, Morocco is a constitutional monarchy. The monarch appoints the prime minister and the cabinet. Legislative authority is vested in a chamber of representatives elected for a six-year term and comprising 306 members, of whom 206 are directly elected by universal adult suffrage and the remainder by an electoral college composed of local councillors and representatives of professional bodies.

Morocco was the only Maghrib state to send troops as part of the US-led coalition in the Gulf, although it had been emphasized that the 1,500-strong force would have a purely defensive role. On 28 January 1992 a general strike had been successfully called as a show of pro-Iraqi solidarity by three trade unions and supported by five opposition parties. According to a report in *El Pais* on 20 February 1992, a group of 13 Islamic clerics denounced the government's attempts to control the content of their sermons; they claimed that 22 *imams* had been dismissed in recent months on account of their pro-Iraqi preaching.

The Moroccan government was strongly criticized for the arbitrary detention of political opponents and the common use of torture on detainees. In a report of 27 March 1992 the human rights organization Amnesty International claimed that 1,500 people had been detained in past months, many of them in connection either pro-Iraqi demonstrations. The government, however, denied the allegations.[29]

Algeria

The French process of the assimilation of a colony was perhaps nowhere so comprehensive and palpable as in Algeria. No other country in the world of Islam faced such a concentrated effort to destroy its basic social and cultural order. The aim was to turn it into an integral part of France. It can only be compared with the Czarist and Stalinist assimilation of Islamic society and culture in the Central Asian Republics of the USSR, where the Russians destroyed, in the true sense of the term, the socio-cultural and religious order of the Muslims by a systematic and deliberate policy of annihilation. The Algerian freedom movement's first priority was to define the meaning of being an Algerian—a process to which Islam had a significant contribution to make. The Islamic factor in the awakening of Algerian nationalism was expressed in the career of one of the earliest nationalist leaders, 'Abd al-Hamid ibn Badis, popularly known as Ben Badis (1889-1940). He stressed the Islamic aspect of emerging Algerian nationalism. He said, 'History has taught us that the Muslim people of Algeria were created like all others. They have their history, illustrated by noble deeds. They have their religious unity and language. . . . This Muslim population is not France, it cannot be France, it does not want to be France.'[30]

After World War ll, when the process of the liquidating European colonial empires had begun, the French authorities resorted to a brutal policy of suppression and oppression against the nationalist uprisings in Algeria. This gave rise to the extremist groups whose prime objective was the political drive for independence. They were less concerned than earlier nationalist leaders with the reform or revival of Islam. The ideology was less important than the immediate goal of emancipation from oppressive foreign rule. But Islam was not completely ignored; it supplemented and reinforced the drive for political freedom. 'Islam was a vital force in providing the symbolism and emotion of the Algerian revolution. It was complementary to, rather than competing with, nationalism.'[31]

Ben Bella, who became the founder of the independent state of Algeria in 1962, was aware of the role of Islam in building his new nation. He identified Algeria as an Islamic country by taking symbolic Islamic actions: for example, when Algeria held its first national reception at the United Nations in New York in 1962, Ben Bella refused to serve alcoholic beverages, saying, 'even if it is custom, I am not going to do it. Algeria is a Muslim country. She will offer hospitality according to her own traditions.'[32]

Recent tragic developments in Algeria

Algeria gained independence, as we have already stated, at a heavy cost against the French atrocities during a five-year war of liberation. Algeria lost about one million people. After independence in 1962, Algeria enjoyed economic prosperity in the 1970s and 1980s. The founding president, Ben Bella, was over-thrown in a coup in 1965. In the 1990s Algeria started experiencing difficulties with a population of about 26 million people of whom 70 percent were below the age of 30.

Public disillusionment with years of official corruption and mismanagement, hastened the birth of a rightist movement in Algeria. Fierce riots in 1988 forced the National Liberation Front (FLN), the old guerrilla organization that since independence had run Algeria as a one party state, to promise the establishment of pluralism. Multiparty national elections, the first in Algeria's history, were held in December 1991. However, when it became evident that the rightist front, the Islamic Salvation Front (FIS), would win by a landslide, Algeria's military regime abruptly cancelled the vote, banned the FIS and declared a state of emergency. FIS leaders went under-ground and launched a terrorist campaign that has already claimed hundreds of lives. Algerian President Muhammad Boudiaf was gunned down in 1992 as he was delivering a speech; he might have been a victim of terrorists, though the FIS denied responsibility for his murder.

Since Boudiaf's assassination, Algeria has been in a virtual state of siege. Tanks and security forces maintain a high profile in Algiers and the surrounding area. Police continually patrol smaller towns, as well as neighbourhoods such as El Harrach, where sympathy for the FIS is known to run high. Yet the government has been unable to intimidate Algeria's homegrown Islamic forces or to snuff out terrorism by arresting or driving FIS leaders into exile. Terrorism 'comes in waves', admits Mohammad Hardi, Algeria's Minister of the Interior. 'Every time we act, (the terrorists) react. Every time we increase our level of effectiveness, they increase theirs.'

Unlike in Egypt, Western tourists have not been a target so far. But almost everyone associated with the ruling elite or the professions has been: civil servants, government ministers, lawyers and journalists, among others. The government's inability to halt the almost daily attacks has given the terrorists a romantic aura in the eyes of Algeria's young and poor. 'They can hit any time', boasts one teenager in Bab El Oued, an Algiers neighbourhood where every grimy wall bears the scrawled graffiti of the FIS. 'You don't know where they come from or where they go.'

Often they disappear into the so-called Triangle of Fear, a stretch of fruit and vegetable farms that extends some 30 miles southward from Algiers. Tanks and armoured personnel carriers guard a major crossroad on the highway that runs from the Triangle to the city of Oran, 200 miles to the west. Young soldiers stop every truck and every other car that comes through the crossroad. On Fridays, the Muslim holiday, police surround the main mosque in Blida, the Triangle's largest town, to ensure that mass demonstrations do not break out after prayer services.

Officials say it is impossible to know how many Algerians are active FIS supporters. Many of those who sympathize with the FIS do so more as a political protest than out of religious zeal: Algeria still has a secular tradition, particularly among its Westernized middle class. But that is cold comfort, considering the damage the government's 15-month-old crack-down against terrorism has done to Algeria's suffering economy.[33]

Talk of Reforms

Concerned by its poor image abroad and its deep unpopularity at home, Algeria's military-backed High State Council has promised to renew the democratic process it abrogated in January 1992. Gen. Khaled Nezzar, who heads the military regime, has proposed talks with opposition parties. President Ali Kafi has promised that before the end of the year he will dissolve the council and hold a popular referendum on 'change'. He also has promised to have a transitional government as well as economic reforms to make Algeria more hospitable to foreign investors.

Many Algerians are sceptical. The authorities talk about their good intentions, but that is not enough, says Omar Belhouchet, publisher of *El Watan*, Algeria's most prominent independent daily. (Belhouchet himself was the target of a failed terrorist attack.) They will have to make more concessions before the forces of democracy trust them. Even if that should happen, Algeria may never recapture the sense of promise and possibility of its first days of independence thirty years ago.[34]

Libya

Libya, considered a part of greater Maghrib, is unique in the world of Islam. The Libyan monarchy, overthrown on 1 September 1969, had a long history behind it. It began with Muhammad ibn al-Sanusi (1780-1859). He was the founder of an Islamic reform movement known as the Sanusiyyah, like the Wahhabi in Saudi Arabia and that of the Mahdi in Sudan, which gathered together various peoples who today live in Libya, Chad and western Egypt. The objectives of the Sanusiyyah movement were to set up an Islamic state and to purify Islamic practices and tradition. During the period of European colonialism, the Islamic regime in Libya was conquered by Italy, and by 1930 Italy had fully established its rule. As a result of Italy's defeat in World War II, Libya regained its independence in 1951. King Idris, a descendant of the founder of the Sanusiyyah, ruled Libya until 1969, when a group of young army officers, under the leadership of Mu'ammar Qaddafi, took power.

Qaddafi has become a highly controversial figure in the contemporary world, both among Muslims and non-Muslims. He has introduced a 'Third way' or 'Third International Theory' which is based he claims, on 'the spiritual precepts emanating from the heart of our sacred book the Noble Quran'. Qaddafi has written a Green Book, like Mao's Red Book, in which he elaborates his 'Third Way' for solving the problems and meeting the challenges faced by the Islamic world.

Qaddafi's hero was Gamal Nasser of Egypt whose ideology was, as we have already seen, pan-Arab, and not Islamic. Region, not religion, was Nasser 's main emphasis. Qaddafi is also a believer in pan-Arabism but he is equally enthusiastic about Islamic unity. His Green Book comprises three parts:

(i) 'The Solution to the Problem of Democracy';
(ii) 'Solution to the Economic Problem : Socialism'
(iii) 'Social Basis of the Third International Theory'.

Although Qaddafi claims to base his ideology on Islamic principles, he has departed from an important source of the Islamic law, the *shari'ah*; he does not include the *Sunnah*, the sayings and practices of the Prophet Muhammad in his Green Book.

He rejects the *Sunnah* on the grounds of it being inauthentic. Qaddafi has developed his own version of Islamic law, disregarding a vital part of that law and as such his version of Islamic ideology is rejected by many schools both inside and outside Libya. Qaddafi's main sources are the Quran and his own Green Book. Qaddafi limits the Quranic injunctions to the individual's personal life while his

Green Book contains elaborate provisions for a socialist system for Libya. He claims that socialism and true Islamic principles are not contradictory, but this is not entirely correct. While Islam enjoins a just and equitable socio-economic order, which may be compared with modern socialism, it permits private ownership of land and other property. Qaddafi has abolished the private ownership of land. Libya's name has been changed from the Libyan Arab Republic to The Socialist people's Libyan Arab Jamahiriya. Certain reforms have been introduced: for example, night clubs, gambling and drinking alcohol have been banned—these are not permissible in an Islamic state. The activities of foreign missionaries have also been banned. As a further step towards the islamization of Libyan society, in 1971 a law commission was set up to bring the existing laws of Libya into conformity with the injunctions of the Quran. However, Qaddafi's islamization of his society is based on his own interpretation of Islam which is, in many respects, not in conformity with the standard practices of Islam as defined by either the Shi'ah or the Sunni school. Qaddafi follows his own brand of Islamic principles. But there can be no denying that under Qaddafi Islam occupies a central place in Libya's socio-economic as well as its political order; the interpretations may be different, but in Islam interpretation through the process of individual judgement (*ijtihad*) and consensus *ijma'*) are permissible as long as clear and unambiguous injunctions of the Quran are not violated. Qaddafi cannot be accused of violating the fundamental principles of Islam in his various socio-economic reforms. His popular slogan is *al-fath* (victory, which means the beginning of Libya's revolution in 1969); it implies an 'Islamic Revolution and the glorious Quran is the *shari'ah* of our new socialist society.'[35]

Like some other Arab countries, such as Saudi Arabia, Libya has considerable oil resources. When Qaddafi came to power in 1969 Libya was already a rich country because of its oil resources, and when oil prices soared in the 1970s Qaddafi had enormous wealth at his disposal. He gave all-out support to the causes of the Palestinian people which was quite natural and justified. However, Qaddafi's alleged support for acts of terrorism (hijacking civilian aircraft, etc.) in the name of 'exporting' Islamic revolutions to other Muslim countries cannot be condoned. Islam could not allow such tactics. Islam strictly enjoins the rule of law and there is no room for terrorism or lawlessness in Islam. If Qaddafi has encouraged such acts, as is widely believed in the West and in some other Muslim countries, then he is guilty of violating the true spirit of Islam of which he claims to be a great champion.

In recent years, Libya under Qaddafi is experiencing severe strains and stresses with the Western powers—Britain, France and the USA—for its failure to hand over two Libyans who are allegedly accused of destroying a Pan-Am aircraft which killed many passengers; the Western powers imposed sanctions against Libya, increasing its economic plight. Earlier, in the 1980s President Ronald Reagan bombed the presidential palace where Qaddafi and his family were staying. It was a crude form of pressure and constitutes an example of the gun-boat policies of the old imperial powers.

Qaddafi is not popular in the Islamic *ummah* but the West's harsh treatment towards Libya is proving counter-productive. Some sympathy is growing in some parts of the *ummah* for the people of Libya.

Notes

1 Annemarie Schimmel, 47, *Islam: An Introduction*.
2 John L Esposito, *Islam and Politics* (second and revised edition), New York, 1987, 100-101.
3 *Ibid.*, 104-105.
4 Akbar S. Akbar, *Discovering Islam: Making Sense of Muslim History and Society*, London, 1988, 148.
5 Fouad Al Farsy, *Saudi Arabia: A Case Study in Development*, London, 1982; 'The Constitution: The Holy Quran' in chapter IV.
6 Ronald R MacIntryre, 'Saudi Arabia', in Mohammad Ayoob (ed.), *Politics of Islamic Reassertion*, New York, 1981, 13.
7 Akbar S Akbar, *op. cit.*, 69.
8 See M Heper and R Israeli (eds.), *Islam and Politics in the Modern Middle East*, New York, 1984, 331.
9 Clyde Haberman, 'As Islam is Revived, Secular Turks Wince', *New York Times*, 26 March 1989.
10 *Ibid.*
11 *Time (Magazine)*, June 28 1993.
12 *Sunday Telegraph* (London), June 17 1993.
13 *Newsweek*, June 28 1993.
14 Tareq Y Ismail, *Arab Left*, New York, 1976, 91.
15 Muhammad al-Ghazzali, *Our Beginning in Wisdom*, translated by Ismail R al-Faruqi, Washington D.C., 1953, 59.
16 See interviews with Anwar Sadat in *al-Nahar* (Beirut), 7 September 1974; *Christian Science Monitor*, 2 July 1976, cited in Heper and Israeli, *op. cit.*, 71.
17 Heper and Israeli, *op. cit.*, 77.
18 See *Islam In Transition: Muslim Perspective*, edited by John J Donohue and John L Esposito, New York, 1987, 131-132.
19 *Ibid.*, 135-36.
20 *Ibid.*
21 Cited in *Ibid.*, 139.
22 Cited in *Ibid.*, 139.
23 *Ibid.*
24 Voll, *op. cit.*, 169.
25 *Ibid.*, 170.
26 Ira M Lapidus, *A History of Islamic Societies*, Cambridge, 1988, 715.

27 Voll, *op. cit.*, 169.
28 *Ibid.*, 214.
29 Based on *Kessing Record of World Events* (UK 1991-93).
30 See Charles F Gallagher, *The United States and North Africa*, Harvard, 1964, 95.
31 Voll, *op. cit.*, 212.
32 Robert Marie, *Ahmed Ben Bella*, translated by Camilla Sykes, New York, 1967, 133.
33 *Kessing Record of World Events, idem.*
34 *Ibid.*
35 Esposito, *op. cit.*, 160.

Chapter V
Islam in the Non-Arab World

Iran

The last chapter looked at the role of Islam in the Arab states and Turkey. This chapter will examine the role of Islam in non-Arab Muslim countries: in south west, south and south east Asia and in Africa, as well as the case of persecuted Muslim minorities in non-Muslim countries.

Modern Iran, as a Western scholar has recently pointed out, inherited from the Safavid period (1501-1722) patterns of state, religious and tribal institutions which have shaped its history to the present day.[1] The Qajar dynasty (1779-1925) was not very dissimilar in its policies from its predecessor, the Safavid dynasty. During the 18th and 19th centuries, the *'ulama'* (the religious teachers) gained great influence and power at the cost of the weak government of the Qajar state, though during several periods there was coexistence between the Qajar regime and the *'ulama'*. But the intervention of the Russians and the British disrupted the delicate balance between state and religion in Iran under the Qajar regime. Ultimately the Russians and the British established spheres of influence in Iran; unlike many other parts of Asia and Africa in the heyday of European colonial expansionism in the 18th and 19th centuries Iran was not made a formal colony. Like the rest of the Muslim world which came under direct European colonial domination, the Iranians agitated against the European presence in their country. The *'ulama'* became the leading opponents of the foreign domination and of the Qajar regime which was seen as collaborating with the foreign powers. The tensions between the ruling Qajar government and the *'ulama'* became acute during the reign of Nasir al-Din Shah when the regime sought to curtail the power of the *'ulama'* and the *'ulama'* planned a *jihad* (holy war) against Russian expansionalist designs. These years saw a preparation for the struggle between the state and the *'ulama'*.[2]

This resulted in the convening of a constituent assembly to bring about a parliamentary system of government by curtailing the powers of the monarch. In 1906 a constitution was adopted which lasted, in theory, until 1979. The growth of constitutional government was supported by the *'ulama'* and pan-Islamists, like Jamal al-Din al-Afghani. The constitution of 1906 provided for a board of *'ulama'* which could veto power over the legislature if any law were repugnant to Quranic injunctions.

Neither constitutional monarchy nor democracy was however, successful in Iran. The Russians intervened in 1911 to destroy the constitutional order and restored the government of the shah. Then followed a period of political instability and confusion between the years of 1911 and 1925. With the collapse of the Czarist regime in Russia, the British virtually controlled the destiny of Iran under the Anglo-Persian treaty of 1919. Internal political instability continued until an army officer, Reza Khan, came to power, first as the head of the army; then in 1925 he declared himself the Shah of Iran, the founder of the Pahlavi dynasty. Reza Shah was removed from his throne during World War II when the British and the Russians forced him to resign and made his son Muhammad Reza Pahlavi, who had not yet reached the age of maturity, nominally king. Ultimately the United States replaced both the Russians and the British as the dominating power in Iran, and remained so until 1979.

The process of modernization which took place under Shah Muhammad Reza Pahlavi from the 1950s until his removal in 1979, and the Islamic forces' reaction to that process, is a highly important development in the relationship between state and religion in a predominantly Muslim country. It illustrates the inherent strength of Islamic forces in the mind of the Muslim; it also shows the grave risks for any regime in a Muslim society in trying not only to modernize, but also to westernize, at the cost of Islamic tradition and heritage. The Shah of Iran wanted to make his country 'the Japan' of south east Asia, or of the Middle East, ignoring the traditions and religious sentiments of the Muslims and their deep desire to preserve and foster their Islamic values and principles. Herein lay the failure of the Shah's attempts to create a modern Muslim state, which resulted in utter chaos, confusion and ultimately a costly revolution.

The Shah of Iran had not officially abandoned Islam, as Kemal

Ataturk sought to in 'secular' Turkey, but he had no regard for Islamic values and traditions. Personally he was arrogant and a strong believer in an authoritarian system: he did not tolerate opposition, ruthlessly suppressing any voice of dissent by all means, including the indiscriminate use of his secret service, SAVAK.

As a cabinet minister in the Pakistan Federal Government before the creation of Bangladesh in 1971, the present author had the opportunity to observe the Shah's policies and attitudes and to compare them with those of the Saudi kings. Both countries are predominantly Muslim in population; both were monarchies; both gained enormous wealth from oil revenues. The Saudi monarchs have achieved progress and modernisation of their country while maintaining the Islamic values and traditions. The Saudi monarchy keeps close contact with the people, valuing their cherished cultural and spiritual heritage. In contrast, the Shah of Iran kept his distance from his people and showed no sensitivity to their cherished cultural and spiritual tradition. He surrounded himself with top military officials and a Westernised urban elite who had no contact or knowledge of the deep-rooted feelings and aspirations of the vast majority of the rural population.

The Shah of Iran applied himself vigorously to building a powerful military machine in a strategically important area. Under successive US administrations from the 1950s Washington gave the Shah the 'green light' to pursue his grand military designs and the so-called modernisation of the urban areas of Iran. The vast majority of the rural population was ignored. Iran under the Shah was an example of contradiction and conflicts between a small urban elite and the vast majority of the people in a developing third world country and a deeply religious society.

In 1963 the Shah of Iran proclaimed his much publicized 'White Revolution'. (In the same year Saudi Arabia announced Prince Faisal's ten-point programme of pragmatic socio-economic reforms based on Islamic tradition.) Announcing the significance of his 'White Revolution', in a major policy speech to the Iranian legislature (a controlled body under an authoritarian system), on 6 October 1967, the Shah made no significant reference to Islamic tradition. He ignored the strength and depth of the feelings of his people for Islamic tradition. No plan or programme of social or economic reforms can succeed unless it takes proper account of the aspirations and sentiments of the people for whom the reforms are meant. The Shah was surely sincere in making Iran a progressive, modern state and a militarily stronger power. These aims were no doubt commendable and Iran did make some progress under the Shah.

In the 1960s Iran, Pakistan and Turkey formed a grouping for regional development purposes known as the Regional Cooperation for Development (RDC). These countries were also members of the American-sponsored military alliance, CENTO (originally known as the Baghdad Pact). There were frequent meetings among the top civil and military officials of the three countries. There were also summit meetings among the heads of state of the three countries. Pakistani presidents, Ayub Khan (1958-69) and Yahya Khan (1969-71), had frequent meetings with the Shah of Iran. During this period in the 1960s and in 1970, the present author held important government posts in Pakistan (first as Director-General [research] in the Pakistan Ministry of Foreign affairs and then as a member of the cabinet until February 1971), and therefore had the opportunity to read unpublished minutes and records of the dialogues between the heads of state of Iran, Pakistan and Turkey and the top military and civilian officials of these countries. What was most striking about these documents was the attitude of the Shah of Iran and the Iranian officials towards Islam. Although Turkey is officially a secular state, the Turkish leader and officials did not make the type of derogatory remarks about Islam that the Iranians made. Similarly, the Iranians showed a disparaging attitude towards Pakistan as an Islamic state. The Iranian's attitude towards the religious groups in their own country was one of complete contempt, if not hostility. They failed to appreciate the deep-rooted sentiments of the rural population of their own country and the growing influence of the religious teachers or *ayatullahs*, as the higher religious leaders in Iran are known. The Shah, in his discussions with Pakistani presidents, Ayub Khan and Yahya, betrayed an attitude of indifference, if not contempt, to the role of Islam in nation-building. He and his ruling elite's contention was that Iran was there before Islam, Iran can do away with Islam and Iran shall survive without Islam.[3] It showed a colossal ignorance of the political dynamics of their own country.

The Shah unwisely sought to identify his rule with the pre-Islamic Persian empire. Though his father was a military officer without any 'royal' or 'blue blood', the Shah began to consider himself the descendant of a pre-Islamic imperial dynasty that had lasted for over 2000 years. In 1971 the Shah observed the '2500th anniversary' of the Iranian empire, declaring himself the descendant of an ancient royal family which had been in existence long before the advent of Islam in the 7th century. There was a grand celebration attended by a large number of foreign heads of state and of government: but religious groups in Iran were greatly offended by its subtle attempt to separate Islam from the ruling regime. Like the Czars of Russia, the Shah could not see the writing on the wall.

With this total disregard for the values and traditions of the people, the Shah proved to be a failure and had to quit his throne in disgrace and humiliation. In contrast, King Faisal was successful because his ten-point plan reflected both the Saudi people's aspirations (based on their religion) and the modern scientific and technological needs of his country. There is still the misconception, both in the West and among the Western-educated Muslim elite, that progress or modernization and a return to the principles of the Quran are not compatible. This assessment is not correct. The Muslim concept of a progressive, modern, developed, equitable, just and fair socio-economic and political order has to be evolved and worked out in accordance with Islamic tradition and values. As already explained, in Islam there is no separation between the spiritual and temporal spheres of human life. In an Islamic society material progress or development must be achieved in the context of Islamic tradition, otherwise it is doomed to fail. The case of the Shah of Iran provides a vivid illustration of the inherent strength of Islamic tradition in modern Muslim nation states. The sooner this is accepted the better for the people of these states and for the Western world if it wishes to win the goodwill and friendship of the world's Muslim population of nearly one billion. In a Muslim society, the path to progress, modernization, democratic order and the realisation of an ideal and fair society lies in the true spirit of Islam.

Islam must not be judged by any particular country or any particular leader or leaders. Islamic ideology must be judged by only one source—the will of God as revealed in the Quran and practised by the Prophet Muhammad.

The Iranian revolution was the product of the authoritarian and secular rule of the Shah of Iran (1941-79). He and his father failed to recognise the strength of the religious feelings of the Muslims of Iran. As a result an explosive situation was gradually developing underground, occasionally boiling over into wide-spread conflict between government and society (as in 1948-53 and again in 1960-63). The Western powers, in particular the United states, gave unqualified support to the Shah without taking into account the deep-rooted and centuries-old religious sentiments and traditions of the people of Iran. The result was the Islamic Revolution of 1979. We can only hope that the true Islamic spirit of tolerance, peace and universal brotherhood ultimately triumph in the predominantly Muslim country of Iran.

Afghanistan

Afghanistan is a highly traditional country, 99.5 percent of whose population is Muslim. The state of Afghanistan was founded in 1747 and Islam has been a factor in both the public and personal lives of the Afghans. Unlike neighbouring Pakistan or Iran in the post-Shah era, the Afghan regime has not publicly designated their political order as Islamic: but no political regime, monarchy, dictatorial republic (1973-8), or even the communist regime that had been in power since 1978, could disregard Islam as a factor in Afghanistan's socio-political order. Even the communist constitution of the puppet regime in Kabul declared Islam the 'state religion' of the country.

When one Muslim country after another fell to the expansionist designs of colonial European powers in the 18th and 19th centuries, Afghanistan somehow managed to escape from total domination by any European power. Both Czarist Russia and the British (for the security of the Indian empire) wanted to subjugate Afghanistan, or at least keep it as a buffer between them, but due partly to its geographical location and largely to the strong sense of independence of the people of Afghanistan, it did not become a fully-fledged colony of any European power. Though the British, after their repeated failures to conquer Afghanistan, gained some control over the country's foreign policy, internally the Afghans maintained their freedom from direct foreign domination.

Afghanistan had a long history of military empires. The Durrani dynasty, which continued until 1973, was established by a powerful tribal chief in the 19th century. A member of the Durrani dynasty, Amir 'Abd al-Rahman (1844-1901), consolidated the tribal groups and organised modern Afghanistan. In order to meet the growing threats from the Russians, 'Abd al-Rahman made peace with the British, who recognised him as the king of Afghanistan in return for control over Afghanistan's foreign policy. The British government treated Afghanistan as a buffer state between Russia and their Indian empire. Rahman died in 1901 and was succeed by his son Habib Allah, who was killed in 1919 in mysterious circumstances. Afghanistan enjoyed internal stability and peace during this period (1901-19). There was, however, resentment over the dominant British influence and a resistance movement was backed by religious leaders, notably Mahmud Tarzi (1865-1933), a follower of the great pan-Islamist, Jamal al-Din al-Afghani. Tarzi's daughter was married to Habib Allah's son, Amanallah, who became king of Afghanistan after the murder of his father in 1919.

Amanallah's reign (1919-28) was significant for the history of modern Afghanistan. He began a modest process of modernisation of the highly traditional Afghan society. Though Amanallah never went so far as the Shah of Iran, and though he did not dissociate himself from religious groups, yet his allegedly Western reforms alienated some extremist groups. When the king and his wife visited England (during this visit Amanallah secured full independence from British control over his country's foreign policy), the tribal religious leaders prominently displayed pictures of the Afghan queen driving in the state coach with the English monarch, George V, and shaking hands with him—which was, according to the mullahs, not permissable for a Muslim lady under Islamic tradition, albeit a narrow interpretation of Islam. On his return from his European tour, King Amanallah was faced with a major revolt, the causes of which were both religious and tribal. The king was unable to suppress the revolt and had to flee the country in 1928, spending the rest of his life in exile in Rome. The failure of Amanallah to carry out his modest reforms without challenging the basic principles of Islam was a sad chapter in the history of modern Afghanistan. His departure was followed by a period of total chaos and confusion; finally a member of the royal family Muhammad Nadir, backed by the army, suppressed the revolt and became the king of Afghanistan. Nadir's reign (1929-33) was noted for a 'policy that was committed to Afghan independence and open to gradual modernization but he avoided reforms that would anger the conservatives. He cooperated with great tribal notables and worked to placate the religious leaders.'[4] He was thus successful in bringing internal stability and political cohesion to Afghanistan. By the time of his death, his son Muhammad Zahir was to become the new king without any power struggle. The succession was smooth and peaceful.

King Zahir continued his father's cautious policy of modernization until he was overthrown in 1973. He introduced reforms only when he was sure that they would not upset the delicate balance between the government and the religious establishments. At the end of World War II, when the British empire was liquidated and a new Muslim country, Pakistan, was established, Zahir challenged the validity of the international boundary line (the Durand line) which had been established by the British between the new state of Pakistan and Afghanistan. By the mid 1950s Pakistan, the largest Muslim country, and also an Islamic state, entered into a number of American-sponsored military pacts, both bilateral and multilateral, including CENTO and SEATO. Pakistan also gave the Americans valuable military bases near the Russian border, one of which was the Badabar Base, where the U2 incident originated.[5] Pakistan's pro-Western policy, prompted mainly by the need for security in relation to India, made Moscow furious. Following the old myth of 'my enemy's enemy is my friend', King Zahir turned to Moscow for support in his disputes with Pakistan over the Durandline. The

Kremlin leaders responded quickly to Zahir, in order to punish Pakistan for her pro-Western policy. In their 1955 tour of India and Afghanistan the Russian leaders, Khruschev and Bulganin, gave unqualified support to Afghanistan's claims over the Durand line.[6]

King Zahir's flirtation with Moscow gave him some immediate diplomatic boosts, but his policy led to a process of penetration and subversion of Afghan society by the USSR—Afghanistan's close neighbour. The Russians gave economic and military aid to Kabul. More significantly, a new Russian-influenced and Russian-trained middle class emerged in Afghan society: they began a subtle process of Marxist-orientated modernisation and reforms, which culminated in the emergence of a powerful communist party in a predominantly Muslim country. The communists were careful not to challenge Islam and its tradition openly; and they continued to pay lip service to Islam.

King Zahir was overthrown by his cousin, Daud, who had also been his prime minister since 1953, in a bloodless coup in 1973. Daud abolished the monarchy and declared himself the president of the 'Republic of Afghanistan'.

Daud was a constitutional dictator. The 1963 constitution, proclaimed during the reign of King Zahir, had reaffirmed Islam as the state religion, and Daud followed the same path of giving Islam a definite role in the country's political order. No law which was repugnant to the basic principles of Islam was to be valid. A 'modernising Islamic process', begun under the monarchy, continued to be followed by the new republic. Daud was alleged to be moving away from Moscow and closer to Iran and the United States: this alienated the emerging communist forces which had been growing, thanks to Kabul's pro-Russian foreign policy and the Soviet penetration into Afghan society with the help of the communist party of Afghanistan, known as the Peoples' Democratic Party of Afghanistan.

Islam as a political factor in Afghanistan had a very paradoxical history. Islam was never challenged openly, even by the Soviet-orientated urban elite or the ruling authority. But during the 1950s and 1960s, Islam was gradually losing support among the increasingly powerful urban elite whose ideology was either nationalism, prompted particularly by the dispute with the Islamic Republic of Pakistan, or a veiled socialism inspired by the Russian-trained middle class. In their initial public appearances on the political scene, the urban intellectuals 'emerged as Islamic modernists rather than Afghan nationalists. Their efforts, therefore, were concentrated on changing the content of the dominant Islamic discourse rather than introducing a novel (nationalist) discourse . . . The modernists interpreted Islam as the way to scientific and technological development, equality of the citizens before the law, wholesale reform of the state institutions and anti-imperialism.'[7]

This is the background to the rise of the communist regime in Afghanistan's traditional and deeply religious society. We shall discuss its significance along with the 'Islamic Revolution' in Iran and 'Islamic Democracy' in Pakistan under President Zia-ul-Haq in Chapter VIII.

Islam in South Asia: Bangladesh, Pakistan and India

The Muslims of the subcontinent are noted for their strong attachment to Islam and its ideology both in their public and private lives. They also have strong bonds with the Islamic *ummah*. They have never tired of showing their unqualified and consistent support and extending their fullest cooperation and assistance to the hopes and aspirations of the world of Islam; they make no distinction between Arab and non-Arab Muslims, nor between Asian, African or western Muslims. They are noted for their zeal and enthusiasm for the unity and universal brotherhood of the Islamic *ummah*.

Islam entered the South Asian subcontinent about thirteen centuries ago when the Arab general Muhammad b. Qasim occupied Sind in 712 AD. The Muslims ruled the subcontinent for about six centuries, until the Mughal Empire became fragmented and the subcontinent, like many other areas of the Afro-Asian world, fell prey to the colonial expansionism of the European powers in the 18th and 19th centuries. India became the 'jewel' of the British crown and the British monarch acquired the title of emperor as a result of the establishment of the British empire in India; the British monarch's representative, the viceroy, remained the supreme lord of the British Indian empire until 1947. Before the British left India in 1947, they divided the empire into two sovereign independent states: the India Union and the Muslim state of Pakistan (which at that time included the present day Muslim state of Bangladesh.)

Pakistan

The role of Islam as a nation-building force and its place in Muslim independent countries can be best illustrated by the Indian Muslims' struggle for a separate state of their own where they hoped to cherish and foster their spiritual and cultural heritage.

Sir Muhammad Iqbal, the post-philosopher of Indian Muslims, said: 'It cannot be denied that Islam regarded as an ethical ideal plus a certain kind of policy—by which expression I mean a social structure regulated by a specific ethical ideal—has always been the chief formative factor in the life-history of the Muslims of India.' Iqbal made this statement in 1930, when he first gave expression to the vision of a 'new world' for the Indian Muslims by proclaiming that the future of the Muslims, with their distinct cultural and spiritual urges, lay in a separate state.[8]

What led the Muslims to demand a separate state? Why could they not be fused into a single nation with the Hindus with whom they had lived for centuries? Like the creation of any other national state, Pakistan's birth was conditioned by many factors—political, economic, sociological, psychological—operating at a particular time and place. It would perhaps be over simplification to look for a single factor or cause. Yet the fact remains that the *raison d'être* of the emergence of Pakistan as an entity, independent of the rest of India, has been the recognition of the distinction in the rights, interests, and cultures of Hindus and Muslims considered as separate nations. Quaid-i-Azam Mohammad Ali Jinnah, the founder of Pakistan, declared in 1944 that, by any definition or test of a nation, Muslims and Hindus were two major nations. Pakistan was claimed as a homeland for Indian Muslims on the principle of the right of self-determination.[9]

Pakistan's Experiment of an Islamic Democratic State (1947-71)

The role of Islam in building a socio-political structure was widely discussed in Pakistan when it came into existence in 1947. The first prime minister, Liaquat Ali Khan, predicted that Pakistan would be 'the laboratory of practical Islam'. Speaking to the Constituent Assembly, he said, 'Islam expects its followers to build up a society for the purpose of the good life, as the Greeks would have called it,' and emphasized 'the essential principles of Islam, including the principles of democracy, freedom, tolerance and social justice' in building the new society.

The founder of Pakistan, Mohammed Ali Jinnah, fully shared the view that the broad principles of Islam should be incorporated into the constitution. He claimed: 'Islam and its idealism have taught us democracy; it has taught equality of men, justice and fair play to everybody. It is the indwelling spirit and the history of the nation from which constitutions are made. As Aristotle would say, a constitution is a kind of life and a form of government is the expression of the kind of life which the state is designed to foster. The constitution of a country should try to reflect the ideals on which people want to base their political life; it should try to implement the objectives which embody the aspirations of the nation. A constitution, in order to be successful, should take into consideration the morals and attainments of the people for whom it is meant.'[10]

This is the basic justification for incorporating Islamic ideology into the constitution of Pakistan, but its inclusion has not led to abandoning democratic institutions. By giving Islamic ideology, what Professor Smith calls a 'twentieth century interpretation', the framers of the constitution could absorb all the essential ingredients of a democratic government—equality, universal franchise, representative institutions, and freedom of speech, the press, and of movement—into the Islamic constitution of Pakistan. The constitution of Pakistan is 'Islamic via Democratic'. By enacting a democratic constitution the Pakistanis have integrated democracy into their religio-social ideal. On 23 March 1986, after nine years work, Pakistan had framed a constitution proclaiming Pakistan an Islamic Republic in which the principles of freedom, equality, tolerance and social justice as enunciated by Islam should be fully observed. Despite the many divergent concepts of the character of an Islamic constitution, in the end the framers of the constitution were successful in developing one which was a commendable synthesis of modern needs and Islamic principles. While some of the extremist *'ulama'* and a few ultra-secularists were disappointed, the public in general welcomed the Islamic character of the constitution.[11]

Pakistan's experiment with an Islamic democracy suffered setbacks in the 1950s and 1960s. The democratic process was destroyed by a powerful group of civil and military officials who had faith neither in democracy nor in Islamic ideology. The so-called civilian heads of the state, Governor-General Gholam Muhammad and President Iskander Mirza, turned the democratic process into a farce and put the Islamic provisions of the constitution into cold storage—though they never dared to challenge Islamic ideology openly or publicly. Then followed a period of martial law: the first military regime, under General Ayub Khan, lasted from 1958 to 1969, and the second period of martial law from 1969 to 1971. Democracy was formally buried and Islamic provisions were maintained only to satisfy the religious sentiment of the people of Pakistan—these provisions were not implemented.

The result was tragic. The great unifying force of Islam was not utilised to keep East and West Pakistan together; with the failure of democracy, the people of East Pakistan lost all control in the affairs of the country. The result was growing tensions and conflicts between East and West Pakistan. As power was concentrated in a small but powerful ruling elite composed entirely of West Pakistani civil and military officials, the people of East Pakistan had no share in the decision-making process. Their revolt against the ruling clique of West Pakistan culminated in 1971 in a nine-month civil war, which resulted in the dismemberment of the largest Islamic country. East Pakistan became a new state, Bangladesh, and West became the 'new' and smaller Pakistan.[12]

As we have already stated, in Bangladesh, the founder of the country, Mujibur Rahman, was keen to placate his bosses in New Delhi. India had played a vital role in the dismemberment of Pakistan, not out of love for the Muslims of Bangladesh, but to destroy the ideological Islamic foundation of Pakistan. The prime objective of India's foreign policy since 1947 has been to weaken and if possible to destroy the largest Islamic state. The civil war in Pakistan in 1971 gave India that great opportunity. Mujib, out of 'gratitude' to India, or more accurately out of his stupidity, eliminated Islam from the 1972 constitution and, following India's example, declared Bangladesh a 'secular state'.

The period between 1958 and 1972 had been a sad and disappointing era in the history of the Muslims of the South Asian subcontinent. But by the mid-1970s, new regimes emerged in both Bangladesh and Pakistan which restored Islam to its proper place in the political and social order of the two countries. In Pakistan, a grand process of *Nifazi-i Nizam-i Islam* began under a devoted Muslim ruler, Muhammad Zia-ul-Haq. In Bangladesh secularism was formally buried by the two post-Mujib regimes (1975-81 and 1982-90). Islam has again been revived in Bangladesh by two military rulers, Zia-ur Rahman (1975-85) and H M Ershard (1982-90). Islam has been declared the state religion, reflecting the aspirations of the Muslims of Bangladesh.

Indonesia

In South East Asia there is also a large number of Muslims. Malaysia, which we like to consider as approaching an 'Ideal Non-Arab Muslim State', will be dealt with below. Here we describe Islam in Indonesia which is today the largest Muslim country in terms of population.

Islam entered Indonesia during the 13th century through Muslim port city-states, the earliest of which was Pasai in north Sumatra. A number of small Muslim city-states developed from the 13th to the 17th century in the areas which constitute Indonesia today. These small states were mainly trading centres and they were noted for local rivalries and cultural differences. The Dutch East India Company, like the British East India Company, took full advantage of the tensions and rivalries among these smaller states and finally established its colonial authority over the whole territory that now comprises Indonesia. The Dutch rule lasted until 1942 when Japan 'liberated' Indonesia from colonial rule and established her own hegemony there. Indonesia declared independence after the defeat of Japan in World War II. The Dutch, backed by Britain and Australia, made desperate but unsuccessful attempts to regain the former colony. Indonesia became an independent state when, under Indonesian military pressure and United Nations' political pressure, the Dutch finally recognised Indonesian independence in August 1950.

As in many other parts of the Afro-Asian world, the nationalist movement in Indonesia in the 20th century comprised both secular and Islamic forces. The formation of the Javanese secular cultural organisation, Budi Utomo (Noble Endeavour), in 1908 was a significant event in the nationalist movement. A Muslim counterpart to Budi Utomo—Muhammadiyya was formed in 1912. These two organisations could be compared with the Indian National Congress and the All-India Muslim League in the South Asian subcontinent—the former secular and the latter its Muslim counterpart. But unfortunately for the Muslims of Indonesia, there were no leaders of the stature of Muhammad Ali Jinnah, the founder of Pakistan, and the Indonesian Muslims' aspirations to establish an Islamic state in Indonesia were not successful. The nationalist leaders, Sukarno and Mohammad Hatta, were Muslims, but their orientation was Western secular nationalism rather than Islamic nationalism.

In addition to Muhammadiyya, there appeared two other Muslim organisations: Sarekat Islam (Islamic Federation) in 1912 and Nahdat ul-Ulema in 1926. Sarekat was divided into factions: a left wing and an Islamic wing. The Islamic wing formed the first Islamic political party, the Indonesian Islamic Party (PSII). Disunity among the Islamic forces and lack of great leaders were responsible for the failure of Islam to become the dominant force in the freedom movement in Indonesia. In 1943 another Muslim political party was founded, with Japanese encouragement—Japan wanted to strengthen the Islamic forces to utilize anti-colonial sentiments among the Indonesian Muslims. The aim of the new party, Masjumi, was 'to unify and coordinate the whole of the Muslim movement'.[13] But the fate of Masjumi in gathering Indonesian Muslims together was no better than other Muslim organisations and parties. They could not effectively challenge the secular nationalist movement's charismatic leaders.

State Ideology and Islam

By 1945 the Japanese realised that the end of World War II and their defeat, was not far off, so they set up a committee of sixty-two members to plan the constitutional framework of Indonesia. The committee bitterly debated state ideology. The secularist nationalist and the Islamic groups confronted each other on the issues of the relationship between the state and religion (Islam) in defining state ideology. Mohammad Hatta (who subsequently became the first vice-president of the Republic, with Sukarno as the president) pleaded for the separation of state and religion, while the Islamic groups wanted to give Islam a positive place in the political order of the republic.[14] Finally Sukarno proclaimed his 'five principles' of the state ideology (*Pancasila*): belief in one God, nationalism, humanism, social justice, and democracy. Sukarno realised that Indonesia could not endorse the concept of an Islamic state: so here was the reference to 'belief in one God'. At one stage he went further and agreed to add, after 'belief in God', 'with the obligation for adherents of Islam to practise Islamic law' and he proposed a further concession by providing that the president 'be born Indonesian and a Muslim' in the document known as the Jakarta Charter. But these concessions to the Islamic groups were opposed by the non-Muslim members of the committee as well as by the secular-orientated Muslims, and they were dropped; however, 'belief in God' was expanded to 'belief in the one and only God', which is the most fundamental principle of Islam as laid down in the first *kalimah*.

The reaction of the Islamic groups to the state ideology that was finally approved was one of great resentment and anger. They revolted against the new republican regime headed by Sukarno and Hatta, and, in some provinces there were armed uprisings against the republic. The revolt began in West Java where a Muslim leader, Kartosuwirjo, proclaimed 'an Islamic state of Indonesia' with himself as *imam*, the head of the Islamic state. *Dar al-Islam* (the domain of Islam) was proclaimed in other parts of the country. Unfortunately the Islamic revolt coincided with the Dutch 'police action' against the republic in December 1948. Sukarno made an all out effort to preserve the unity and independence of the republic against the Dutch military, rousing the national sentiments of the people, both Muslim and non-Muslim, against Dutch aggression. The people gave support to Sukaro's national struggle to preserve independence rather than to any ideological battle over the religious issue. The attempts to establish an Islamic state in Indonesia were unsuccessful for many reasons. According to Donald K Emerson: 'Had the devout been a great majority, they could have grown an Islamic state in independent Indonesia organically, 'from below', by making official what was customary; on the contrary, practising Muslims were in a minority inside a lax and syncretic majority, especially in Java, the nation's demographic, cultural and political core. Lacking an effective mass base, Muslim politicians lobbied in constituent and consultative assemblies from the 1940s onward, hoping to create an Islamic state artificially by legislative fiat. They failed . . . the provinces who sporadically waged holy wars fared no better.'[15]

This ended a sad chapter of the Muslim struggle to establish an Islamic state of South East Asia.

Islam after Independence era (1945-92)

Indonesia began its political career with a parliamentary democracy, and the first general election was held in 1955. Of the Muslim parties, Masjumi had better prospects, but in fact gained only 45 seats. The Nahdat ul-Ulema cooperated with Sukarno's nationalist party, while the Masjumi party went into the political wilderness, in desperation giving its support regional revolts (alleged to be aided by the CIA) in Sumatra and Sulwawesi, directed against Sukarno's pro-leftist foreign policy. The Masjumi was pro-Western and anti-communist. The revolts were crushed and Sukarno banned Masjumi in 1960. Sukarno began a 'guided democracy' in the late 1950s and 1960s. There is no scope for ascertaining the peoples' wishes or preferences under such disguised authoritarian systems as 'guided' or 'controlled' democracy. Sukarno remained in power until 1965 when an abortive communist coup introduced army rule, with general Suharto as president. The Masjumi party and the Islamic groups expected a better deal from the new regime because of their common opposition to the communist forces. But Suharto continued the secular policy of his predecessor and the 'guided democracy' of an authoritarian system.

What are the prospects of the Islamic forces in the largest Muslim country? Will there be an emergence of a radical Islamic regime in Indonesia in the near future? Indonesia, under both Sukarno and Suharto, has not shown any special enthusiasm for the unity of Muslim countries worldwide. Sukarno, with Nehru of India, Tito of Yugoslavia and Nasser of Egypt, was one of the founding fathers of the non-alignment movement. Neither Sukarno nor Suharto had any special sentimental attachment to the growth and development of the Islamic *ummah*, though Sukarno forged special links with Pakistan in the later stages of his rule and Indonesia has been a member of the OIC. But Indonesia cannot be described as a dynamic force in the activities or policies of the world of Islam. Does this mean that Islam has no prospects in Indonesia? The answer is difficult and complex.

It would be a grave mistake to write off the forces of Islam in Indonesia. Islam has been dormant in the country's political order and foreign relations, but the Indonesians are pious and good Muslims. The present author during a visit to Indonesia saw the widespread and regular observance by the Indonesian Muslims of the five pillars of Islam.

Suharto may be a secular army general, but who can predict that there may not emerge a Muslim military leader in Indonesia who will encourage the revival of Islam as a political factor? It was a military general in Pakistan, the late Zia-ul-Haq, who introduced the far reaching and comprehensive process of Islamization in Pakistani society and government. In Bangladesh, it was two military rulers who buried secularism and made Islam the state religion. There are many instances of military leaders in Muslim countries contributing to the cause of Islam. Who could, for instance, predict that the powerful secular government of the Shah of Iran would produce a revolutionary Islamic regime in Iran? So though Islamic forces today are weak in Indonesia and the present secular military regime is stable, there cannot be any certainty that the Islamic resurgence which has captured the imagination of the vast majority of Muslims all over the world could not make an impact on the largest Muslim state of the Islamic *ummah*.

Islam in Africa

It is neither possible nor fair to attempt a full account of Islam in a whole continent in just one section of one chapter. In our discussion on Islam in Africa, we will focus on general trends, not because Africa is unimportant in the history of contemporary Islam, but due to lack of space and time. We hope to produce a special work on Islam in Africa in due course: Islam has great potential in the newly independent countries of Africa, some of which have predominantly Muslim populations. Current trends towards self-assertion in the Islamic *ummah* have reached the African continent, and the resurgence of Islam of the 1970s and 1980s has had an impact in Africa. Great changes are taking place in Africa: the European colonial empires have gone and since the mid-1960s a large number of new African states have emerged. In many of the newly independent African countries, Muslims constitute an overwhelming majority of the population (e.g., Mauritania, Senegal, Guinea, Mali, Niger); Muslims also form majorities in Nigeria, Sudan and Tanzania, and there are substantial minority Muslim groups in other African countries such as the Ivory Coast, Ghana and Sierra Leone.

Through the 19th century Muslims penetrated the African continent 'as traders, missionaries and warriors.'[16] The expansion of Islam in Africa was halted by European colonial rule but, even during the colonial era, the spread of Islam by peaceful means did not end.

Spencer Trimingham, who has written extensively on Islam in Africa, divides Islam in Africa into seven 'cultural zones' which he identifies by the 'pre-existing geographical and cultural background of the inhabitants and the historical aspects of the penetration and impact of Islam.' The seven cultural zones are: Mediterranean Africa; Western Sudan; Central Sudan; Eastern or Nilotic Sudan; North-Eastern Ethiopic zone; East Africa. Mediterranean Africa is further subdivided into Egypt and the Maghrib, making seven zones in all.[17]

Ira Lapidus points out that, whereas Islam entered the Middle East and the Indian subcontinent by conquest and by state regimes, Islam was spread in Africa by Muslim merchants, teachers and settlers. He divides Islamic societies in Africa into three main regions:

> (i) the Central and western Sudanic belt, settled from the origins of Islam until the 18th century—this region was the centre of a succession of Muslim empires.
> (ii) Guinean Savannah, Senegambia and Mauritania, settled from the 13th to the 19th century and an area of Muslim *jihads* and state formation in the 18th and 19th centuries.
> (iii) Eastern Sudan, the East African coast and the hinterlands of Ethiopia, Somalia, and Kenya. Islam entered this third zone from Egypt, Arabia and the Indian Ocean region.[18]

The colonial powers left behind states which have only territorial unity: the peoples of these newly independent countries are extremely divergent, ethnically, linguistically and in their customs and ways of life. There is religious diversity, though Islam is predominant in several newly independent African countries. Because of the diverse nature of African societies, Islam in Africa, except in Mediterranean areas, shows the strong influence of regional culture, tradition, customs etc. There are common religious rituals, but Islam's political influence is not as great as in some parts of the world. In many cases, Islam was adjusted to local traditions and circumstances, though without sacrificing the fundamentals of Islamic teaching. The influence of Islam is, however, significant in several African countries, notably Sudan, Mauritania, Senegal, Nigeria, Niger and Somalia.

Islam's entry to Africa included some other methods. The ways of Islam in Africa had more than one route.

John Esposito speaks of 'Jihad revivalist movements' in Africa. He states: 'A series of Jihad revivalist movements led to the establishment of Islamic states such as those of Uthman Dan Fadio in Nigeria (1754-1817), the Grand Sanusi in Libya (1878-1859), and the Mahdi of the Sudan (1848-1885). A distinctive characteristic was its sufi leadership—reformist, militant and politically orientated charismatic heads of sufi orders. Their posture was in striking contrast to the syncretistic, passive, non-worldly image of mystic orders whose missionaries had brought Islam to much of Africa. Although much of the success of African sufism had been attributed to its openness to cultural synthesis, blending Islam with indigenous beliefs and practices, reformers now attempted to bring sufism into conformity with the demands of Islamic law, in order to stamp out what they regarded as idolatrous customs that had led to social and moral decline. Sufism was not suppressed but redefined, emphasizing a spirituality that incorporated militant activism with its willingness to fight and die to establish Islamically oriented states and societies. Prayer and political action were joined together in the earthly as well as the heavenly pursuit of the divine.'[19]

The Sanusi and Mahdi Movements and Islam in Africa

Esposito gives an account of the Sanusiyyah and Mahdi movements and their impact on the spread of Islam in Africa. He states that, born in Algeria, Muhammad 'Ali b. al-Sanusi (1787-1859), or, as he came to be known, the Grand Sanusi, studied in Cairo and Makkah, where he earned a reputation as a scholar of law and *Hadith*. He rejected the political fragmentation of Muslims resulting from tribalism and regionalism and reasserted the need for Islamic unity and solidarity. A student in Makkah of Ahmad b. Idris, the renowned scholar of Prophetic traditions and a revivalist sufi, al-Sanusi followed in the footsteps of this great reformer in calling for the purification of sufism and much of Islamic law, which, he believed had been distorted by *'ulama'* interpretation. This and his claim to be a *mujtahid* (an independent interpreter of Islam) alienated him from many of the *'ulama'* and sufi leaders. Al-Sanusi moved from Arabia to what is modern-day Libya after the death of his teacher and established the Sanusiyyah brotherhood, a reformist and missionary movement that created a network of settlements across central and western Africa.

The Sanusi programme pursued a path of militant activism. It involved the unification of tribal factions in the name of their common Islamic brotherhood and the establishment of sufi centres, or lodges, which served as places of prayer and instruction as well as of military training and social welfare. They were committed to both the creation of an Islamic state and the spread of Islam. Although not hostile to the outside world, descendants of the Grand Sanusi resisted European colonialism. His grandson led the Sanusi resistance to Italian colonial rule and at independence became King Idris I of Libya.[20]

The Sudan

In contrast to the Grand Sanusi, Muhammad Ahmad (1848-85), the founder of the Mahdiyyah in the Sudan, proclaimed himself Mahdi in 1881; when the Mahdist forces finally triumphed over Egyptian forces in 1885 an Islamic state was established in the Sudan which existed until 1899.[21]

The Sudanese republic deserves special attention in discussing the rule of Islam in modern African countries. We shall, therefore, take the Sudan as an illustration of the influence of Islam in the modern African state.

Islam entered the regions which constitute the modern state of the Sudan from Egypt. The first Muslim influx took place in the 9th century and its people have been mainly Muslim since then. By the 19th century the Sudan had a long history of Muslim rule, a substantial Muslim population and the development of Islamic institutions. The evolution of Islam in the Sudan is closer to that of the Middle East and the Maghrib than in other parts or regions under the Egyptian hegemony of Muhammad 'Ali (1820-30). A reformist movement like the Wahhabi in Saudi Arabia emerged in the Sudan, the Mahdi movement.

Organized by Shaykh Muhammad Ahmad (1848-85), a pious member of the Sammaiyah order, which had been established in 1800 by Shaykh Ahmad al-Tayyib, the Mahdi's objective was 'restoration of the true Islam'. Shaykh Muhammad Ahmad declared himself Iman or Mahdi and rose against Egyptian rule. He drove out both the Egyptians and the British (who had occupied Egypt in 1882 and established 'Anglo-Egyptian co-domination' over the Sudan in 1885) and set up an Islamic state, Mahdiyyah, which was defeated by Anglo-Egyptian forces in 1895. The Anglo-Egyptian co-domination was revived in 1899 and lasted until 1955. In 1956 the Sudan became an independent state.

The Sudan is a huge but extremely poor country. The northern part is predominantly Muslim, while in the southern provinces are substantial Christian and animist minorities. There are acute tensions between the Muslim-dominated north and the non-Muslim south which created tremendous problems of national integration. Like most of the former British colonies, on becoming independent in the mod-1950s the Sudan experimented with the British parliamentary system, which, however, proved to be a failure. In 1958 the first military regime took power under General Ibrahim Abbud. The military regime lasted from 1958 to 1964 when General Abbud was forced to quit. Then followed a period of civilian coalition government (1964-69), which failed to solve the country's desperate economic problems and the regional-cum-religious tensions between north and south, which led to a second military regime under Colonel Gaafar Nimeiri, who remained in power until 1985.

In the early years of his rule, Nimeiri was firm with the Islamic parties and with the communists. He tried to make peace with the non-Muslim southern provinces by recognizing their African identity and autonomy. The southern provinces were opposed to 'Arabism' and 'Islamization', but Nimeiri realised that he must also recognize the strength of the Islamic forces which the Mahdists represented. In foreign policy Nimeiri wanted closer ties with Egypt and followed a pro-Western policy. He also sponsored large-scale agricultural development projects along the Nile.

By the mid-1980s, Nimeiri could no longer afford to ignore the growing influence of Islam, particularly among university and college students who, inspired by the resurgence of Islam which had begun at the end of the 1970s, became vocal in demanding the Islamization of Sudanese society and its political order. Nimeiri moved closer to the Islamic forces, reconciling the Mahdists. Changes to Islamic law, constitutional and legal changes were sought as was the increase of the Islamic content of Sudanese society and government. However, the Islamic revival led to further tensions and conflicts between north and south. The country's economic problems were also acute, and charges of corruption and maladministration were widespread. Introducing Islam as a political or social force to a modern state requires following the true spirit of Islam, not merely declaring Islam as the state religion or making the *shari'ah* the law of the land. Islam enjoins strict tolerance, fairplay, social and economic justice to all citizens, Muslim or non-Muslim. Nimeiri did not have the stature to use the broad principles of Islamic justice, equality and fairplay to establish a harmonious community in which different religious, ethnic and racial groups could live together. He left office in 1985, leaving his successor, Prime Minister Sadiq al-Mahdi, to face great challenges and huge socio-economic problems. as well as regional and religious tensions.

It was said of Prime Minister al-Mahdi that he belonged to two worlds.[22] He is the great-grandson of Muhammad Ahmad b. al-Sayyid 'Abdullah, who routed the Anglo-Egyptian forces in 1885. His great ancestor Mahdi was a warrior-priest of Islam, the spiritual leader of a fierce Islamic revival. On the other hand, he was educated at Oxford University, and during his exile in the 1970s spent considerable time there lecturing on Middle East politics. In his three years as head of the first democratic government in the Sudan for 16 years, he was unable to bring himself to give up Islamic law, the mere threat of which perpetuates the north-south civil war, now in its sixth year.

A new coalition government led by Prime Minister al-Mahdi was formed on 25 March 1989; the previous government had to resign because of pressures from the army, which wanted either peace with the rebels in the south or stronger measures to crush the rebellion. Prime Minister al-Mahdi seemed to be torn between his personal loyalty to Islam and a pragmatic need for rapprochement with the rebels in the south.[23]

Al-Mahdi was overthrown in a military coup on 30 June 1989. The new regime has promised a referendum on the issue of the *shari'ah*.

Recent Developments in the Sudan

The military regime, headed by Lt. Gen Omar Hassan Ahmed al-Bashir, which came to power in 1989, is confronted with great challenges and issues. Apart from the religious rift between the Islamic northern part and the non-Muslim southern area, the Sudan is immersed in a serious economic situation, culminating in a famine.

A total of thirty-one army and police officers were executed in the wake of an alleged coup attempt on 23 April 1990 against the military government headed by Lt. Gen. al-Bashir.

Bashir described the 'coup' as the work of 'the alliance in coalition with the outlaws'—references to the signatories of the National Democratic Alliance charter, drawn up in October 1989 by political parties, trades unions and professional associations, and to the southern rebel grouping, the Sudanese People's Liberation Army (SPLA).

In the continuing civil war, there had been heavy fighting of late around the government-held garrisons of Yei and Rumbek in south western Sudan. Convoys carrying supplies to the area were attacked by the SPLA as part of its effort to control the roads to the main government base at Juba. Both sides claimed substantial victories.[24]

The human rights organization, Africa Watch, published a report on 18 March 1989 which dfscribed the Sudan as 'a human rights disaster.'

The report claimed that more than 500,000 people had been killed in the civil war and resulting famine, with both the SPLA and the government using starvation as a weapon, while thousands of women and children in the south had been sold into slavery. The report added that human rights violations in northern Sudan had increased dramatically since the June 1989 coup which brought Bashir to power, with purges in the judiciary, civil service and the army, the banning of trades unions and the torture of hundreds of political detainees.

Earlier, the United States government had banned all further economic and military aid to the Sudan.

On 8 February 1991 Bashir signed a decree, passed by the Revolutionary Command Council (RCC), dividing the Sudan into 9 states, subdivided into 66 provinces and 281 local government areas. New state governments would be responsible for local administration and some tax collection, with the central government retaining control over foreign policy, military affairs, trade, the economy and other key sectors.

This regional reorganization was presented by the military government as a devolution of power away from the centre and therefore as a move towards resolving the conflict between the predominantly Muslim north and the largely non-Muslim south. In the south, the SPLA had since its emergence in 1983 demanded the abolition of Islamic *shari'ah* law and the restoration of local autonomy.

A decree signed by Bashir on 1 February 1991 introduced a new penal code based, as was the previous one, on *shari'ah* law, which was to come into effect on 22 March 1991, but which did not apply to the three southern regions (now states).

In an Independence Day speech on 1 January 1992, Lt. Gen. al-Bashir announced the formation of an appointed 'transitional parliament' to pave the way for democracy until the election of assemblies.[25]

The fate of the largest and most conspicuous Muslim state in Africa is uncertain and bleak. The Muslims and Christian 'peace talks', as begun by the military rule of al-Bashir, is still far from any meaningful solution of the religious conflicts between the northern Muslims and the southern non-Muslim population.

The Sudan is listed as so-called 'fundamentalist' and there is the risk of it being listed among the countries encouraging 'terrorism'. We can only hope for the best for the Sudan and its people, both Muslim and non-Muslim.

Recent Trends in Islam in Africa

A Muslim interpreter of Islam in Africa has pointed to the recent trends in Islam in Africa. He writes, 'Islam entered into the African continent in the seventh century CE, long before the start of the Hijra. By the twelfth century, Arabs and Persians had established themselves in a string of fortified trading settlements, many on island sites. A mixed Arab-African population developed along the coast speaking a distinctive language, Swahili. Two Arab explorers, Ibn Haukal, a twelfth-century native of Baghdad, and Ibn Battuta, born in Algeria in 1304, revealed throughout their works the secrets of the 'Dark Continent'.'[26]

Muslims were a majority compared with Christians in the African continent. According to a conservative Western source, the total Muslim population in 1900 was 34,531,292 out of 107,854,260, i.e., 32 percent, when Christians were 9,938,448, i.e., only 9.2 percent. Even in 1968 they were a majority. T B Irvine writes: 'Africa itself, with over 300 million people, is an Islamic continent (1968), since the clear majority, 180 million, are Muslims.'[27] Recently Christianity in Africa is growing faster than in any other continent. A Vatican spokesman said that in 1901 there were 1.1 million Catholics in all of Africa, making up about 1 percent of the continent's population. In 1985, Catholicism was gaining 2 million adherents every year and there were 65 million Catholics in the continent, some 16 percent of the total population of Africa.

The census figures very recently started showing Muslims as a minority community. Out of 59 independent African countries, 21 were Muslim majority countries. Similarly, based on the same conservative Western estimates, the total Muslim population of the mid-1980s was 189,728,390, i.e., 41.2 percent, whereas the Christians were 44.2 percent. How could the Christian, which was a minority community a few years ago, go up to a level and status of a majority religious community composing 44.2 percent of the total? These figures seem questionable to say the least.[28]

The explanation may be found in the colonial period, when Christianity spread under the umbrella of the colonial masters. Until very recently, most of the Muslim world was under the domination of Western, Christian powers. Even after independence, the courses followed by both faiths are continuously crisscrossing each other.

In the words of a Christian writer: 'The Christian colonial powers not only deprived Muslims of political freedom, but also made every effort to undermine their faith and culture. The missionaries not only served the interests of colonial powers, but also took advantage of

Muslim ignorance, of the Muslim need for educational, health, cultural and social services, of every Muslim stress and crisis, of their economic dependence, political division and general weakness and vulnerability. These missionary services have served purposes other than holy—proselytism, that is, adding members to the Christian community for reasons other than spiritual.'[29] (*International Review of Missions*, vol. LXV, no. 260, October 1976; David Kerr, pp. 458-9).

In concluding our brief survey of Islam in Africa we may raise the question: what does Islam mean to African Muslims? Bosworth Smith, in his *Mohammedanism in Africa* (1887), identified areas of the African social world in which Islam was establishing its influence. He noted that the adoption of Islam by traditional Africans increased their understanding of hygiene and made them aware that covering one's physical nakedness was also a step towards covering one's spiritual nakedness before God. He summed up his view of the Islamic impact in Africa by saying: 'As regards the individual, it is admitted on all hands that Islam gives to its new Negro converts an energy, a dignity, a self-reliance and self-respect which is all too rarely found in their pagan or their Christian fellow countrymen'[30]—an excellent and far-sighted assessment of the influence of Islam in a neglected continent. The advent of Islam has given African countries new hopes, new aspirations and a sense of belonging to a world-wide community based on equality and justice to all, irrespective of colour, race, language, sex or religion.

Islam in the United States

There are about 5 million Muslims in the United States of America. They include converts and immigrants, among whom there are professionals such as doctors, faculty members, engineers and lawyers. On the other hand, there are factory workers, workers in restaurants, grocery shops, taxi drivers, etc. It is impossible to generalise about the growing number of Muslims in the Unites States. Broadly speaking, we may categorize them into two groups, the immigrants—thousands of Muslims who have come to settle in the United States from a large number of countries, Asian, Arab and European—and the Afro-Americans, who have converted to Islam in growing numbers.[31]

American Muslims are experiencing both exhilaration at the opportunity to increase their numbers and develop their institutions, and dismay as they continue to experience intimidation, discrimination, misunderstanding and even hatred. It is increasingly important, therefore, to take a fresh look at some of the ways in which they have succeeded in creating a distinct identity and establishing an Islamic community in North America. The dramatic growth in the number of Muslims in the United States has come about at a time when anger is rising among many American citizens towards Muslims overseas, as well as hostility and discrimination against American Muslims. The situation of Muslims in America must be understood in terms of the dynamic of their relationship to their American environment and its influence on the development of Islamic ideas throughout the modern world.[32]

Interest in the Muslims of America has grown in relation to their increasing presence in urban areas, as well as the development of their distinctive institutions across the country. These include more than 600 mosques/Islamic centres, two Islamic colleges, scores of parochial day-schools, several hundred weekend schools, women's organisations, youth groups, and professional and civic organizations. The leadership of the Muslim community has been predominantly in the hands of lay volunteers concerned about the maintenance of their heritage and the perpetuation of the faith by the next generation. In the last decade they have been able to organize several printing presses, book distribution centres and national and regional denominational magazines to help guide the faithful in maintaining Islamic beliefs and practice in what is often an alien environment.[33]

The history of Islam in the United States is not only a story of immigrants searching for economic opportunities in a strange land. It is also the experience of conversion by a small but growing body of indigenous men and women in American society who have discovered a new way of life and a new belief system that fills a void in their spiritual lives. Islam has also received support from students visiting the United States since the 1930s.

The evolution of both the immigrant and indigenous segments of the Muslim *ummah* in America reveals two tendencies. Whereas the majority of indigenous and immigrant Muslims have embraced an Islam that is colour-blind, a pocket of heterodox and sometimes orthodox Sunni Muslims still remains, especially among Afro-Americans, who see Islam as an ideological weapon in the fight against white racism.

The constituent elements of this community are immigrants from virtually all parts of the Muslim world and native Americans who converted to Islam (or as they themselves like to put it, they 'return to their natural religion (*fitrah*)'. The history of the immigrant segment of the emerging Muslim community goes back to the last century, as does the rise of Islam among native-born Americans. However, Islam among Americans became a national phenomenon only in the 1960s.

Among Muslims in the Afro-American community, ethnicity is virtually synonymous with race. Because of this peculiar situation in the black community, two tendencies have developed among converts to Islam which can be called the assimilationist and simulationist tendencies towards Islamization. The assimilationist approach is what makes the American Muslim convert totally, change his way of life so that he adopts an Islamic name, an Islamic code of dress to reflect the cultural origins of those who introduced him to Islam, an Islamic code of ethics, and an Islamic consciousness which negates a great deal of what he was previously socialized to accept as American culture. The assimilationist Afro-American Muslim begins to see his membership of the Muslim community as an alternative, and sometimes superior, identity to his original ethnic identity.[34]

American foreign policy has had a profound influence on Muslim identity and on the ways in which Muslims choose to participate in the American process. US dealings in the Middle East over the last forty years appear to have alienated the majority of its Muslim citizens. The last decade has been a particularly difficult period for Muslims as they have tried to function in an atmosphere charged with hostility. As a result they have sought to frame their identity in a number of ways, their choices resulting in special sets of characteristics, perceptions and attitudes.[35]

Arab Muslims have become increasingly aware of the power of the Israeli lobby, which to them appears to have 'hijacked' the American government and subverted it to Israeli interests. Other Americans who have experienced the power of the lobby share this view. To some Washington experts it is quite evident that America is unable to execute an independent foreign policy in the interests of the United States. Former Assistant Secretary of State Richard Murphy grumbled that American policy is controlled by Israel and its allies, whose approval is necessary before any action can be taken. Identifying Jordan as a friend in need of American assistance against outside anger and terrorism, he acknowledged that this assistance can be provided only when we are able to persuade Israel that the security of Jordan is in Israel's interest. Donald McHenry, former US ambassador to the United Nations, expressed a similar opinion when he acknowledged that the Israeli lobby prevents the United States from freely pursuing its own national interests in the Middle East.[36]

Persecuted Muslim Minorities

There are about three million Muslims scattered in countries with non-Muslim majorities and in 'communist' countries, such as the demised USSR, where they are the object of both persecution and prosecution.

In Africa, the Muslims of Eritrea in Ethiopia have been fighting for their survival for decades. Similarly, the Muslims in the Philippines are engaged in armed conflict with the government in Manila over self-rule. The people of Palestine, particularly those living in the occupied Arab territories of the West Bank and Gaza Strip, are struggling against the Israeli government to preserve their basic human rights and the right of self-determination.

Muslims in the Soviet Union

Czarist Russia was one of the four major European powers, together with Britain, France and Holland, to conquer a large number of Muslim territories. When, after World War II, the Western colonial systems or imperialism were crumbling as the result of nationalist uprisings among Afro-Asian peoples, the Soviet Union at the United Nations pretended to be a great champion of the peoples struggling against foreign domination. While the colonial empires of Britain, France and Holland, and even of Belgium and Portugal, withered away, the Czarist empire in the Muslim territories of Central Asia was kept in tact by communist Russia until its demise. There was, perhaps, nowhere in the world a more successful process of colonization as in the Central Asian republics of the USSR. There were about 55 million Muslims in communist Russia, who constituted the world's fifth largest population (after Indonesia, Pakistan, Bangladesh and India). According to some estimates, Muslims will make up one quarter of the former Soviet Union's population by the end of the present century.

What was the fate of this large concentration of Muslims in an officially atheist state? We may begin by referring to the attitude of Marxist-Leninism towards Islam. In the eyes of the Soviet rulers, science and religion, Marxist-Leninism and religious ideologies, are incompatible and irreconcilable. In their campaign against Islam, the Soviet rulers resorted to two types of argument. The first is valid for all religions and need not be repeated here beyond stating that religion, according to Marx, is the 'opium of the people', a reactionary and anti-scientific ideology giving a fanciful and fallacious notion of society. However, Islam was the special target of vilification by the Soviet authorities; Islam was represented as a primitive and fantastic religion, a chaotic mixture of Christian, Jewish and pagan doctrines, founded by a member of the feudal trading classes of Makkah. 'For centuries Islam has been the servant of all imperialists, first of the Arabs, Persians, Afghans and Turks and now of the British and the

American.'[37] Examples demonstrating the hostility of the Russian communist party to Islam can be cited indefinitely. Thus the Quran is accused of codifying injustice and inequality, and Islamic law is presented as a collection of laws among the most unjust that the world has ever seen.[38] It is, therefore, no wonder that the Muslim population of the USSR continued to suffer the same, if not worse, persecution under the communist regime as under the Czars. According to Muhammad Safwat el-Saqqa Amin, Assistant Secretary-General of the Muslim World League (a Saudi-based Islamic philanthropic organization), the Muslims of the Soviet Union had experienced very hard times. The Russians killed thousands, even millions, of Muslims in 1917; they displaced millions in 1921; more than two million suffered death in 1926 when the communists confiscated their livestock according to communist principles: they died of starvation. The communist rulers have also divided Muslims into numerous nationalities in order to scatter them.[39]

The above account may be coloured by the author's deep feelings of sympathy for the oppressed Muslims of the old Soviet Union, but accounts of the misfortunes of Muslims who fell victim to 'red colonialism' is corroborated by many other impartial sources. As *Time*, in its special issue on 'The New USSR', 10 April 1989, pointed out: 'most of the country's 26,000 mosques and 24,000 religious schools were shut down. The vast majority of Islamic teachers were either killed or imprisoned. During World War II Stalin forcibly deported to Siberia entire populations of Muslims who were suspected of disloyalty.' Stalin's oppression and suppression of the Muslim populations of the Soviet Union can only be compared to Hitler's persecution of the Jews. Both cases are the worst examples of ruthless and systematic suppression of people for their religious faith.

However, religious faith can never be destroyed permanently. We now see Islam regaining its voice in the Central Asian republics of the old USSR. The present author had the opportunity of visiting Tashkent, Samarqand and other Muslim areas of the Soviet Union when he went there as a member of Pakistani President Ayub Khan's entourage during Ayub's first state visit to the neighbouring communist superpower in April 1965. One particular incident gave a unique demonstration of the inherent strength of Islam in the minds of Muslims in the Soviet Union, despite seventy years of suppression and oppression. President Ayub, during his visit to Samarqand, visited the grave of the great hero of the Muslim world, Timur Lang (Tamberlane), and in accordance with Islamic ritual, he prayed for the soul of the Muslim hero. He offered what is known in Islam as the *fatihah*, prayer for the dead. As soon as Ayub and members of his entourage began the *fatihah*, thousands of Soviet Muslims, particularly the young people, joined Ayub in a spontaneous outburst of religious feeling. The Soviet minister and the protocol officers who accompanied Ayub were visibly annoyed by this display of religious sentiment. They told the Pakistani delegation, 'This prayer was not part of our programme.' Ayub's answer was, 'When you have invited a Muslim to a graveyard of a great Muslim hero, it was bound to happen.' The Soviet officials grudgingly accepted Ayub's explanation of his prayer for Timur. During the tour of the Central Asian cities, Ayub was given a hearty reception by Soviet Muslims. The members of the entourage, including the present author, had the chance to talk to Muslims, who embraced them and expressed their determination to maintain their loyalty to Islam and its great tradition.

When the Russians attacked their Muslim neighbour, Afghanistan, in December 1979, and sent more than 100,000 soldiers to occupy Afghanistan, many of the Soviet soldiers were Muslims from the Central Asian republics. However, the Kremlin leaders soon realised their mistake in employing Muslim soldiers to carry out such aggression against Muslims of another country, so the Muslim soldiers were replaced by European Russians. The Afghan war continued for more than half a decade, during which period the Russians committed all kinds of atrocities against the civilian population of Afghanistan—an implied threat to the Muslims of the neighbouring Central Asian republics. The Pakistani president, Zia-ul-Haq, the chief architect of support for the freedom-fighters of Afghanistan told the present writer on 14 August 1988, just three days before his death, of the impact of the Soviet atrocities in Afghanistan on the minds of Soviet Muslims. Zia also expressed the firm hope that after the forced withdrawal of Soviet forces, the people of Afghanistan, given a free choice, would opt for an Islamic state as it was Islamic ideology which was the driving force behind the high morale of the Afghan fighters. Zia's expectations were that three Islamic republics (Iran, Pakistan, and the third emerging in Afghanistan)—all adjoining the borders of the Central Asian republics of the USSR—would be a great source of inspiration to the oppressed Muslims of the Soviet Union. There was no fanaticism or 'fundamentalism' in Zia's dream of an Islamic revival around the Central Asian republics. He hoped that it would help the persecuted Muslims of the Soviet Union to lead a 'free life in a free society'. Is there anything wrong or sinister in such wishes for the emancipation of a large group of humanity who had been suffering for the last sixty years under an authoritarian system? Zia expressed the same hope to the American scholar S Harrison when he told him, '[Afghanistan] will be a real Islamic state, a part of a pan-Islam revival, that will one day win over the Muslims in the Soviet Union.'[40] It is most tragic that a liberal paper like *The New York Times* took exception to the pious hopes of Zia; but *The New York Times*, together with many free presses in the West, never tired—rightly—of expressing sympathy and concern for another persecuted religious community in the Soviet Union: the Jewish community had become a major issue in USA-USSR dialogues in recent years and, again, rightly and with justification. If one oppressed religious group gets support and sympathy, why is another, and larger, religious group—the Soviet Muslims—denied the same help and concern for their legitimate aspirations and their fight for basic human rights, including the right of conscience? Are they not part of that humanity whose causes the United States has always championed? President Bush told the young graduates of an American university: 'You are graduating into a exciting world where the opportunity for peace, world peace, lasting peace has never been better . . . our country, America, was founded on these values.'[41]

Why should the 55 million Muslims of the Soviet Union be excluded from this vision of a free world? There is nothing to be afraid of in a real Islamic awakening. Islam must not be identified with one ruler in Iran or Libya. Islamic and Judaeo-Christian traditions have many things in common, and share common values and ideals. Islam, like the Judaeo-Christian tradition, is incompatible with closed and authoritarian orders as they exist in communist systems. The Muslims of the old Soviet Union survived sixty years of suppression by the communist regime; that regime itself has now crumbled. The inherent strength of Islamic forces in this region, as in the rest of the Islamic world, will triumph. The sooner the West, particularly the United States, realizes this simple truth, the better for a real understanding between the Islamic *ummah*, consisting of some one billion people, and the free societies of the West. Persecution and oppression have never succeeded; this is the verdict of history and it has provided inspiration for the Muslims of the USSR.

The fate of Muslims in other communists countries, including China, is also very sad. We have chosen the case of the Muslims in the Soviet Union for two reasons: firstly, the USSR had the largest concentration of Muslims in an atheist communist country; secondly, the degree of persecution in the Soviet Union, especially during the Stalinist era, was quite ruthless. Lack of space does not permit us to examine the cases of other communist countries, but this should not be misconstrued as a lack of concern.

However, in our discussion of oppressed Muslim communities we must make some reference to China (PRC). As in other communist countries, Muslims and Islam are the targets of victimization particularly during the era of Mao. This suppression turned ugly during the Cultural Revolution (1966-76). It was reported that Muslims were paraded in the streets with pigs on their heads or around their necks. Mosques were demolished. During the Cultural Revolution, Muslims were publicly humiliated, sometimes even tortured.

During the post-Mao period (1976 to the present) the situation improved somewhat, but still Chinese Muslims do not enjoy freedom of religion or a free life in a free society—this is not found in any communist country where human rights and values are not respected. The present author went to China in the late 1980s and early 1990s. He offered the Friday prayer in a mosque in Beijing and talked freely with Chinese Muslims. Things have improved and the spirit of Islam is unbowed.

Muslim Minorities in 'Secular' India: Communal Riots

The long struggle of the Muslims in India to establish a state of their own succeeded on 14 August 1947 when Pakistan emerged as the largest Muslim state in the Islamic *ummah*. However, Indian Muslims' joy and celebration over their success in establishing a home was overshadowed by the unprecedented and brutal sufferings inflicted on those millions of Muslims who were left behind in India after the partition of the sub-continent. The majority Hindu community of India, which opposed the creation of Pakistan, began a ruthless genocide against helpless Muslim minority groups who were scattered over parts of 'new' India and who could not be integrated into Pakistan because of geographical considerations.

Communal murder, on a scale unprecedented in India, began in August 1947. It was not the type of rioting that used to occur at regular intervals in the major cities of the sub-continent. It was nothing less than a war of extermination against the Muslim minority of east Punjab and in a number of adjoining princely states. These massacres have been described in detail; fair and impartial accounts of the Punjab massacre have been given by British and foreign authors. One of the most reliable of the many accounts was that published in *The Times* (London) on 25 August 1947:

> 'A thousand times more horrible than anything we saw during the war', is the universal comment of experienced officers, British and Indian, on the present slaughter in East Punjab. The Sikhs are on the war-path. They are clearing eastern Punjab of Muslims, butchering hundreds daily, forcing thousands to flee

> westward, burning Muslim villages and homesteads, even in their frenzy burning their own too. This violence has been organised from the highest levels of Sikh leadership and it is being done systematically. Some large towns like Amritsar and Julladhpur are now quieter because there are no Muslims left. Appalling atrocities have been committed; bodies have been mutilated; none has been spared—men, women or children.

The communal riots in India, at the time of partition, were a great tragedy—about one million people lost their lives. In Pakistan, particularly in West Punjab, there were communal riots resulting in loss of life of non-Muslim minorities. Though these riots, both in India and Pakistan, are to be condemned and are very sad, it is yet understandable because the partition of India produced the bitterest feelings in both countries; passions were extremely high; religious hatred and age-old, deep-rooted hostile attitudes between the Hindus and Muslims became prominent—all these factors were responsible for the riots immediately after the partition of the sub-continent in 1947. Lord Mountbatten's hasty and somewhat ill-planned process of the transfer of power also bears some responsibility for the events of 1947.

Yet the continuous yearly communal riots in India since 1947 are deplorable and tragic. India claims to be a 'secular country'; some of its national leaders might genuinely believe in secularism but there has hardly been a year when there was no communal riot in so-called 'secular' India. Muslims have died annually (except in 1971 when India was engaged in dismembering Pakistan and trying to prove that it really cared for the Muslims of Bangladesh) for no other reason than that they are part of Islam. In an age aspiring to religious tolerance, India has failed to protect its religious minorities.

The most recent example is the demolition of a six-hundred-year-old mosque—Babri Mosque—and the subsequent killing of Muslims in 1992-93 on a large scale. The world's press and world opinion were shocked and expressed doubts about Indian secularism. The growing rise of Hindu extremist parties who openly preach hatred against Muslims and Islam is also deplorable.

The brutal suppression and oppression of the Muslims in Kashmir is another example of India's arrogant attitude towards Muslims. They were given international assurances by the United Nations—to which India was a party—to have a plebiscite to ascertain their wishes, whether they wanted to remain with India or to form a Muslim state of Pakistan. India broke away from that UN-sponsored pledge.

The Indian government resorted to brutal methods to suppress the demand of the people of Kashmir for the right to self-determination.

During the last forty-five years the Indian government has employed all kinds of suppressive methods against the Muslims of Kashmir.

Since 1992, there has been a popular uprising in Kashmir, demanding the promised plebiscite and thereby the right to self-determination. Many had expected that with the liberation of eastern Europe, as a result of the withering away of the Soviet empire, the people of Kashmir would also be liberated. When India did not respond to the world-wide trends of peaceful settlement in the post-Cold War era, the Muslims rose and revolted against India's continued occupation of Kashmir—against which there were three Indo-Pakistani wars. Then began a process of suppression and oppression of Kashmiri Muslims. The atrocities in Indian-held Kashmir since the most recent popular uprising constitutes a blackspot in the present era. It has been condemned by most of the human rights organizations and the OIC. The world press has given great coverage of India's suppression of the Kashmiris in which the old, sick, children, women—even pregnant ones—were not spared. There were cases of gang rape of women, the destruction of Muslim houses and property, including places of worship. Like the people in the Arab territories under Israeli occupation, the Muslims of Kashmir are also engaged in a bitter and costly fight to gain their freedom and to foster and preserve their cherished Islamic tradition. If history provides any guide, the people of Kashmir will ultimately succeed. In the meantime, the Islamic *ummah* should acknowledge the brave Muslims of Kashmir. Kashmiris will be able to live a 'free life in a free society' in due course.

A Persecuted Muslim Minority: Bosnia

Our account of persecuted Muslim minorities in non-Muslim states must take note of the current genocide in Bosnia-Herzegovina, which was carved out of the former Yugoslavian federation in the early months of 1992. In recent months, the gruesome details of the killing of Muslims in Bosnia has captured the headlines of the world's press. The current Bosnian tragedy has caused the lives of 137,000 dead or missing, and perhaps more than 2 million have been uprooted from their homes. It is a result of 'ethnic cleansing' carried out by Bosnian Serbs and Croats. This has been compared, and rightly so, with Hitler's holocaust. The world community made a vow that the holocaust would never be repeated and unfortunately it is happening in Bosnia.

Bosnia-Herzegovina was one of the six republics which formed Yugoslavia. The present state of Bosnia-Herzegovina is bordered in the east by Serbia, in the north and west by Croatia and in the south east by Montenegro. Its area is nominally about 51,000 square kilometres. It is almost landlocked with a short coastline of 20 kilometres with no harbour. The name Bosnia derives from the Serbo-Croat for the river Bosna; Herzogovina stems from the German *Herzog*, meaning duke, a title held by its ruler in the 15th century.[42]

Modern Yugoslavia was established in late 1920. During World War II, Hitler occupied Yugoslavia and when he was defeated, a new liberated government under Marshal Tito was formed in 1945. Tito ruled with an iron hand until his death on 4 May 1980. With the death of Tito and the demise of the Soviet Union, multinational Yugoslavia headed towards disintegration. Bosnia's population of some 4 million was composed of 43 percent Muslims, 31 percent Serbs, 17 percent Croats and 8 percent Hungarians.

During this period of turmoil after Tito, Bosnia-Herzegovina became an independent state in 1992. Its separate entity as an independent state was recognized by the United Nations, including the USA and the European Community.

The people, including Muslims, were delighted at their independence, but their joy was short-lived and bitter ethnic conflict between Muslims, Serbs and Croats culminated in the present holocaust. Although Muslims constitute over 40 percent of the population they became the target of atrocities at the hands of Serbs and Croats.[43]

In spite of figuring prominently in the world's press and other news media, the persecuted Muslims received little except sympathy and tears. The Western powers, including the USA, have not yet been able or willing to affect the continuing tragedy. Even the Muslim world and its organization, the OIC, have talked loudly, but without tangible action. The foreign ministers' conference of the OIC, held in Pakistan in July 1993, at last decided to send troops from the OIC countries under UN auspices. But we are not sure whether the promised troops will reach Bosnia. The US president, Bill Clinton, made many promises and assurances during his presidential campaign, describing former President George Bush's policy as 'weak'. However, as *The New York Times* pointed out on 21 June 1993, he in turn dramatized the 'weakness' by calling for stronger action and then abandoning it. According to *The New York Times*, Clinton's political advisers were against American involvement in Bosnia as the American people did not want it. But *The New York Times* rightly commented, 'the failure to lead on their painful problem—to act against murderers' aggression—will haunt him for the rest of his political life.'

From our account of about 300 million persecuted Muslims of the world, the situation can only be remedied if the Muslim countries forge unity on the basis of Islam and its ideology by following the Islamic principles of universal brotherhood. The *ummah* can protect the legitimate rights of suffering Muslim minorities, be it in Bosnia, Kashmir, Palestine, or for that matter anywhere.

Notes

1 Ira M Lapidus, *A History of Islamic Societies*, Cambridge, 1988, 782.
2 *Ibid.*
3 Based on the author's reading of unpublished documents of the government of Pakistan.
4 John Obert Voll, *Islam: Continuity and Change in the Modern World*, Boulder, 1982, 192.
5 For details, see G W Choudhury, *India, Pakistan, Bangladesh and the Major Powers: Politics of a Divided Subcontinent*, New York, 1975.
6 See G W Choudhury, *Pakistan's Relations with India*, London, 1968.
7 See Ashraf Ghani's 'Afghanistan: Islam and Counter-revolutionary Movements', in J L Esposito (ed.), *Islam in Asia: Religion, Politics and Society*, New York, 1987, ch. 4; Oliver Roy, 'New Political Elite of Afghanistan' (unpublished), Afghanistan-Iran-Pakistan Workshop, 31 October, 1988, MIT Centre for International Studies.
8 See Sir Muhammad Iqbal's presidential speech at the Annual Session of the All-India Muslim League, 29 December 1930.
9 For details, see G W Choudhury, *Pakistan's Relations with India*, London, 1968, introduction.
10 See the debates of the First Constituent Assembly of Pakistan, 1947-56, Karachi, Government of Pakistan Printing Press.
11 See G W Choudhury, *Constitutional Developments in Pakistan*, London, 1969.
12 See G W Choudhury, *The Last Days of United Pakistan*, Bloomington, repr. Karachi, 1993.
13 Lapidus, *op. cit.*, 768.
14 For details, see Anthony H Johns, 'Indonesia: Islam and Cultural Pluralism', in J L Esposito (ed.), *Islam in Asia: Religion, Politics and Society*, New York, 1987, ch. 9.
15 Donald K Emerson, 'Islam in Modern Indonesia', in Stoddard *et al.*, *Change and the Muslim World*, New York, 1981, ch. 16.
16 *Ibid.*, 875.
17 J S Trimingham, *The Influence of Islam upon Africa*, New York, 1968.
18 Lapidus, *op. cit.*, ch. 20 and 21.
19 J L Esposito, *Islam, the Straight Path,*, New York, 1989, 118-19.
20 *Ibid.*, 119-20.
21 *Loc. cit.*
22 Jane Perlez, 'Sudan Leader of Many Hats and Two Worlds', *The New York Times*, 14 March 1989.
23 See *The New York Times*, 26 March 1989.
24 *Kessing Record of World Events*, 1990-1992.
25 *Ibid.*
26 Mozammel Haque, 'The Need for a Revival of Islam in Africa', *Islamic Quarterly*, London, 3rd quarter, 1992.
27 *Ibid.*

[28] M Haque, *loc. cit.*
[29] Cited in *ibid.*
[30] Cited in Sulayman S Nyang, 'Sub-Saharan Africa: Islamic Penetration', in Stoddard *et al.*, 147-48.
[31] See Yvonne Haddad, *The Muslims of America*, New York, 1991.
[32] *Ibid.*, 3.
[33] M Arif Ghaynr, 'Muslims in the United States and Visitors', cited in *ibid.*
[34] Sulayman S Nyang, 'Convergence and Divergence in an Emergent Community. A Study of Challenges Facing US Muslims', in *ibid.*, ch. 16.
[35] See 'American Foreign Policy in the Middle East and Its Impact on the Identity of Arab Muslims in the United States', in *ibid.*, ch. 15.
[36] Paul Findley, 'The American Political Process and the Middle East Policy', *American Arab Affairs*, spring, 1986.
[37] Cited in A Benningsen and C Lemercier Quelquejay, *Islam in the Soviet Union*, London, 1967, ch. 12.
[38] *Ibid.*
[39] This account was given after the visit of Mr Amini to the Central Asian Republics of the USSR in 1982 in his *Muslims in the Soviet Union*, New York, 1982.
[40] *The New York Times*, editorial, 3 April 1989.
[41] *The New York Times*, 25 May 1989.
[42] K M Mohsen, 'The Bosnian Crisis', unpublished paper at a seminar held in Dhaka, 6 July 1993.
[43] *Ibid.*

Chapter VI
Towards an Ideal Non-Arab Muslim Country: Malaysia

A near ideal Muslim state has emerged where the basic Islamic values and tradition are cherished and valued and simultaneously a highly successful modernising process is going on.

Malaysia under the dynamic leadership of the prime minister, Dr Mahathir Bin Mohammad, who is a believer in Islam and Islamic heritage and who also turned his country into a model for development, provides a unique example of the synthesis of Islam and modernization.

Before we discuss the case study of Malaysia, let us consider Islam in South East Asia. Here there is a large concentration of Muslims. However, unlike the Middle East, the Maghrib or the South Asian subcontinent, there is little 'noise' or pretention about Islam's role in the political order of their countries.

The relationship between Islam and society or state in South East Asia is complex and sometimes baffling. Islam in South East Asia has a history of about seven centuries. There are five nation states in the region: Indonesia, Malaysia, Thailand, Singapore and the Philippines—which originally formed the Association of South East Asian Nations (ASEAN); a sixth member, Brunei, has now joined the ASEAN. Of the six, Indonesia, Malaysia, and Brunei have Muslim majorities; in Singapore, Thailand and the Philippines Muslims constitute minorities. Perhaps, nowhere else in the Muslim world is Islam so compromised by indigenous cultural traditions as in South East Asia.

Islam in SouthEast Asia has become an indigenized tradition which is firmly embedded in the socio-economic and political context of the last seven centuries of South East Asian history. The nature of Islam in South East Asia is also highly varied and syncretic. Notwithstanding all these variations and adjustments to regional cultures and traditions, Islam is a powerful political force in contemporary South East Asia.

Malaysia: Basic Data
Area: 329,758 sq km.
Population: 16,921,000 (1988).
Capital: Kuala Lumpur.
Languages: Bahasa Malaysia (official); English widely used and Chinese, Tamil and Iban spoken by minorities. Religion: Islam (about 53%), Buddhism (about 19%), Hinduism, Christianity and Animism.
Average life expectancy: 70 years (1988).
Armed forces: 114,500 (1989).
GNP per capita: US$1,920 (1988).
Currency: Ringgit or Malaysian Dollar (US$1.00 = 2.7068 ringgits as at June 11, 1990).

The Federation of Malaysia, consisting of the 11 states of peninsula Malaysia and the two states of Sarawak and Sabah situated on the northern coast of the island of Kalimantan (Borneo), is an independent member of the Commonwealth and a parliamentary monarchy.

More than half of Malaysians are Muslims and Islam is the official or state religion. But the multi-racial state of Malaysia is not designated as an Islamic state. Islam occupies an important place in Malaysian society and government. Malaysians follow the true spirit of Islamic toleration to other religions as taught in the Quran and as practised by the Prophet of Islam, Mohammad. In the constitution of al-Madinah, which may be called as the first Islamic state in the history of Islam, Mohammad implemented religious toleration and left behind the finest example of religious toleration. By allowing freedom of religion, Malaysia has demonstrated the true spirit of Islam.

Malaysia has given expression of the dynamic concept of Islamic law (*Shari'ah*) and by stressing the virtues of knowledge, particularly in the spheres of science and technology, Malaysia has provided an encouraging example of the complimentary aspects of Islam and modernization.

Malaysia is also a multi-party parliamentary democratic state, again illustrating that Islam and free institutions must go hand in hand. The Malaysian government and its people are not fanatics; they want a peaceful co-existence with the followers of other religions, again demonstrating a fundamental teaching of Islam.

When an extremist group in Kelantan state in northern Malaysia and its leader Nik Aziz Nik demanded a rigid form of the Islamic provisions in the country's constitution, the Malaysian prime minister, Dr Mahathir, while addressing Malaysian students in London, rightly pointed out that: 'Islam is a flexible faith that allows religious practices to be adapted to local situations.'

The prime minister, Dr Mahathir, in a recent speech before the Malaysian Academy of Science stated his country's attitude towards Islam and he also emphasised the dynamic aspects of Islam:

> Islam is a progressive religion. There are no injunctions against the acquisition of knowledge as long as it is not intended for evil. I believe that the many challenges and difficulties that we face can be overcome if we adhere closely to the true teachings of Islam. It was the adherence to the true teachings that led to the Golden Age of Islam. It was during this age that the various branches of science flourished as a result of the work of Muslim scientists. But when superstition and narrow interpretations of the teachings took over, the glorious age faded. For as long as we be submit to this kind of interpretation, for so long will we be subservient to others.
>
> It is my earnest hope that your deliberations (at the Islamic Academy of Science) will result in a better understanding of the problems and issues facing the Muslim scientists political forces.[1]

A notable feature of modern Malaysia is the unique International Institute of Islamic Thought and Civilization, 'The Beacon of the Crest of A Hill', which is organized by the International Islamic University of Malaysia.

This important Institute was established by the Malaysian government to:

> . . . possess the ideological continuity to perform its functions and to serve the community in Malaysia as well as in the entire Muslim World. It will help in inspiring others to develop and establish genuine Islamic institutions.
>
> The islamization of present-day knowledge is a method of interpreting facts and creating and producing meanings—both individual and social—out of the metaphysics of Islam.

The aims and objectives of ISTAC are as follows:

i) to conduct and promote studies and research on Islamic thought and civilization involving conceptual analyses, clarifications, elaborations and definitions of Islamic key concepts relevant to the cultural, educational, scientific and epistemological problems encountered by Muslims in the present age.

ii) to supervise graduate and postgraduate studies and research in ISTAC with the objective of training scholars and intellectual leaders in the efforts to restore the Islamic civilization to its rightful place in the modern world.

iii) to develop itself to become one of the institutions in the Muslim world whose objectives shall be the creation of an Islamic philosophy of science, which are both pre-requisites for the gradual reconstruction of Islamic civilization.

iv) to conduct research and studies on Islamic civilization in the Malay world.

v) to conduct research and studies on methods and contents of the various disciplines and academic courses for implementation at the International Islamic University with the objective of integrating the sciences in all faculties of the University

vi) to provide for the present need for creative intellectual efforts that will help bring about the reconstruction of Muslim civilization.

vii) to provide an Islamic response to the intellectual and cultural challenges of the modern world and various schools of thought, religion and ideology.

viii) to study the meaning and philosophy of Islamic art and architecture, and to provide guidance for the Islamization of the arts and art education.

ix) to publish the results of its researches and studies conducted from time to time for dissemination to the Muslim world.

x) to establish a reference library as a means of attaining its objectives.

xi) to conduct all forms of research relating to Islam as determined by the Director.

xii) to hold conferences and meetings for the reading of papers and the delivery of lectures and for the acquisition and dissemination of knowledge.

xiii) to support the activities of the University in the promotion of Islamic education and research.

xiv) to cultivate, develop and maintain contact and association with other institutes, universities and bodies engaged in Islamic activities and periodically to conduct dialogues, seminars and conferences with other foreign and local organizations established with similar objectives.

xv) to re-establish the Islamic worldview in the science and in the domains of education relevant to the social forces of human development and the future growth of the *ummah*.

xvi) to assist in the efforts towards achieving the general objectives of the University in re-establishing the primacy of Islam in all aspects of knowledge as a continuation of the tradition of Islam in the pursuit of knowledge and truth as enshrined in the University's objectives.[2]

With these introductory remarks, we will examine Islam in Malaysia.

The status of Islam as a political factor is stronger in Malaysia than in Indonesia. Islam is the state religion in Malaysia and an essential aspect of the identity of Malaysian Muslims, as it is for Muslims of the South Asian subcontinent and the Middle East, and Islam is deeply entrenched in Malaysian Muslim society and politics. According to the constitution of Malaysia, 'Malay means a person who professes the Muslim religion, habitually speaks the Malay language, conforms to Malay customs'. This definition is a reflection of the strength of Islam in a multi-racial, multi-religious country where Muslims barely constitute a majority. The combined strength of religion and ethnicity has a great impact on the role of Islam in Malaysian politics. 'The Malay Muslim', according to Fred von der Mehden, 'although he takes considerable pride in being part of the World of Islam, has a certain parochialism and ethno-religious nationalism.'[3]

The country's ruling party, the United Malay National Organization (UMNO) and its leader Tunku Abd al-Rahman, also the first prime minister of independent Malaysia, was skilful in maintaining the delicate balance of loyalty of the Malay-Muslim and of other ethnic groups—the Chinese and Indian parties. The UMNO leadership has presented itself as a moderate party to retain the confidence of both dominant Islamic groups as well as of the minority ethnic groups. This has not been an easy task and it has required skilled statesmanship. The National Front, composed of UMNO and Chinese and Indian-dominated parties, has been successful in maintaining the delicate balance between religion and ethnicity in Malaysian politics though it has faced challenges from extreme parties of both left and right (e.g., the Pan-Malayan Islamic Party, PMIP or PAS).

During the 1970s there was greater stress on the role of Islam in the politics of Malaysia. While PMIP began to campaign for an Islamic state and the Islamic law, the Islamic revival dominated three major groups. The Malay Muslim Youth League (ABIB), founded in 1971 and led by Anwar Ibrahim demanded reforms on the individual level 'to bring practices in accord with the Quran and on the social level to bring about a just Muslim collective order.' A second group, Darul Argam, is dedicated to living by Quranic principles and a third, the Tabligh, which has its origins in the Indian subcontinent, also stresses adherence to Islamic values and traditions in Malaysian society. The rise of these new Islamic forces, according to Ira Lapidus, 'threatens to upset the delicate balance which preserves the cohesion of the Malaysian state.'[4] The UMNO-led Malaysian government has responded to new pressures from the Islamic groups by taking a number of steps to increase the role of Islam in Malaysian society and government. The other major ethnic group, the Chinese, reacted negatively to these recent trends. The government has to move slowly and cautiously to avoid the kind of riots that took place in 1969.

Recent Developments in Malaysia and its Growing Involvement in the Islamic Ummah

The Malaysian prime minister, Mahathir Bin Mohammad, by profession a medical doctor from the state of Kedah, is universally known to be the architect and builder of modern Malaysia flanked by its astounding economic development on one side and its astonishing cultural refinement on the other.

Malaysia, under the dynamic leadership of Prime Minister Mahathir, has achieved outstanding success in the development of roads, highways and bridges, cities and towns, ports and shipping, industrial estates and agricultural farms, forests and plantations, power generation and distribution, telecommunications, etc.

A proud son of the soil, Mahathir has led Malaysia from one interesting phase of development to another in his avowed mission to advance the development of his country in the same pattern as that of Japan and South Korea.[5]

The prime minister stressed a common theme during his visits to Bangladesh and Pakistan in February 1993, and to Uzbekistan and Iran, in April 1993. Muslim countries must unite and stand together with the rest of the Third World.

The Prime Minister's message was: 'Muslim countries should interact more and cooperate more economically and politically. It is the division among us—not held together by a strong common purpose—that causes us to be easily divided by others . . . We should concentrate on common issues that can unify us while avoiding issues that tend to divide us.'[6]

He said the enthusiasm shown towards suggestions for linking such regions as the Economic Cooperation Organization (ECO)—Iran, Turkey, Pakistan, the Central Asian republics and Afghanistan—with other regional organizations in the Middle East and ASEAN was a positive indication.

Dr Mahathir told them that Muslim nations were weak politically and economically and were unable to unite because they were divided by the ethnic, sectarian, ideological and personal differences of leaders. 'It is only when Muslim nations are economically strong and politically united that they will gain the respect of others and be able to influence world events,' said Dr Mahathir.[7]

Malaysia was playing a more and more vigorous role in the OIC (Organization of Islamic Countries). At the meeting of the OIC foreign ministers in Pakistan in April 1993, the Malaysian foreign minister urged fellow Muslim countries to take strong measures to protect the Muslims of Bosnia.

Malaysia was seeking a ruling by religious officials on whether troops sent by Islamic nations to protect Bosnian Muslims qualify as a holy war. Defence Minister Jajib Tun Razak said: 'The operation, which is aimed at saving lives, certainly meets the criteria of a Jihad' (using the Arabic word for holy war).

He announced that the cabinet had approved a plan to send 1,500 troops to the war-torn region of former Yugoslavia to protect six Muslim enclaves besieged by Serb and Croat forces. Najib said the government was now seeking the views of the National Religious Council which oversees Islamic affairs.

'The declaration is likely to be made once we get the go ahead to despatch the troops,' Najib told a news conference.

Those dying in the course of protecting Muslims would automatically be martyrs if religious officials term the Bosnia operation a *jihad*.[8]

The Malaysian foreign minister, Abdullah Badawi, returning from a special ministerial meeting of the OIC in Islamabad , said Iran had offered to send 10,000 troops, Pakistan 3,000, Bangladesh 1,220, Tunisia 1,000 and the Palestine Liberation Organisation 1,000.

The Malaysian government and political leaders condemned the US attack on Iraq in June 1993. Several Malaysian political and social organizations have condemned the United States for its attack on Iraq's intelligence headquarters in retaliation for an alleged plot to assassinate former President George Bush.

UMNO Youth, in criticising the assault, said the US had acted as the international policeman, investigator, judge and executor. Its

International Bureau Secretary, Mustapha Yaakub said in a statement that the US continued to apply pressure on Baghdad even after the conclusion of the Gulf War and its actions were not made under the auspices of the United Nations.[9]

Notes

[1] See the text of the Prime Minister, Dr Mahathir's speech at the Sixth Academy of Science Conference on August 10, 1993 at the Islamic Centre, Kuala Lumpur, Malaysia.

[2] See *A Brief History and Philosophy of the International Institute of Islamic Thought and Civilization*, 3, 32, 37-41.

[3] Fred R van der Mehden, 'Malaysia: Islam and Multi-Ethnic Politics', in J Esposito (ed.), *The Voice of Resurgent Islam*, New York, 1987, chapter 8.

[4] Ira M. Lapidus, *A History of Islamic Societies*, New York, 1988, 782.

[5] *Illustrated News Weekly* (Dhaka), 2 April 1993.

[6] *New Straits Times* (Kuala Lumpur), 18 April 1993.

[7] *Ibid.*

[8] *The Morning Sun*, 29 July 1993.

[9] *New Straits News*, 29 June 1993.

Chapter VII
The Islamic Theory of International Relations

Islam is for a universal order, an international system based on universal brotherhood and on the moral values and principles as laid down in the Quran. Like many other aspects of Islam, the Islamic theory of international relations is grossly misunderstood and misrepresented. Islam is depicted as the 'religion of the sword' which enjoins *jihad* (holy war) against non-believers. The world, according to a narrow and traditional interpretation of the classic Islamic theory of international relations, is divided into two parts: (1) *Dar al-Islam*, areas where Muslims are rulers and free and where the *Shari'ah* prevails; (2) *Dar al-Harb*, those parts of the world which are beyond the jurisdiction of *Dar al-Islam*. It is alleged that Islam enjoins its believers to carry out *jihad* until the *Dar al-Harb* is integrated into *Dar al-Islam*. Even if there is any peace or temporary period of coexistence between *Dar al-Islam* and *Dar al-Harb*, it should not last for more than ten years.[1] Islam is depicted as a militant ideology, like orthodox Marxism-Leninism, which is bent on world conquest to bring the whole world under its domination. Professor Bernard Lewis betrays his misconception about the Islamic theory of international relations when he states: 'Between the Muslims and the rest of the world there was, therefore . . . a religiously and legally obligatory state of war, which could only end with the conversion or subjugation of all mankind. A treaty of peace between the Muslim state and a non-Muslim state was juridically impossible. The war could not be terminated, it could only be interrupted, for reasons of necessity or expediency, by a truce.'[2] This view may be compared to the medieval Christian doctrine which involved 'an implacable and unending war against those who are not Christians.'[3]

However, neither Christianity nor Islam, presented correctly and in a proper perspective, justifies such a state of perpetual war. This type of misconception arises when certain terms like *jihad*, *ummah* (the world community), *Dar al-Islam* and *Dar al-Harb* are quoted out of context, or taken from one particular source of a particular period. Islam, being a dynamic force, has demonstrated its flexibility and capacity of adjusting to the changing circumstances and changing requirements of the world of Islam. Before examining the contemporary theory of international relations in Islam, we will try to explain some of the fundamental terms mentioned above.

The Islamic theory of international relations centres around the Quranic concept of *ummah*. The word *ummah* appears sixty-four times in the Quran. The primary meaning of the word, as Muhammad Asad states, is 'a group of living beings having certain characteristics or circumstances in common.'[4] The word *ummah* is used in the Quran in more than one way: to connote excellence, way, length of time, a group and a people.[5] Islam envisages an international order which is a commonwealth of nations and which accepts racial diversity and ever-changing geographical demarcations only for facility of reference and not to limit the social horizon of its members. The Quran says, 'Mankind! We created you from a single [pair] of a male and a female, and made you into nations and tribes that ye may know each other, not that ye may despise [each other], verily. The most honoured of you in the sight of God is [he who is] most righteous of you. And God has full knowledge and is well-acquainted [with all things].' (Surah 49: 13).

Yousef Ali, commenting on this verse, writes that the designation of mankind into tribes, races and nations are convenient labels by which we may know certain differing characteristics. Before God, they are all one and most honour is given to the one who is most righteous.[6] This concept of *ummah* was elaborated by Sir Muhammad Iqbal when the Islamic world stretched from Senegal in the west to Bandung in the east. The original idea of *ummah* during the time of the Prophet Muhammad and his four immediate successors could not be applicable to the 20th-century world of Islam consisting of so many national states.

Does the concept of a nation state come into conflict with the universality and unity of the Islamic community? According to Iqbal, Islam stresses the fact that religion is not national, racial or personal, but purely human. Territory as a geographical concept does not come into conflict with Islam. In the Quran, the term *ummah* is used instead of *qawm*, which means nation, because whereas 'many nations can belong to a community of faith, a nation does not necessarily include a community . . . being non-racial, non-linguistic and non-territorial, Islam furnishes a model for human unity.' Finally, Iqbal says, 'by accepting nationalism, the Muslim states cannot cease to be Islamic because so long as the Muslims believe in *tawhid* (unity of God), and prophethood of Muhammad (peace be upon him), they do not step out of the fold of Islam . . . uniform spiritual atmosphere in the world of Islam would facilitate the "political union" of Muslim states.'[7]

This view of compatibility between the Islamic concept of *ummah* and modern nation states is, however, opposed by many Muslim scholars. Ali Muhammad Naqavi, for instance, holds the view that Islam and nationalism are two opposite poles: 'Nationalism and Islam have two opposite ideologies, schools and ideas and independent goals and programmes.'[8]

With the vast demographic and geographical expansion of the world of Islam, we must find a broader and more dynamic concept of the *ummah*. Under the prevailing international order, which had emerged since World War II—the rise of two superpowers and their world-wide competition for greater influence and role at the cost of each other until recently, European colonial empires, being liquidated and giving rise to a large number of Afro-Asian independent countries, including nearly sixty independent Muslim countries—the old concept of *ummah* was not a working proposition. As the Quran lays down so much scope for the meaning and connotation of the concept of *ummah*, it must be adjusted to the dynamics of the contemporary international order.

In the context of present-day world politics, the idea of establishing a single *ummah* by means of *jihad* is also untenable. What is the true significance of *jihad*? Does it only imply war and physical force to achieve the objectives for which the Quran enjoins the duties of *jihad* for its believers? The concept of *jihad* is much wider than this.

Interpreting the Quranic verse relating to *jihad* (Surah 19: 23), Yusef Ali states:

> It [*jihad*] may require fighting in God's cause as a form of self-sacrifice. But its essence consists in (1) true and sincere faith which so fixes its gaze on God that all selfish or worldly motives seem paltry and fade away and (2) an earnest and ceaseless activity, involving the sacrifice (if need be) of life, person, or property in the service of God. Mere brutal fighting is opposed to the whole spirit of *jihad*, while the sincere scholar's pen or preacher's voice or a wealthy man's contributions may be most

> valuable forms of *jihad*.[9]

Jihad is not only an outward act; it is also an inward one to strengthen oneself and correct one's own mistakes. Thus *jihad* does not necessarily imply waging a war. Abu Sulayman explains the significance and the true spirit of *jihad* by pointing out:

> For man to carry out his responsibility as the custodian or vicegerent of Allah on earth, he has voluntarily to exert his utmost efforts to bring his behaviour in line with guidelines revealed in the Quran and *Sunnah* to man by Allah, the creator and sustainer of the whole universe. This exertion of the self in all directions, in every effort and act, personal and collective, internal and external, is the essence of *jihad* and *'ibadah* (obedience to Allah in the choice of the right path) in the Islamic sense . . . Clearly *jihad* is supposed to run through all phases of a Muslim's life as it is his duty in every possible way to do good to the world and prevent harm. This can, of course, include combat on the battlefield but to equate *jihad* exclusively with war is to be bound only be some aspects of historical experience of the classical period and to misread the historical experience of the early Muslims.[10]

It is a great shame that, in spite of such a clear explanation of the spirit of *jihad*, it has been misinterpreted by scholars like Majid Khadduri as an injunction by God that Muslims should 'fight polytheists until they say: there is no God but God.' He further alleges that in Islamic legal theory *jihad* is a permanent obligation upon believers to be carried out by a continuous process of warfare, psychological and political, even if not strictly military, until, *Dar al-Islam* overcomes *Dar al-Harb*.[11] He does, however, concede that *jihad* in the broad sense of the term did not necessarily mean war or fighting, even though a state of war existed between Islamic and non-Islamic countries, since expansion of the *pax Islamica* might be achieved by peaceful as well as by violent means. *Jihad*, he adds, 'was equivalent to the Christian concept of the crusade.'[12]

We may sum up by saying that *jihad* implies an obligation on the part of Muslims to spread the message of the Islamic concept of an international order which is based on the principles of justice, equality and fair play, where people are enabled to lead a free life in a free society. It is a gospel of peace, not of war. It implies respect for human dignity, human rights, freedom of religion and conscience, not coercion. The Quran lays down: 'We sent thee as a mercy for all creatures' (Surah 21: 107), and 'God forbids you [Muslims], not with regard to those who fight you not for [your] faith nor drive you out of your homes, from dealing kindly and justly with them. For God loveth those who are just' (Surah 60: 8).

How should Muslims strive to attain this Islamic international order? In this age of nuclear weapons, of two superpowers—until recently—with two conflicting ideologies, communism and capitalism, Islam can contribute greatly to world peace by upholding its broad principles of universal brotherhood and tolerance. The newly independent Muslim countries of the contemporary world need not look to the West or to the communist world for their progress, development and modernization. Islam can meet the emerging challenges and requirements of modern science and technology. The new national Muslim countries cannot, however, make any progress, individually or collectively, unless they are united. The basis of the unity for the Muslim countries must be only one factor—Islamic ideology. The Islamic *ummah* of today must have the same source of inspiration and guidance as laid down in the Quran and as practised by the Prophet Muhammad. Those broad and flexible principles are applicable today as they were fourteen centuries ago. But in order to meet the challenges and requirements of the modern age, Islamic ideology must be given a dynamic interpretation. There is no difficulty in achieving this objective because Islam is a dynamic force capable of proper interpretation and adjustments without sacrificing the fundamental principles of the Quran. The fundamentals are broad and universal. The Quran was not meant for any particular age or a particular country or group of countries. We have a broad vision which Muslim scholars must interpret adequately by using *ijtihad* (individual judgement) and *ijma*' (consensus).

The first step in the revival of Islam as a factor in contemporary world affairs is unity among the newly independent countries of the world of Islam. The unifying bond cannot be any 'ism' borrowed from Washington or Moscow or Beijing. For Muslims it is Islamic ideology which can enable them to establish a model international order, and history shows that such an order was established in the early days of Islam. If the modern generation doubts the efficacy of Islam, that is due, as pointed out by a learned commission in Pakistan, to the lack of appreciation of the universal applicability of Quranic teaching and a lack of knowledge of Islamic history. The remedy lies, the commission adds, in acquainting oneself with the principles of Islam and with Islamic history and not in discarding them.[13] Those who say that the Muslim world can solve its problems by 'secularism' or 'socialism' or 'regionalism' are wrong. The salvation of the modern *ummah* lies in drawing inspiration from the Quran and the practices of the Prophet.

Pan-Islamism

Toward the end of the 18th century, the Ottoman sultans, 'Abd al-'Aziz and 'Abd al-Hamid II, made some serious efforts to initiate a Pan-Islamic movement. The Ottoman constitution of 1876 proclaimed the goal of Pan-Islamism. 'Abd al-Hamid II gathered around him men of Arab origin (the Arabs were most numerous and important non-Ottoman people in the empire), mostly identified with orders of mystics who became the protagonists of the movement, and they used the language of the holy book of Islam, the Quran, to propagate the ideas of Pan-Islamism.[14]

The movement for Pan-Islamism received powerful support from a group of dedicated reformers led by the famous and dynamic Jamal al-Din al-Afghani. The core of Pan-Islamism 'is the common faith of Muslims. From Morocco to the Philippines this unity in faith has power amidst remarkable political, social and cultural diversity; it is so even amidst the sectarian divisions built into the Islamic heritage by faith itself, not to mention those arising from outside pressures.'[15]

Al-Afghani was born in 1839 in Sa'dabad, Afghanistan; along with his colleagues, Muhammad 'Abduh (1849-1905) and Rashid Rida (1865-1935), as stated earlier (Chapter III), he contributed greatly to the intellectual foundation of pan-Islamism in the late 19th and early 20th century. They 'played a fundamental role in the formulating of an Islamic response to the twin problems of domestic development and Westernisation. Their doctrines—formulated at a time when European pressure on the Islamic world had reached new heights with the Russo-Turkish War (1877), the French occupation of Tunis (1881) and the British occupation of Egypt (1882)—were to have a lasting effect on social and political thought in the Islamic world, and one which can be seen into the present day.'[16]

Afghani's primary concerns were with the disunity, corruption and weakness of the Islamic world in the face of Western imperialism. He attributed the causes of this sad state of affairs in the Muslim world to the Muslim leadership which, according to him, allowed superstition and ignorance to replace reason and enlightenment in the guidance of society. He asserted: 'Religion and science cannot disagree, if it appears as such, we must employ exegesis. Ignorance and rigidity are so abundant among those who don the cloak of the ulama that they allege that the Quran contradicts scientific facts . . . The Quran disavows such allegations. The Quran must transcend contradictions with real science.'[17] Afghani sought to bring a synthesis between Islamic thought and Western science and technology (as did Sir Muhammad Iqbal later in India). Afghani advocated radical reforms, if not revolution, against the corrupt Muslim leadership of his time. This brought him into conflict with the regimes in Afghanistan, Egypt, Persia and Turkey. He then moved to Paris in exile and established a society, *Jamiyat al-Urwa al-Wathqa*, whose objective was Islamic awakening and revolution. His publications also preached his ideas of Islamic reforms. He seemed to have been influenced by Salafiyyah thought, a movement founded by an earlier Islamic thinker and reformer, Ibn Tayminah. From the 17th to the 19th century a number Salafiyyah writers developed the doctrine into a significant political force which had an impact on the Wahhabi movement in the Arabian peninsula, the Shawkani movement in the Yemen, the Sanusi movement in Libya and the Mahdi movement in Sudan: all these movements had the common objective of unifying Muslims with the help of Islamic ideology.

Afghani's colleague and follower Muhammad 'Abduh began a revolution in Egypt in 1832, after the failure of which he was also exiled in Paris where he joined Afghani's secret organization and contributed to its publications. He also started advocating reforms in Islam with the twin objectives of strengthening Islamic ideology and increasing its capabilities of fighting against Western imperialist domination.

Rashid Rida was a follower of 'Abduh. As we have already stated, he studied in Syria until 1897, then moved to Cairo where he began a journal, *al-Manar*, in which he preached the political and social reformist ideas of Afghani and 'Abduh. He also supported the Wahhabi doctrine.

In spite of some differences in their emphasis and styles, there were certain common key issues which engaged the attention of these three great Islamic reformers: (1) to what extent did the external power and internal welfare of the Islamic world depend on the religious character and moral code of the *ummah*? (2) What role did the lack of scientific progress play in Islamic weakness *vis-à-vis* the West? Were modern technology and scientific inquiry compatible with Islam? (3) What political reforms were needed to strengthen the Islamic world? (4) To what degree was Islam compatible with nationalism?[18]

These issues, to which the three great Islamic reformers gave serious thought and made valuable contributions, are still vital issues facing the leaders, intellectuals and writers of the Muslim national states of the contemporary period. We must address ourselves to these vital questions in order to revitalize and revive the spirit of Islam.

The fundamental centrality of Islamic unity and Pan-Islamic cooperation in the works of Afghani and 'Abduh reduced nationalism to a secondary element. They regarded the Islamic *ummah* as a superior basis for cohesion. Indeed they considered European nationalism, based as it was on cultural and racial homogeneities, as an essentially divisive force. The Islamic community, on the other hand, was based on moral commitment that protected all members, even non-Muslims. As an article in *Al-Urwa Al-Wathqa*, the Paris-based journal, said: religion 'is the strongest bond that unites the Arab and the Turk, the Persian and the Indian, the Egyptian and the Moroccan.'[19]

It would, however, not be correct to say that Pan-Islamism, as a movement seeking political power to challenge the European domination of the Islamic world, was a great success, as visualized by Afghani and his colleagues and followers. The European colonial empires continued to survive until the end of World War II. The movement for liberation against European rule was waged by a number of forces, both secular and Islamic. In our survey of Islam in modern nation states we have shown the role of Islam as force in national liberation movements in the period between the two world wars; and we have shown that even where the nationalist movements were led by the Western-educated urban élite, the role of Islam as a nation-building force was not excluded. Even in cases where Islam was not the main driving force, it did supplement and support the causes of the liberation forces.

After World War II, when a large number of Muslim nation states emerged, there was again, as we have already pointed out, wide discussion about the place of Islamic ideology in consolidation and in modernization of these newly independent countries. There have been varying degrees of the role of Islam as a political factor in the modern nation states. Some countries, like modern Turkey, opted for 'secularism'. Some other Middle Eastern countries stressed 'Arabism'—regionalism—in the process of national reconstruction, development and modernization. Some countries, like Saudi Arabia and Pakistan, assigned Islam as the supreme force in the process of national development and modernization.

Secularism in Turkey, Arab regional nationalism and the so-called Islamic socialism of Nasser in Egypt and of the Ba'th regimes in Syria and Iraq, the 'White Revolution' in Iran and the 'guided democracy' in Indonesia could not, however, solve the gargantuan socio-economic problems of these countries nor forestall external threats and pressures. The creation of Israel in 1948 in the heart of the Muslim world and the Zionist expansionist designs of Israel, the penetration of neo-Western domination, the persecution of Muslim minorities, particularly in communist Russia and 'secularist' India, continued. Muslim leaders and thinkers continued and are still continuing to look for ways and means to safeguard the vital interests of nearly one billion Muslims scattered all over the globe. Serious attempts have been made to bring unity and cohesion among Muslim countries, to revive the old spirit of an Islamic *ummah*.

Islam as a Factor in International Relations

In order to reconstruct the Islamic theory of international relations, Majid Khadduri writes that we should recall that Islam is a political community endowed with a system of law designed to protect the collective interests of Muslims as well as to regulate their relations with the outside world. The Muslim aspiration to form a bloc in the international community has a long history. Pan-Islamism, led by Jamal al-Din al-Afghani, was a move forward, but this aspiration of the world of Islam was thwarted, though not destroyed. Muslims did not give up their aspirations of unity in terms of the religious and cultural rehabilitation of the total community or *ummah*.

In a sense, Pan-Islamism was not a new force but as old as Islam itself. The bond that binds the Muslim peoples is extra-racial, extra-territorial and extra-political. Iqbal, as we have already stated, envisaged 'an international Islam' when he preached that 'Islam was neither nationalism nor imperialism' but a 'commonwealth of nations which accepts the racial diversity and the ever-changing geographical demarcations only for the facility of reference and not for limiting the social horizons of its members.' Iqbal was of the view that nationalism in Muslim countries would be welcomed 'so long as it was not separated from Islam.'[20]

The need for closer union among Muslim countries was imperative, though it was not fully appreciated in certain Muslim countries. Pakistan (including Bangladesh) and Saudi Arabia, however, continued to stress the need for closer understanding and cooperation among Muslim countries. These countries have made consistent efforts to develop institutional means for greater cooperation among Muslim countries. This aspect of the policy of countries like Saudi Arabia, Bangladesh and Pakistan has deep roots in their history, originating from a common heritage and socio-economic bonds. The Muslims of the south Asian subcontinent, having identified themselves with the hopes and aspirations of the Muslim world, persisted in this approach after gaining their independence in 1947, and the same aspirations have also guided Saudi Arabia.

The 1967 Arab-Israeli war was a terrible blow to the Muslim world, resulting in the military conquest of large territories of the Muslim countries of Egypt, Jordan, and Syria. It demonstrated the main weakness of the Muslim world: lack of unity and cohesion. The consistent and persistent Israeli military adventures against the Muslim countries of the Middle East, and the persecution of Muslim minorities in non-Muslim countries, constituted great challenges for the world of Islam. It also gave a new impetus to reach unity and cohesion among Muslim countries. Muslims could no longer afford to ignore the urgent need for unity and understanding among themselves. It was in this new atmosphere of crisis and urgency that the leaders of Muslim countries, Arab and non-Arab, met at the first Islamic Summit in 1969 at Rabat, Morocco. This was the first manifestation of the great Islamic community straddling the world from Indonesia in the east to Senegal in the west, and constituting one-fourth of the world's population. This unique gathering of the heads of states and governments of Islamic countries was a big step in the realization of the goal of the Islamic *ummah*. Muslims from all over the world were gathered to seek solutions to the challenges facing the world of Islam. It also epitomized the inherent unity, integrity and strength of the Islamic community.

The result was the OIC—the Organization of the Islamic Conference—we now give a *resumé* of earlier attempts made by Muslims to create an international Islamic forum or organization. Though those attempts were not successful at that stage of the political and social development of the Muslim world, the history of these attempts will show that the unifying strength of Islam was never dead, even in the most distressing circumstances and environments. In order to appreciate a present-day Muslim international organization like the OIC, we must trace its past history: we cannot appreciate the present without the past.

Early Attempts at Pan-Islamic Ideals

The idea of a Muslim congress—*al-Mu'tamar al-Islamiyyah*—has a long history. Late in the 19th century, Muslims under European colonial rule and separated by distance, language and history began to think in terms of a world Muslim congress. There were some irregular sessions of the Muslim congresses between the two world wars. 'These were the earliest occasions on which Muslims, assembled from various parts of the Muslim world discussed and resolved on issues of common concern. They were perhaps the broadest attempt by a group of subject peoples to ward off the West.'[21] However, these gatherings were of little practical significance, nor were they followed by any specific actions, either in creating any organization or in the pursuit of any coordinated policy.

The idea of an Islamic assembly or Muslim congress figured in the writings of the Islamic reformists, Afghani, 'Abduh and Rashid Rida, to whose thought and writings we have referred earlier in connection with pan-Islamism. Through their publication *Al-Manar*, they propagated the idea of a Muslim congress, and *Al-Manar* raised the issue in 1898.

This reform is consistent with the creation of an Islamic society, under the auspices of the caliph, which will have a branch in every Islamic land. Its greatest branch should be in Makkah, a city to which Muslims come from all over the world and where they fraternize at its holy sites. The most important meeting of this branch should be held during the pilgrimage season, when members (*a'da'*) from other branches in the rest of the world come on pilgrimage. Thus they can bring back to their own branches whatever is decided, secretly and openly, in the general assembly (*al-mujtama' al-'amm*). This is one of the advantages of establishing the great society at Makkah rather than Dar al-Khalifah [Istanbul]. There are other advantages, the most important among them being the distance [of Makkah] from the intrigues and suspicions of [non-Muslim] foreigners, and security from their knowing what there is no need for them to know, either in part or in whole.

Sultan 'Abd al-Hamid did not like the idea of having the congress held in Makkah because he considered it a threat to his authority as the head of the Ottoman empire, but *Al-Manar* continued to preach the idea of a Muslim congress.[22]

The idea also received encouragement from another influential Muslim thinker, 'Abd al-Rahman Kawakibi (1854-1902). In his famous Arabic work, *Umm al-Qura*, published in 1900, he made forceful pleas for some kind of Islamic grouping; he termed the Muslim Congress the Congress of Islamic Revival (*Mu'tamar al-Nahdah al-Islamiyyah*). His ideas were influenced by 'Abduh and Rida. Some clandestine meetings of this congress took place, and a charter for a Congress of Islamic Revival was drawn up. This was at a time when the tensions between the Turks and the Arabs in the Ottoman empire had already erupted, and Sultan 'Abd Al-Hamid did not like Kawakibi's ideas in the context of the Arab awakening against Turkish rule. He tried to persecute Kawakibi for his views. In spite of 'Abd al-Hamid's hostile reaction, Kawakibi's book *Umm al-Qura* attracted wide attention.[23]

Another adventurer in the utopian idea of a Muslim congress or

Islamic assembly in the early 20th century was a Crimean Muslim, Ismail Gasprinski. Though he was a stranger to the heart of the Muslim world and though he lacked the charismatic qualities of Afghani or some of his colleagues, yet Gasprinski created a great deal of interest in the idea of an international Muslim gathering, both in Cairo and Istanbul. His Turkish newspaper, *Tercuman*, was used to propagate a general Muslim Congress. Rashid Rida, himself a great exponent of a Muslim Congress, termed Gasprinski's initiatives a 'usurpation'.

The real difficulty was that at this stage of their political development, and struggling under European colonial rule, Muslim countries were not yet in a position to respond positively and constructively to the calls of these early dreamers and thinkers for an effective Islamic international grouping. Another limiting factor was the consistent and persistent opposition of Sultan 'Abd al-Hamid to the idea of any such Islamic gathering, particularly if it were at the initiative of a non-Turkish Muslim thinker or leader. He was always apprehensive of the Arab awakening involved in such moves.

However, the contributions of these early Muslim thinkers showed that the concept of an Islamic unity or *ummah* had always inspired Muslims scattered all over the globe, 'from Fez to China', each representing a different cultural identity but all sharing broader and more lasting bonds based on Islam and its ideology. Muslims were already engaged in formulating the foundations on which lasting Muslim unity could be built.

The Post-Ottoman Caliphate Era to the Emergence of Independent National Muslim States

The disappearance of the Ottoman caliphate in May 1924 confronted the Muslim world with new and unexpected problems and challenges. According to Sir Hamilton Gibb, the Muslims had three alternatives. First, 'The pure Modernist toyed with the idea of creating a new kind of caliphate.' Gibb puts Iqbal into this category—which is not correct. Iqbal, as we have shown, was not a 'pure modernist', but a strong believer in 'dynamic' Islam. Second, 'The secularists and more nationalist Muslims' were engaged in creating 'national units' on 'modern Western lines'—this is a partial truth, even the 'more nationalist Muslim' could not afford to ignore the Islamic forces altogether. The third alternative, according to Gibb, was 'the revival of Mahdism, the assertion that the Muslim world must be purified and reunited by the sword.'[24] This is an unfair and distorted interpretation of Mahdism. The difficulty with many orientalists like Gibb is that they judge Islam, Islamic tradition and Islamic people according to preconceived notions and set ideas. Any Muslim groups or Islamic doctrines which do not fit in with their Western ideas and standards are termed 'fundamentalist', or 'militant' and bring the condemnation that Islam is 'the religion of the sword'. The sooner these preconceived ideas and outlook of Western scholars are changed the better. With full and mutual understanding, there is vast scope for cooperation between Islam and the West, which are not inherently contradictory or hostile.

Turning back to our account of the growth of international Islamic groupings, we find a new era in the post-Ottoman caliphate period. The abolition of the caliphate in 1924 led Muslims in different parts of the Muslim world to think seriously about ways and means to fill the vacuum caused by the Turkish leader, Kemal Ataturk, in abolishing the caliphate. In the Indian subcontinent a mass movement in favour of the caliphate began under the leadership of two dynamic brothers, Muhammad Ali (1878-1931) and Shawkat Ali (1873-1938), who gained support from the leader of the Indian national liberation movement, M K Gandhi. As a result of this cooperation between Gandhi and the Ali brothers, the caliphate movements became a really big event which threatened the British Raj in India. The Muslims of the South East Asia/Indonesia/Malaya periphery were also deeply concerned over the fate of the caliphate. 'It was hard for most Muslims to conceive the existence of the community without the institution of caliphate.'[25] The issue led to the first general Islamic Congress, held in Cairo, in May 1926. Representatives from several Arab countries of the Middle East, from the Indian subcontinent, Indonesia, Malaya, and several other countries, participated in the conference. As most of these Muslim countries were at that time under colonial rule, the representatives came as unofficial delegations and not as official delegations from any government. Muslims from Turkey, Iran, Afghanistan and Russia did not attend the conference. The main issue before the conference was the question of the revival of a new caliphate in accordance with the Islamic law, the *shari'ah*. As the meeting was held in Egypt, the Egyptian king, Faud (1920-36), had the ambition to become a new caliph, but his move was not acceptable to the rest of the community. The Saudi king, Ibn Saud, who had established his control over the holy cities of Makkah and al-Madinah, was not enthusiastic about the Egyptian king as a new caliph. Saudi Arabia did not send a delegation to the conference as they were not interested in an Egyptian-dominated caliphate which might want to acquire some form of seniority over the holy cities of Makkah and al-Madinah. The Egyptian king's pursuit of the caliphate led to the failure of any positive action on the caliphate. The conference simply appealed to the Muslim world to consider how a new caliphate could be established in accordance with the Islamic *shari'ah*.

The next meeting of the Islamic world, the Congress of the Islamic World, was held in Makkah in June 1926. The big issue facing this gathering was no longer the establishment of the *hajj* (pilgrimage). The issue arose as a result of the emerging control by 'Abd al-'Aziz Ibn Saud (1880-1953)—the founder of modern Saudi Arabia—of the Hijaz, where the two holy cities of Makkah and al-Madinah are situated. Anyone who controlled the Hijaz would also be responsible for the management of the *hajj*, one of the five pillars of Islam. Ibn Saud had recently captured Makkah and al-Madinah from the Hashemite Sherif Hossain. But his *de facto* jurisdiction of the two holy cities was controversial; and the Hijazi War had raised a debate over the future management of the *hajj*. In the Indian subcontinent, some Muslim leaders were in favour of an 'international regime' for the Hijaz and consequently the management of the *hajj*, an idea which was advocated by Kawakibi in his book *Umm al-Qura*. The Hijaz had also revived the Egyptian king's ambition to lead the Islamic world by control over the *hajj*.

The issue was very clear, as the question of the caliphate had been at the first Congress of 1924. On 28 April 1926 Ibn Saud sent telegrams to various Muslim leaders and associations, urging them to attend the Congress at Makkah. His appeal was, 'For the service of the two holy sanctuaries and their inhabitants, to secure their future, to increase the means of comfort for the pilgrims and visitors, to improve the holy lands in all respects which all the Muslims in general are for, to fulfil our promises we made and with a view to our wish to see the Muslims cooperating in serving these holy lands.'[26] In the meantime, Ibn Saud was acclaimed by the notables of the Hijaz province in January 1926; he was also recognized by the Western powers. Now he wanted broader acceptance by the leaders of the Muslim world.

The second Islamic Congress approved King Ibn Saud as the custodian of the two holy cities and also entrusted to him the administration of *hajj*. This was the main outcome of the conference, but it also set up a permanent organization—*Mu'tamar al-'Alam*, the Muslim World Congress—which was expected to meet annually at Makkah at the time of the *hajj*. A constitution of the Congress was drawn up, which consisted of thirty-two articles describing its objectives, composition, functions, and other details. The *Mu'tamar* did not, however, meet regularly or annually. Like its predecessor of 1924, the second Islamic Congress of 1926 also failed to produce a permanent Islamic body.

The third Islamic Congress took place in Jerusalem in December 1931. This conference was devoted to discussing the fate of the Muslims of Palestine and protecting the Muslim holy places in Jerusalem. The third conference was initiated by the grand Mufti of Jerusalem, Indian *Khilafat* leaders and leaders of some other Muslim countries. The British government, whose authority over Palestine was at that time in accordance with the Mandate of the League of Nations, had already declared its decision to establish a Jewish state or homeland in Palestine. The reaction of the Muslim world was one of great resentment. 'Secular' countries such as Turkey, however, considered the Congress's defence of Palestine as valueless and an exercise in using religion in politics.

Yet the conference met and passed resolutions demanding the protection of Muslim holy places in Jerusalem, such as the Aqsa Mosque, upholding the causes of the Muslims of Palestine and opposing the creation of a Jewish state in Palestine. Because of the worldwide Muslim interest over the fate of Palestine, the third conference had greater publicity and more coverage in the Muslim press. The conference also passed resolutions condemning French policy in North Africa (Maghrib) and Italian activities in Libya. The third Islamic Congress also decided to set up an executive committee of the *Mu'tamar*, consisting of twenty-five members. It was further decided that the *Mu'tamar* should convene every two years—though it did not meet until 1949.

We have already stated that in the 1940s and 1950s attempts to forge Islamic unity, or to set up an international Muslim body, made little headway because of the opposition from some Arab countries (e.g. Egypt under Nasser and secularist Turkey and Iran). However, countries like Pakistan (including present-day Bangladesh) and Saudi Arabia took a number of initiatives to set up some Islamic international organizations and conferences. The first international Islamic Economic Conference was held in Karachi, Pakistan, in 1949. The second Islamic International Economic Conference was held in Tehran, Iran, in 1950. A conference of all religious scholars of Islam was held in 1952 in Karachi at the initiative of the Grand Mufti of Palestine, Amin al-Husaini, who advocated unity in the world of Islam: 'Modern scientific research and discoveries have shortened distances. In these circumstances even the most powerful nations of the world cannot remain in isolation.' Then he referred to the Western bloc, led by the USA, and the communist bloc, led by the Soviet Union. He lamented: 'only the Muslims in the face of so many difficulties and problems have so far failed to form themselves into an *ummah*.'[27]

Our survey of the early efforts of the great Islamic reformists and the first few Islamic congresses gives a rather discouraging and disappointing picture of the progress towards the formation of an *ummah*. Why did the Muslims fail to translate their cherished dream of an Islamic *ummah* into reality? Did Muslims fail to present a cause which could be effective enough to overcome regional and other differences in the world of Islam? There was no dearth of able thinkers and dynamic leaders, yet the differences between the Muslims of different parts of the world of Islam failed to create a permanent international organization founded on Islamic ideology. The so-called 'secularists' and 'socialists', or regional nationalists, were not yet prepared to rise above petty differences and forge unity on the basis of Islam.

However, the works of the early reformists and the holding of Islamic congresses were not without some desirable results. They demonstrated at least the tenacity of Muslim adherence to the concept of a united world of Islam, which ultimately triumphed after about three decades of Muslim countries' gaining independence from colonial rule in the 1940s and 1950s. As the 1960s began, new and more vigorous attempts to foster and develop bonds among the Muslim countries of the contemporary world began to emerge. The Saudi crown prince, subsequently King Faisal, began a new series of attempts to create an international Islamic organization. The *Mu'tamar* held its fifth and sixth conferences in 1962 in Baghdad and in 1964 in Mogadishu. Faisal wanted to contain Nasser's Arab nationalism with Pan-Islamism. He toured a number of Muslim countries, including Pakistan, Iran, Jordan, Sudan, Turkey, Morocco, Guinea, Mali and Tunisia, to advance the idea of an Islamic *ummah*. Faisal, like the leaders of Pakistan, was genuinely interested in developing a Muslim awakening in favour of Islamic unity. In the meantime, Saudi Arabia had set up a philanthropic organization, *Rabitah al-'Alam al-Islami* (the Muslim World League). This new organization was set up at an international Islamic Conference held in Makkah in May 1962. The conference's aim was to combat Nasser's radicalism, socialism and veiled secularism.

The whole situation was dramatically changed after the 1967 Arab-Israeli war, which was a disastrous episode in the history of Islam. Israel achieved a crushing defeat of Egypt, Jordan and Syria and occupied large territories of the three Arab countries. Zionist expansionism gave a rude shock to the entire Muslim world, particularly the occupation of Muslim holy places in Jerusalem, including the third holiest Muslim site, al-Aqsa mosque. The whole Muslim world was profoundly shocked when the Israeli authorities apparently condoned extensive fire damage to al-Aqsa mosque on

21 August 1969. The religious sentiments of the entire Muslim world were roused against this crime. The former Mufti of Jerusalem, Amin al-Husaini, sent urgent calls to all Muslim states to hold an immediate Muslim summit conference to discuss this grave provocation. King Faisal renewed his call for an Islamic summit conference, which could no longer be ignored. Many Muslim countries joined King Faisal's initiative. Tunku Abdar Rahman of Malaysia also raised his voice in favour of an Islamic summit. In the changed circumstances, Arab leaders, like Nasser, could no longer ignore the initiatives of Saudi Arabia, Pakistan and other Muslim countries which had been advocating such an Islamic grouping for the past two or three decades. Finally the first Islamic summit was held in Rabat, Morocco, on 22-25 September 1969. The present author, then a cabinet minister in Pakistan, was following the rapid developments towards the formation of an Islamic international order from close quarters and took an active part in formulating the plans and programme of the proposed Islamic organization. A dream of the Muslim world was being fulfilled after a long period of preparation and struggle—a process which had many setbacks but ultimately triumphed in the formation of a new vision of an *ummah*. 'Islam in its principles, values and goals pertaining to international relations is still capable of guiding successful and constructive external relationship.'[28]

Notes

1 For this type of distortion of the Islamic theory of international relations see Majid Khadduri, *War and Peace in the Law of Islam*, Baltimore, 1955.

2 Bernard Lewis, 'Politics and War' in Joseph Schacht and C E Bosworth (eds.), *The Legacy of Islam*, London, 1974, 175.

3 See Martin Heper and Raphael Israeli (eds.), *Islam and Politics in the Modern Middle East*, New York, 1984, 108.

4 Cited in Abdullah al-Ahsan, *OIC: The Organization of the Islamic Conference*, Handen, USA, 1950, 2.

5 For different uses of the term *ummah* see the following verses in the Quran: Surah 16: 120, 42: 8, 43: 23, 13: 45, 11: 8, 7: 159, 7: 164, 28: 23, 3: 104, 16: 92, 23: 34, 35: 24, 2: 134, and 23: 52.

These references are given in Abdul Hamid A Abu Sulayman, *The Islamic Theory of International Relations: New Directions for Islamic Methodology and Thought*, Handen, USA, 1987.

6 Abdullah Yusuf Ali, *The Meaning of the Glorious Quran*, Cairo, n.d., vol. 2, 1677.

7 Sir Muhammad Iqbal's concepts of the Islamic *ummah* and modern Muslim nation states were eloquently explained by his son, Dr Javid Iqbal, in a paper entitled 'Islam, Pakistan: Iran and Gulf States' given at the International Conference, Bellago Conference Centre, Lake Como, Italy, 13-18 August 1985.

8 Ali Muhammad Naqavi, *Islam and Nationalism*, Tehran, 1984, parts 7 and 8.

9 Ali, *op. cit.*, 444.

10 Abu Sulayman, *op. cit.*

[11] Majid Khadduri, 'The Islamic Theory of International Relations' in J Harris Proctor (ed.) *Islam and International Relations*, London, 1965, 28.
[12] *Ibid.*
[13] See the Report of the Constitution Commission of Pakistan (1960-61), headed by the Chief Justice of the Supreme Court of Pakistan, Government of Pakistan Press, Pakistan, 1961.
[14] T Cuyler Young, 'Pan-Islamism in the Modern World: Solidarity and Conflict Among Muslim Countries' in Proctor (ed.) *op. cit.*, 194-219.
[15] *Ibid.*
[16] Tareq Y Ismael and Jacqueline Ismael, *Government and Politics in Islam*, London, 1985, Chapter 2.
[17] Quoted in *Ibid.*
[18] *Ibid.*
[19] Cited in *Ibid.*
[20] See Javid Iqbal, *op. cit.*
[21] Martin Kramer, *Islam Assemblies: The Advent of the Muslim Congress*, New York, 1986, viii.
[22] Cited in *Ibid.*, 28.
[23] For details of these early Muslim congress and assemblies, see *ibid.*, which gives a comprehensive account of what is termed 'Islamic Assembly.'
[24] H A R Gibb, *Modern Trends in Islam*, Chicago, 1945, 112-13.
[25] Abdullah al-Ahsan, *op. cit.*, 11.
[26] Quoted in Martin Kramer, *op. cit.*, 107-108.
[27] Cited in al-Ahsan, *op. cit.*, 15.
[28] Sulayman, *op. cit.*, 141-2.

Chapter VIII
The Resurgence of Islam

A mounting religious fervour or resurgence of Islam has been sweeping the Muslim world. Muslims all over the world, from Indonesia in the East to Senegal in the West, are rediscovering their spiritual roots and reasserting the political power of the Islamic way of life. The resurgence of Islam has become the subject of great debate in the West, among orientalists, political leaders, the intelligentsia and students. The phenomenon is still unfolding and sometimes may even appear bewildering, but no serious student of contemporary world affairs can afford to ignore it. There are divergent interpretations of the Islamic revival as a political force in world affairs. However, one aspect of this powerful reawakening among Muslims seems to be clear: its main urge is the rejection of what is regarded as alien to Islamic values and a vigorous search for renewed strength from Islamic ideals and principles. There is a new realization in the world of Islam that the era of the last two centuries, during which the Muslim world had been oppressed, colonized, remained backward and lost its initiatives, has, at last, come to an end and a new era of unity and inward strength based on the broad teachings of Islam has dawned on the Islamic community.[1]

The late president of the Islamic Republic of Pakistan, General Mohammed Zia-ul-Haq, was rightly chosen as the spokesman of perhaps 900 million fellow-Muslims at the 1980 session of the General Assembly of the United Nations. Explaining the new spirit in the Islamic world, he said: 'Living in different customs and political systems, speaking different languages and dialects, Muslims all over the world retain the abiding sense of Islamic affinity. It is this unity in diversity which is the hallmark of the Muslim *ummah*, or the commonwealth of Muslim nations.' The Islamic Conference, of which president Zia was then Chairman, constitutes a concrete manifestation of the urge of the Muslim *ummah* 'to re-establish its historic role as a factor for peace and progress and to reassert the overriding unity of the Muslim peoples scattered over the globe.'[2] On another occasion, President Zia described the resurgence in the Islamic world by saying: 'In the world of Islam today, a new awakening, a new awareness, a new mood and a new vision'[3] can be found.

However, Muslims' desires and urges for unity, for 'peace and progress', have been grossly misinterpreted and misunderstood. It has been seen as a 'quantum leap backward', as a return to the intolerance, and bigotry of the medieval period.[4] As explained by Professor Edward Said of Columbia University, much of this gross misunderstanding is due to the fact that the West has always divided the world into two imaginary sections; the orient and the occident. This misconception, which Professor Said calls 'orientalism', has existed as a kind of daydream that could often justify Western colonial adventures or military conquests. Orientalism, he points out, is based on 'Western fear, desire, dreams of power, and of course, a very partial knowledge' and has led to 'more myths, detailed ignorance and more ambitions than any other perception of difference.'[5] Islamic unity is not directed against any country or any bloc. Islam is a religion of peace. It preaches tolerance, universal brotherhood and it does not permit its ideology to be imposed on others by force. Islam believes in the principle of peaceful coexistence. To quote President Zia again: 'We do not wish to impose our ideology on others and similarly we would not tolerate others imposing their ideologies on us.'[6] In fact, there should not be any conflict or contradiction between Islam and Western values and tradition. As Dr Zbigniew Brzezinki, President Carter's National Security Advisor, points out, there is really no reason why Americans should be hostile toward an Islamic renaissance. It is a religious phenomenon rooted in certain basic values which are not alien to the Christian tradition, yet, instinctively, many Americans are perplexed by this development. Zia explained the true spirit of the Islamic message of peace and universal brotherhood. He stated:

> The credentials of the Muslims to be able to play a role in helping to promote peace and harmony among nations are provided in the statement of human rights and duties by the Prophet in his last sermon on Mount Arafat, which is as fresh and relevant today as it was 1,400 years ago. On that occasion the

Prophet said:
'Hearken to my words, O men . . .
'The Arab is not superior to non-Arab; the non-Arab is not superior to Arab. You are all sons of Adam, who was made up of dust . . .
'The vengeance of blood practised in the days of Ignorance is prohibited, and blood-feuds are abolished.
'Verily, you should consider each other's blood, property, and reputation, inviolable unto the Day of Judgement.'

If this be the message, then should not the present resurgence of Islam and the reawakening among the Muslims of the world be a welcome phenomenon? It should be welcomed as a revitalizing force that could bring peace to a weary world and hope to a distraught humanity. It is not a religion that forces itself on the others. The Quran explicitly reminds us: 'There is no compulsion in religion.'[7]

Thus, without obstructing, and its own imperceptible ways, Islam can act as a catalyst in rousing the conscience of the international community.

The world of Islam is confident that the era of stark materialism, which bred imperialism, colonialism and injustice in all its forms, is finally over, and cannot be brought back. As they enter the 15th century of the *Hijrah*, the Islamic peoples, who have rediscovered their pride in their religion, their great culture and their unique social and economic institutions, are confident that the advent of this century will mark the beginning of a new epoch in which their high ideals of peace, justice and the equality of man, and their unique understanding of the universe, will once again enable them to make a worthy contribution to the betterment of mankind.

The current Islamic resurgence, whether in Afghanistan, Iran, Malaysia, Pakistan, Saudi Arabia, the Sudan, has no doubt, local, regional and ethnic differences, but beneath these local diversities, it is all inspired and influenced by the broad teachings and message of Islam which is trans-sectarian and trans-national. The resurgence is based on the fundamentals of Islam and not on the Western concept of 'fundamentalism'. It is based on Islam as 'an all-embracing system of life—a faith as well as an ideology and programme of life.[8] Despite two centuries of Western colonial rule and suppression and oppression of the Muslim world, Islam is still a vibrant and dynamic faith. It gives Muslims all over the world a sense of spiritual reinforcement and a new source of a wakening and reassertion. The resurgence of Islam in the 1970s and 1980s in Muslim countries has become a major factor in global politics. It is watched and reviewed by both Western and the old communist countries, by both superpowers, the USA and the demised USSR—the former for its security and economic interests in the strategically important areas of the Middle East, the Persian Gulf, South-West, South and South-East Asia, while the Kremlin leaders are concerned over its potential in the Central Asian Republics, since more than 50 million Muslims who live there are likely to be affected by this re-awakening of Islam. As Professor R Stephen Humphreys writes:

> The events of recent years have demonstrated anew how readily the religion of Islam can be transformed into a political ideology of enormous scope and force. Such a situation is hardly unexampled, of course; it has occurred countless times in the course of Islam's 14 centuries. Still, it is hard to think that a movement of this kind has ever been simultaneously so intense and widespread as is the case today. Moreover, even experienced students of the Muslim world have been surprised by the appeal of Islamic ideology to the technocratic elite—that is, to precisely those professionals, scientists, bureaucrats, and military officers whom it had been supposed were committed to one or another secular vision of society and for whom religion seemed at most a matter of personal belief and morality.[9]

There have been various interpretations and explanations of the current resurgence in Islam. What has led Muslims to turn to Islam in reconstructing their political, social, economic and international order? Since the 1970s many scholars, writers and political leaders, both Muslim and non-Muslim, have offered various explanations for the unique resurgence in the world of Islam. No one factor or interpretation can adequately explain this recent trend in the Islamic *ummah*.

Western colonial rule and domination in most Muslim countries came to an end by the beginning of the 1960s. The newly independent Muslim countries, with a few exceptions, such as Pakistan (including present-day Bangladesh), Malaysia, and some of the older Muslim countries which had not been under direct colonial rule, such as Afghanistan and Saudi Arabia, opted for a Western political and socio-economic order. In the 1950s and 1960s the call for Islamic solidarity on the role of Islam in nation-building was not fully appreciated in many newly independent Muslim nation states. The Islamic forces were overshadowed by other imported or alien political ideas and movements such as Arab nationalism, Afro-Asian solidarity (the 'Bandung spirit'), the non-aligned movement and even socialist ideas such as those of the Ba'th party in Syria and Iraq. When

Pakistan or Malaysia or Saudi Arabia tried to call for Islamic solidarity, it was denounced by Arab leaders, such as Nasser of Egypt and Bourguiba of Tunisia. We have already referred to Pakistan's several abortive attempts in the 1950s to form a union of Muslim countries on the basis of Islamic solidarity. Similarly, when in 1964 King Faisal of Saudi Arabia made a plea for an Islamic conference to contain the Arab regionalism of Nasser he was denounced by the Egyptian leader, who sought to vilify the Saudi king's initiatives as 'conservative' and 'serving Western imperialist interests'. But the inherent strength of Islam ultimately triumphed over the secular forces. After three decades of experience, Muslim countries came to realize that there is no scope for 'secularism' in Islam. Modern secularism is basically a Western phenomenon and has no place in Islam. Western traditions and values could not serve the basic aspirations and hopes of the Muslim world. It is this disillusionment with Western values and tradition which has been a prime factor for the resurgence of Islam in the 1970s and 1980s. Neither did the experiment of socialist thought satisfy Muslim desires for a better and fairer political and socio-economic order in their countries.

Some Western writers have stressed oil revenues as the major factor in the Islamic renaissance. 'The boom in oil exports has, more than anything else, caused the recent Islamic resurgence. The controlling of oil has brought new wealth and power, greatly enhancing the Muslim self-image. For so long Muslims were poor and weak; today a highly visible portion of the Muslim world enjoys an unprecedented affluence and influence. Further, these massive infusions of oil wealth have deeply disrupted normal life, causing Muslims to turn to the familiar Islam.'[10] But this is superficial, a theory of the first look. If oil wealth is the prime factor, how does this explain the Islamic upsurge in South Asian Muslim countries like Bangladesh and Pakistan, or in African Muslim countries like Sudan where there is no oil wealth and where some of the African countries are extremely poor?

The *raison d'être* of the resurgence of Islam in the Muslim world is the inherent strength of religion in the minds of Muslims; they attach great significance and importance to Islamic ideology in both their private and public lives. The recent resurgence has emerged in different parts of the Muslim world in different circumstances: in some cases it has had to assert itself against a dictatorial regime, as in Iran, while in countries like Saudi Arabia, Pakistan, Bangladesh, and Malaysia, it has the active support of the ruling authorities.

Another case is the *jihad*, holy war, of the Afghan freedom-fighters against the mighty military force of a superpower (the then USSR). In the Israeli-occupied Arab territories, the Palestinian freedom-fighters are waging *intifadah* against an oppressive and brutal regime; their material weapons are only bricks and stones. Yet in all these movements, the real strength is provided by a dynamic ideology which has inspired Muslims all over the world in their struggle against all forms of injustice and suffering. The same ideology has also acted as a beacon for the Islamic *ummah* for the last fourteen centuries, in their aspirations to establish a just, fair, equitable and free society. Islam is regarded by Muslims as the will of Allah revealed in the Quran and practised by the Prophet of Islam. The vast majority of Muslims believe, and believe genuinely, that Islamic principles must be the guiding factor, the foundation of their political, social and economic order. In order to achieve this supreme objective, Muslims must abide by the Islamic law, the *shari'ah*. The *shari'ah* is not something static and fixed once and for all. '*Shari'ah* is a dynamic process in which the historical stages in the past are available for study and guidance but of which the proper present and future developments are matters of creative extrapolation.'[11]

King Faisal's inspiring comments on the *shari'ah* have already been referred to: the Saudi king rightly pointed out, 'What does a man aspire to? He wants "good". It is there in the Islamic *Shari'ah*. He wants security. It is there. Man wants freedom. It is there. He wants remedy. It is there. He wants propagation of science. It is there. Everything is there, inscribed in the Islamic *Shari'ah*. The common and prime aim of the Islamic resurgence is the application of *Shari'ah* to Muslims' everyday social-political-economic life, in fact, in all spheres of life.'[12] But the *shari'ah* must be given new and dynamic interpretations. The four schools of Islamic law which evolved about eight centuries ago must be thoroughly overhauled in the context of changing times and circumstance. The Quran gives Muslims enough scope and opportunities to interpret its basic principles. The narrow and rigid Orthodox *'ulama'* interpretation of eight centuries ago must be replaced by a proper one. Islam does not allow, as already explained, any compartmentalization of the different spheres of human life. Throughout the Islamic *ummah*, the decade of the 1970s was a period of dynamic development. 'Clearly', as a Western observer pointed out,'Islam was not a dying force and its vitality was shown in a variety of ways that ranged from major revolutions to the reorientation of the dominant ideologies.'[13] Islamic resurgence has its roots deep in the history of the Muslim people.

In a sense, there is an almost continuous chain of Islamic movements operating amongst Muslim people in all parts of the world. The Islamic movements, as Khurshid Ahmad rightly points out, 'despite some local features and indigenous accents, have stood for similar objectives and displayed common characteristics. They have shown unwavering commitment to Islam and great capabilities to face the challenge of modern life creatively . . . The most important aspect of these Islamic movements has been their emphasis on Islam, not just as a set of beliefs and rituals but as a moral and social movement to establish the Islamic order.'[14] The Islamic resurgence that is spreading throughout the Muslim world has one supreme aim: to establish the rule of Islam in its true and broader perspective. Leaders of the contemporary Muslim world such as the late King Faisal (Saudi Arabia), the late President Zia-ul-Haq (Pakistan), Malaysian Prime Minister Dr Mahathir, Neemeltin Erbakān (Turkey), Gulbeddin Hikmetyar (Afghanistan) and the late Ayatollah Khomeini (Iran) have all had the same aim.

Islamic resurgence is a vast subject, which could be the theme of a major work. We cannot, in a single chapter, encompass the whole subject. The preceding pages have indicated the broad aims and the potential implications for the Islamic world as well as for non-Muslim Western and socialist countries. Now we shall discuss five specific case studies to illustrate the dynamic element of the Islamic resurgence: the modernization in Saudi Arabia on the basis of the Islamic law: the experiment of Islamic democracy in Pakistan and the burial of secularism in Bangladesh; the 1979 Islamic Revolution in Iran; and the *jihad* (1979) of the freedom-fighters in Afghanistan against the former superpower (USSR); The emerging grouping in the Belt of the Crescent: ECO. These five case-studies will provide a picture of the contemporary upsurge in the Islamic *ummah* and its world-wide impacts.

A Modernizing Islamic State: Saudi Arabia

In our discussion on the place of Islam in modern Muslim nation states, we referred to the case of Saudi Arabia, a unique example of how a Muslim country can achieve modernization without sacrificing Islamic tradition and basic principles. The ten-point programme of Prince Faisal (subsequently King Faisal), announced in 1962, was an illuminating document on the synthesis of Islam and modernization. The spirit of the programme of the Saudi prince is noted for encouraging dynamic interpretations of the *shari'ah* by resorting to *ijtihad* (individual reasoning and judgement) and *ijma'* (consensus). Faisal said: 'We want our nation to be in the vanguard and not in the rearguard. We do not want our nation to be mere imitators and satellites. On the contrary we are capable of leading, guiding and steering the helm if we hold fast to God's book and His Prophet's *Sunnah*.'[15] Faisal was committed to both preserving Islamic values and promoting modernization, but not westernization, in his country. He launched his programme in the heyday of Nasser's Arab nationalism. Egypt under Nasser was waging an ideological offensive against the Saudis and also intervened military in the Yemeni civil war. Faisal's reply was to insist that in his country Quranic principles must remain as the supreme law governing all, including the king. Many were watching the ideological confrontation between king Faisal's modernization through Islam and Nasser's Arab radicalism or Arab socialism. It was an issue of great significance and the Islamic *ummah* waited to see the outcome of the ideological conflict: which way lay the future for the Islamic world? Before the end of the 1960s, it became clear that the Saudi experiment was more suited to the genius of Muslims; to their aspirations and hopes; to their goal of economic and political stability and progress. King Faisal emerged as a great leader of both the Arab and the Islamic world. Nasserism, or secular socialism, could not solve the huge economic and political problems of the Arab and non-Arab Muslim countries. On the contrary, Saudi Arabia achieved tremendous economic development and social progress. Little more than a generation ago, as Dr Malcolm Peek points out, per capita annual income in Saudi Arabia was one of the lowest in the world. Today it is upwards of $25,000. There is no doubt that this economic progress was greatly facilitated by the enormous wealth that the country's oil was providing. But there are instances which show that, even with oil wealth, a country cannot make the kind of progress achieved in Saudi Arabia: in Nigeria and Indonesia oil wealth failed to achieve economic and social growth. Just over two decades ago there were no public schools for girls. Today most school-age girls are being educated. Only a few years ago most Saudis lived in small towns and villages and many were nomads; now the majority live in large cities and true Bedouins have disappeared. Vast industrial complexes are being built at Yanbu on the Red Sea and Jubail on the Gulf. Despite the vast expansion of the country's university system, thousands of Saudis are now studying abroad, mainly in the United States. Capable young Saudis are now being trained in advanced science and technology in higher educational institutions in the West.[16]

A new phase of modernization and progress has begun in a highly traditional society. However, the Saudi leaders never fail to take Islam into account when shaping their socio-economic plans for modernization. 'In Saudi Arabia Islam plays a more active role in political and social life than in any other Arab state.' King Faisal initiated social reforms, which have been continued by his successors, King Khalid and King Fahd. The Saudi kings have laid the foundation of a responsive governmental machinery by setting up organizations like the Board of Grievances (*Diwan al-Muzalim*) and by maintaining constant touch with the people in accordance with the Islamic spirit. They also started rapid industrial expansion and corresponding social reforms. In a relatively short period, Saudi Arabia has been transformed from a tribal society with a primitive economy into a modern state. In the process of this transformation new institutions have, no doubt, been created, but the Saudi leaders have been extremely mindful of Islamic patterns of life, values and principles. They have been successful in striking a pragmatic balance between modernization and the Islamic tradition. 'Saudi Arabia has the unique advantage of being the birthplace of Islam . . . It is the only surviving Arab state that is the offspring of an Islamic revival movement, Wahhabism. The Saudis have relied on Islam to unify the peninsula, structure the Saudi polity, formulate national policies, decree new innovation, engage learned scholars in national decision-making . . . it thus seems that Islam, a central reality in Saudi life, is not incompatible with a modernizing monarchy.'[17]

Before the end of the 1960s King Faisal began a vigorous campaign against the pan-Arabism of Nasser and of other 'radical' or 'socialist' Arab states by propagating Islamic solidarity and unity—by encouraging pan-Islam, by setting up institutions and organizations for service to the Islamic *ummah* and by holding conferences and meetings of Muslim leaders of both Arab and non-Arab countries. King Khalid and the present monarch, King Fahd, continued this vigorous policy of projecting pan-Islamism and championing the causes of the Muslim world.

The big question facing the present Saudi leadership is, will the pace of modernization, with all its ramifications, affect the Islamic values and principles in their true spirit? This issue is relevant not only for Saudi Arabia, but it also has significance and implications for the entire Islamic *ummah*. The success of Saudi Arabia in achieving modernization by the path of Islam is a source of great inspiration for the rest of the Islamic *ummah* and it has influenced the resurgence of Islam in the 1970s and 1980s. It is a vital matter for the success of the current Islamic movements in various parts of the Muslim world. 'The enormous challenge,' as Dr Malcolm Peek states, 'is to accommodate far-reaching social changes, while keeping the essential core of Arab-Islamic tradition vital and relevant. To be optimistic, one may suggest that Islamic values and religious values generally are not necessarily the impediment to modern nation-building that many Western social scientists have supposed and, indeed, in some cases may be facilitators of change. If the royal family can successfully project its commitment to religious cultural values that gave birth to its rule, if the old informal egalitarianism of the *majlis* can dominate emerging political institutions and if regional and international crisis do not engulf the kingdom, then it is likely that the challenge will be met.'[18]

While discussing the role of Islam in Saudi Arabia, we have pointed out some tensions between the ruling elite and the emerging Western educated professional groups. We expect that the Saudi Arabian monarchy will gracefully evolve towards a liberal and freer socio-economic as well as political order following the examples of the Prophet of Islam and his immediate four successors, the four 'Rightly Guided Caliphs.'

The success of Saudi experiment of modernization through Islam will depend as in any other contemporary Muslim country, on how Islamic laws are given correct interpretation whilst keeping the Quran as the supreme guide.

The Experiment of Islamic Democracy: Pakistan and Bangladesh

We have already referred to the creation of Pakistan as a result of the inherent strength of Islam in the minds of the Muslims of the Indian subcontinent. It was Islamic ideology and the desire of the Indian Muslims to foster and develop Islamic values and tradition that led to the creation of the largest Muslim state, Pakistan (including present-day Bangladesh), in August 1947. The Muslims of the subcontinent made great sacrifices to achieve a homeland of their own where they would be able to lead their lives in accordance with the teaching of the Quran and the practices of the Prophet Muhammad: one million Muslims were killed and ten million uprooted from their homes to achieve the cherished ideological state. It was a unique achievement in the history of Islam in the contemporary period.

Pakistan established an Islamic state in the mid-1950s but the experiment of an Islamic state or an Islamic democracy in Pakistan received serious setbacks with the rise of authoritarian regimes, both civil and military, since 1958. With the eclipse of democracy, the Islamic provisions of the constitution were also put into cold storage and this continued to be so until 1977 when a Pakistani military general, Muhammad Zia-ul-Haq, became president. In Pakistan and in Bangladesh, it was some devout Muslim army generals who revived the Islamic ideology in their countries. In Pakistan, a comprehensive process of Islamization of the country's political, social and economic order was introduced by the late President Zia.

In Bangladesh the first military president, General Zia-ur Rahman, started the process of the burial of secularism and his successor, the former president of Bangladesh, General H M Ershad, finally buried secularism by declaring Islam as the state religion of Bangladesh. The revival of Islamic ideology in Pakistan and Bangladesh in the 1970s and 1980s constitutes an encouraging example of the current resurgence of Islam.

Pakistan

From the very beginning of his military rule, President Zia-ul-Haq stressed giving his country a 'real Islamic state and the Islamic system of working'. In his various speeches between 12 August 1983 and 30 December 1985, when martial law was finally lifted, Zia never missed an opportunity to stress his positive plan for the Islamization of the political and social system in Pakistan. The most novel and outstanding feature of the present-day constitution in Pakistan is the role of Islam in the country's political order.

In the three constitutions (1956, 1962 and 1973) adopted in Pakistan since its inception in 1947, there were some provisions to designate the country an 'Islamic state', but these provisions were more in the nature of an ideal or ideology; there was not any substance to make the political order an Islamic one. But with President Zia the process of *Nifaz-i-Nizam-i-Islam* (Islamization) was an article of faith. The new Islamic provisions, and the measures taken by Zia to implement them, have made Pakistan an Islamic state. The new concept and definition of the Islamic state in Zia's constitutional amendments had given rise to a new and comprehensive ideal of an Islamic constitution in Pakistan.

President Zia-ul-Haq was a practising follower of Islam. He was a devout Muslim following the Quranic principles both in his personal and public life. The present author had the opportunities of knowing him at close quarters. Between April 1987 and 14 August 1988—four days before his tragic death—I had several exclusive and lengthy meetings with him. He sincerely wanted to make Pakistan an Islamic state. But he did not share fully the views of orthodox *'ulama'*, though he did not openly challenge them for the sake of unity of rightist forces as against the secular forces led by Ms Benazir Bhutto.

Zia's faith in a true and dynamic Islamic political order may be substantiated by the fact that a woman could become the first female prime minister in the Islamic *ummah* under Zia's constitution without changing a single article or even a single clause of Zia's constitution. Some of the Pakistani *'ulama'* did not favour the idea of giving women equal political rights and participation in Pakistan's constitution. One may find such reservations in the Ansari Commission headed by a leading Pakistani *'alim*, Moulana Zafar Ahmed Ansari.

It is, however, true that in recent years (after the introduction of Zia's various Islamic provisions) some of the extreme rightist groups have began to agitate for what they term a 'full fledged' Islamic state, demanding strict laws against women, violating, we firmly believe, the status of women in Islam. In some of the Muslim countries, women are unfairly discriminated against in the name of religion.

In our discussion on the status of women in Islam we have expressed the view that if Quranic principles are followed not only in letter but also in their true spirit and meaning, Islam does not discriminate against women. The cardinal principle of Islam is equality of mankind, irrespective of race, colour, sex etc. The only criteria acceptable in Islam for judging any human being is that of virtue and righteousness, not sex, colour, race, religion, etc.

It is, therefore, unfortunate that Zia's honest efforts for an Islamic political order has given rise to narrow and orthodox concepts of some Islamic provisions with regard to women or minorities.

We, however, are confident that the experiment of Islamic democracy as initiated by post-Zia's political leadership, like that of the former Prime Minister Nawaz Sharif, will ultimately triumph and Pakistan's experiment of 'democracy via Islam' will be a great success and source of inspiration for contemporary Muslim countries who are also eager to find out a proper and correct place for Islam in their countries.

Bangladesh

The Muslims of Bangladesh are deeply religious but not fanatical. Their zeal and enthusiasm for Islam and its values are unique. During the movement for the creation of a separate homeland for Indian Muslims in the 1940s, the Bangladeshi Muslims gave the most tangible support to Mohammad Ali Jinnah's call for the creation of a Muslim homeland. Of all provinces which constituted Pakistan in 1947, East Bengal or East Pakistan (now Bangladesh), gave the greatest support to the establishment of the largest Muslim state after the liquidation of the British empire in India. When the Muslims of what was then East Pakistan revolted against the authoritarian ruling elite of Pakistan in 1971, the issues were the political domination and economic exploitation of the East Pakistanis by the West Pakistani rulers composed of top civil and military officials.

There was no debate or controversy over the Bangladeshi Muslims' deep attachment to Islam and its ideology. Yet the founder of Bangladesh, Mujibur Rahman, out of his mistaken gratitude to India for its role in the break-up of Pakistan—India of course, supported Mujib not out of love for the suffering Bangladeshi Muslims, but out of a hostile attitude to Pakistan and to humiliate Pakistan—opted for 'secularism' when he framed the constitution of Bangladesh in 1972. Mujib, however, had no vision to appreciate the fact that a Western concept of secularism cannot be imported to or imposed on a traditional Muslim society like Bangladesh, where the Muslims' attachment to Islam and its ideology have always remained beyond any shadow of doubt.

So when Mujib and his family were assassinated, secularism in Bangladesh, along with Mujib, was buried. The military ruler who came to power in 1975, General Zia-ur Rahman, changed the constitution and abolished secularism in Bangladesh. He also added the words 'in the name of Allah, the Merciful' to the preamble of the constitution. Zia-ur Rahman's successor, President H M Ershad, buried any concept of secularism, even deeper, making Islam 'the state religion of Bangladesh' by an amendment (the Eighth Amendment) on 9 June 1988.

Today Islam is as flourishing in Bangladesh as in any part of the Islamic *ummah*. Bangladesh attaches great importance to its growing ties with the rest of the Muslim world and it plays a dynamic role in the OIC. The Muslims of Bangladesh have always identified themselves with the hopes and aspirations of the world of Islam.

Whenever and wherever there is a violation of the Muslim cause, be it in Afghanistan, Palestine, Lebanon, Bosnia or anywhere else, Bangladesh has never failed to raise its voice. There is a real awakening and resurgence of Islam in Bangladesh which, incidentally, has the second largest Muslim community after Indonesia.

The present author has had many long interviews with both the late President Zia-ur Rahman and the former president, H M Ershad, about the role of Islam in nation-building in Bangladesh. Both showed deep attachment and commitment to Islam and its broad principles in their desire to build a modern, dynamic and economically developed society in Bangladesh. Islam and its ideology have great potential in this new Muslim nation state of South Asia. No power on earth can destroy the inherent strength of Islamic feelings among the Muslims of Bangladesh as in the rest of the Islamic *ummah*.

Islamic Revolution in Iran

The fall of the all-powerful regime of Shah Mohammad Reza Pahlavi (1941-79) and the rise of a revolutionary Islamic Republic in Iran in 1979 is an event of far-reaching and wide significance, not only to Iran, but to the whole world. In the contemporary Islamic resurgence it has turned out as the most startling and controversial phenomenon. On the one hand, the Iranian revolution is described as based on Islam as interpreted by Shi'ite Muslims; on the other, some of the policies and actions of this Islamic revolutionary regime seemed to be repugnant, not only to the West, but also to a large section of the Muslim world. The role of the spiritual leader of the revolution, Imam Ayatullah Ruhollah Khomeini (1900-89), and some of his actions (the alleged approval of hijacking of civilian planes, kidnapping innocent foreigners and keeping them as hostages) are not, we believe, in accordance with the true spirit of Islam whether it is the Sunni or Shi'ite belief. Islam is a religion of toleration, justice and fair play. the Quran does not approve of such things as terrorism or arbitrary execution: Islam puts great stress on the rule of law. Whether all the allegations made against Imam Khomeini are true or fabricated or exaggerated is difficult to prove. Whatever the verdict of history on the role of Imam Khomeini from 1979 to 1989, the fact remains that he organized an earth-shaking revolution whose full implications will continue to haunt not only the Islamic world but the world at large for many decades to come.

The pertinent question, bluntly put by the American magazine *Time*, is: 'how was it possible for an obscure religious fanatic to lead one of the great upheavals of the century?' Even *Time* had to admit: 'like the Soviet Union's Vladimir Lenin, he fomented a revolution from distant exile, then returned to try to bend it to his will . . . like India's Mohandas Gandhi, he mobilized spiritual forces for political ends. Like China's Mao Zedong he attempted to push beyond nationalism to ideological and cultural revolution, believing that by destroying the old order he could create the conditions for the emergence of a utopia.'[19]

A perceptive observer and expert on Iran, Professor William O Beeman, writes about the Iranian leader: 'one person's saint is usually another's demon. There is no one to whom this has applied more poignantly in recent years than Ayatollah Ruhollah Khomeini. There has hardly been a figure in post-World War II history so widely hated and vilified in the United States as Ayatollah Khomeini. Moreover, it has been conventional wisdom in the United States that Iranians really dislike him too and regretted the revolution that brought his brand of Islamic government to power. Yet the paroxysm of grief demonstrated by millions following his death is unprecedented in Iranian history . . . It forces us to ask whether our short-term view of the Ayatollah is not somewhat unbalanced . . . he changed history and set political and historical forces in motion that will be with the world for decades, if not centuries to come'—an assessment which is nearer the truth than the assertion that the Ayatollah's Islamic revolution will crumble like a house of cards in post-Khomeini Iran. 'The revolution that overthrew the Shah', Beeman concludes, 'is proof not only to Iran but to the Muslim world as well that Islam is a vital political and spiritual force in modern times.'[20]

We must leave the verdict on the Iranian revolutionary leader to the future. He was, no doubt, revered by his Shi'ite Muslim followers all over the world as Imam, qualified to be a deputy Mahdi. According to Shi'ite doctrines, there has to be an intermediary between God and man. During Shi'ism's first centuries this role of mediator was played by the twelve Imams, who were regarded as the rightful successors to the Prophet Muhammad and who combined religious and political authority. The Shi'ites believe that the twelfth Imam who disappeared in AD 940 will one day emerge from hiding to establish a purified Islamic state. Many Iranians believe that Khomeini was the deputy of al-Mahdi, or the Twelfth Imam. This concept is not clearly expressed in the present-day constitution of Iran but the concept is embodied in its 5th and 110th principles. The vast powers granted to him under the Islamic constitution of Iran is based on this notion of the Twelfth Imam.

The constitution of the Islamic Republic of Iran reads in part: 'From the view point of Islam, the government does not arise from the notion of classes and mediation among persons or groups but is a crystallization of political idealism based on religious community and concord which provide its organization—which through the process of ideological transformation turns its path toward the final goal (movement toward God)'. Such a 'government of God', to borrow the words of Ayatollah Khomeini, 'perforce is entrusted with the task of shaping all aspects of Iranian life, including the cultural according to the tenets of Islam as interpreted by the Ayatollah and his supporters and embodied in the constitution.'[21]

In the Islamic Republic of Iran politics have been cast in the framework of the fusion of religious and political spheres, according to Shi'ism. In November 1979, the Iranian people approved a constitution through a referendum, ordered by Khomeini, which provides the principle of *vilayat-i faqih*, which means rule by the *jurisconsult*. The constitution provides for a council of the Guardians of the Revolution, half of whose members were chosen by Khomeini himself and the remainder by the supreme judicial council (the highest judicial body of the country under the new constitution). In reality this Council of Guardians of the Revolution was meant to be dominated by the clerics.

> If one applies Mosca's concepts of the ruling class and stratum to Iranian politics, then Khomeini (the Faqih, supreme legal expert), the members of the Supreme Judicial Council, members of the Council of Guardians and those serving as Friday mosque prayer leaders in the major cities (which collectively are represented in a loose corporate body that may be termed the Imam Jum'ah network) constitute the ruling class. The second stratum, which serves as a reservoir for the recruitment of the future members of the ruling class, consists of clerical cabinet members, clerical members of parliament, clerical members of the revolutionary committees, and theological seminary teachers and their most promising students.[22]

The type of Islamic state set up in present-day Iran may be in accordance with the Shi'ite doctrine of Islam but it differs in some vital aspects from the standard concept of an Islamic state in the Muslim world. The constitution of a country must reflect the ideology and spiritual and cultural heritage of the people for whom it is meant. The Quran does not give us any detailed structure of a constitution. It only provides some guiding principles, which we examined in Chapter II. If the majority of the people of Iran approve the constitution as given by Ayatollah Khomeini, who claimed to have based his socio-political and economic order on the principles of Shi'ite doctrine, then we have no comment or reservation about the present-day system in Iran.

The question is: Was the people's approval free and fair? Were any other parties or groups allowed to challenge it? If not, what is the difference between Khomeini's *modus operandi* of ascertaining peoples' will and the plebiscitary democracy of communist countries or of any other authoritarian regimes?

Some of Khomeini's actions and policies, such as creating disturbances at the time of *hajj*, when his followers were shown in television pictures displaying Khomeini's portraits and behaving violently, or when the Iranian government's principal spokesman, the speaker of the Majlis, Hashemi Rafsanjani (at present President of Iran), openly tells people to hijack an American plane or kill some foreigners for their alleged crime against Iran, these actions are not in accordance with the spirit of Islam. Iranians might justify these actions in the name of their Imam or the Islamic revolution but they can never be condoned. Islam is a religion of peace and love, not of violence and hatred. In fact, some of the actions and policies of 'Islamic Revolutionary' Iran have caused disgrace to and misrepresentation of the true spirit of Islam. The current Islamic resurgence, with which the Iranian revolution is no doubt connected, has been grossly misunderstood and misinterpreted as a result of the excesses of countries like Iran under Khomeini and Libya under Qaddafi, who also seeks to justify violence and acts of terrorism in the name of Islam. But these leaders simply commit great injustice and do harm to the noble and humane spirit of Islam as given in the Quran and as practised by the Prophet.

The Triumph of Jihad *in Afghanistan*

The victory of the freedom-fighters (*mujahidin*) of Afghanistan against the might of the armed forces of a superpower is an inspiring chapter in the recent resurgence of Islam. When the Soviet Union committed brutal aggression against a weaker neighbouring Muslim country, Afghanistan, in December 1979, many people thought that it would become a part of the Soviet empire, like the Central Asian Republics of the USSR. A prominent American media person, Dan Rather, the chief anchorman of the US television station CBS, visited the Afghan refugee camps in Peshawar, Pakistan, near the Afghan border. He was talking to the *mujahidin* and they told him: 'We shall never accept the Soviet occupation of our country.' Dan Rather, translating their remarks into English, made his own comments: 'Those people do not know that their country is already lost to the Soviet Union.' Not only the newsman, Dan Rather, but even the US Government under President Carter seemed to have reached the same conclusion. President Carter sent his National Security Advisor, Zbigniew Brzezinski, to the Pakistani president, Zia-ul-Haq, to explore possibilities of helping the Afghan freedom-fighters: the American offer was $400 million US dollars, of which only $200 million dollars was for military aid; Zia, the chief architect of the Afghan cause, rightly tuned down Carter's offer, terming it 'peanuts'. The present author also went to Pakistan during Brzezinski's visit in January 1980, with two letters addressed to President Zia by two prominent Republican senators, Jesse Helms and Orrin Hatch. They were aware of Carter's antipathy towards Pakistan (Carter had stopped all aid to Pakistan, not only military but even economic aid). These two senators urged Zia to come to the United States to discuss the explosive situation in south west Asia which had resulted from the Soviet invasion of Afghanistan. Zia, who knew Carter's attitude towards his country for its alleged attempts to manufacture an

Islamic nuclear bomb, politely declined the suggestion made by the two Republican senators to come the United States at that time. I asked Zia: 'How would you oppose the superpower, the Soviet Union, without the help from another superpower, the United States?' His answer, like a true Muslim, was: 'I cannot sit idle while a fellow brotherly Muslim country is in danger of being a part of the Russian communist empire like another Muslim Central Asian Republic. I believe in the right and just causes of the Muslims of Afghanistan; Allah will help them in saving their country. The entire Islamic *ummah*, including my country, is behind them. The triumph of Islam is sure; it may be slow.' How prophetic were Zia's assertions! The people of Afghanistan began their *jihad* against the mighty Soviet Union with rifles from the era of World War I, but their real strength was their faith in the slogan with which they began their holy war: *Allahu Akbar*, 'God is great'. It is their religion and the strength of Islamic force in their minds which made them ultimately victorious. The Soviet 100,000-strong armed forces had to withdraw from Afghanistan in February 1989 after eight years of fruitless but brutal fighting in which they resorted to all kinds of violent means to suppress the spirit of freedom of the Afghan *mujahidin*. But nothing could dampen the spirit of *jihad* among the Afghan freedom-fighters.

It is no doubt true that the Afghans subsequently received substantial help from the outside world, including the United States after the Republican Reagan administration came to power in 1980. Pakistan, Saudi Arabia and the Gulf countries were the first to come to the aid of the Afghan resistance forces. An extraordinary session of the Foreign Ministers' Conference of the OIC was held in Pakistan in January 1980. The initiative of the conference was taken by Bangladesh, and Saudi Arabia and Pakistan were the principal partners of a comprehensive plan to help the cause of the Afghan Muslims. President Reagan and the leaders of the People's Republic of China also joined the Muslim world in giving help to the freedom-fighters of Afghanistan. The material aid, particularly the courageous and bold help from Pakistan under Zia was, no doubt, of great help to the Afghans in their resistance against the Soviet military. But the most decisive and most inspiring factor was the zeal and spirit of *mujahidin* based on the spirit of Islam. The Islamic spirit, more than anything else, was responsible for the ultimate triumph of the Afghan freedom-fighters.

As a leader of the Afghan resistance groups wrote in *The New York Times*: 'We have been fighting to kick the Soviets out, to depose their puppet regime, and to establish a freely chosen Islamic state. For this we are fighting and dying . . . We started our struggle with the full support and determination of our people and will continue regardless of the wishes or commands of others . . . We don't want to be an American or Soviet puppet . . . There has never been a single instance of our committing a hijack or kidnapping. We don't need to win our struggle with terrorist activities . . . We are right and strong and this is all we need.'[23]

This is a correct picture of the Islamic spirit of the Afghan Mujahedeen and, as long as this spirit is alive with the Muslims of Afghans, no power, not even a superpower, can subjugate their country. The history of Afghanistan has proved that no government can survive in this deeply religious society if it dares to discard Islamic values and tradition. Even the Soviet puppet regime in Kabul, in order to remain in power, had to profess loyalty to the Islamic tradition and Islamic sentiments. On 1 July 1980 Babrak Karmal, then president of the Soviet-backed regime in Afghanistan, said in a speech to the religious leaders: 'You, esteemed scholars and clerics, are the true heirs of the great prophets on the one hand, sincere respect for you is incumbent on the people and state, especially on me. But on the other hand, the basis of your sacred duty, you too have the obligation to guide the people towards peace, happiness, brotherhood, good deeds and search for knowledge.' Karmal went to the extent of declaring that the 'holy religion of Islam and our national heritage are inseparable aspects of national system and national culture.'[24] He even went so far as to call the Soviet intervention an 'act of God'![25] But no amount of propaganda could deceive the *mujahidin* who were determined to overthrow the communist puppet regime in their country and to establish a political order based on Islam. Regardless of who finally will come to power in Afghanistan, after the withdrawal of the Soviet troops, one thing is certain: Islam will be a central force in Afghanistan, as it has always been in its history. There are, no doubt, differences among the various groups of freedom-fighters but they all speak in the name of Islam. It is futile to classify them as fundamentalists and moderates. There are divergent concepts of Islam among different groups, but that should not lead anybody to make the fatal mistake of ignoring the vital role of Islam in Afghanistan. 'The resistance of the Afghan Mujahedeen,' as pointed out by Professor Richard S Newell, 'is essentially by definition motivated by a commitment to defend Islam.'[26] Those who gave support to the freedom-fighters in Afghanistan, particularly, the United States, realize this fundamental aspect of political dynamics in Afghanistan: or they may make the same mistake (as they did in their support of the Shah of Iran) by ignoring the Islamic forces there.

* * *

We have given these case studies of the current resurgence of

Islam, Saudi Arabia, Pakistan and Bangladesh, Iran and Afghanistan, to illustrate the vitality and spirit of the Islamic upsurge which began in the 1970s and has continued in the 1980s. Similar trends are visible in many other parts of the Islamic *ummah*, such as Malaysia, Indonesia, in south east Asia and, of course, in many Muslim countries of the Near and Middle East. Even Turkey, where an attempt was made to separate religion from politics in the Western sense, experienced a revival of Islamic sentiment in the mid-1970s. The National Salvation Party, the junior partner in three coalition governments in the 1970s advocated, with some success, 'a greater role for religion in Turkish life and a closer identification with Muslim, rather than Western states.' Several of the Persian Gulf States have passed laws based on the *shari'ah* to meet the growing Islamic aspirations of the people of the countries of Africa, notably Sudan. We may therefore conclude that a new, strong resurgence has taken place in the world of Islam. The sooner it is appreciated and properly understood by the non-Muslim West and the socialist countries, the better for world peace, cooperation, understanding and stability. There is nothing to be afraid of in this humane and noble resurgence among a huge section of the world population living in about sixty different nation states.

Latest Developments in Afghanistan: The Tragic Civil War

The Afghan freedom-fighters' achievement in compelling the former superpower USSR to vacate their aggression was hailed and acclaimed all over the world as a great feat of the contemporary period.

However, fighting among the various groups of freedom fighters after the withdrawal of the Soviet troops is a tragedy beyond measure. It has caused death and destruction on a vast scale, more extensive and damaging than during the period of the Soviet occupation. Hundreds of people have been killed, homes and hearths have been destroyed: peoples' sufferings have been and still are immense, causing anguish among the well-wishers of the people of Afghanistan.

A number of neighbouring Muslim countries have applied themselves vigorously to put an end of the interime warfare in Afghanistan; in particular, Iran, Pakistan, Saudi Arabia have made serious attempts; a number of 'peace' accords were signed; ceasefires were arranged, only to be broken within days, if not within hours. The most sincere effort was made in Pakistan; a peace accord was made and signed, with the Saudi king and Pakistan prime minister as witnesses; the signing ceremony was held in the holiest Muslim city of Makkah at the house of God, the *Ka'bah*. That accord has not yet been 'formally' broken, but the tragedy is not yet over.

We are, however, confident the unifying force of Islam will move the different ethnic groups and sub-groups to gather and mould themselves into a strong nation. Afghanistan, whose people are noted for a strong attachment to Islam and their freedom, will, we sincerely hope, form a well-knit national state. With Islam as it guiding factor in the country's political and socio-economic sphere, Islamic forces will ultimately succeed.

The Emerging Grouping in the Belt of the Crescent: ECO

Once the great monolith, the Russian empire began to be heading towards disintegration and into an era of political turmoil and instability; the independent minded 'republics' and religious and ethnic groups of the Russian empire raised their voices for self assertion and self-rule. 120 years of Russian rule over its vast empire had been facing new challenges and demands. In the light of the emerging national, religious and cultural ferment in various parts of the Russian empire, some 55 million Muslims of the Russian empire also raised their voices against the ruthless suppression and oppression of their cherished ways of life based on the tradition of Islam. The Russians began to encounter a resistance more subtle, elusive and more determined from its largest and most persecuted minority group, the 55 million Muslim population of the five central Asian Republics and Azerbaijan.

The awakening of the Muslims of the Russian empire had began long before Mikhail Gorbachev's *glasnost*. It is related to the recent resurgence of Islam which, as we have already stated, has been sweeping the world of Islam since the 1960s and 1970s and is still continuing with greater fervour from Indonesia in the east to Senegal in the west. The persecuted Muslims of the Russian empire are also inspired by this new awakening, new awareness, new mood and new vision of contemporary Islamic resurgence. An idea of a grouping of the neighbouring Muslim states of Afghanistan, Iran, Pakistan and Turkey was bound to have a great impact on the Muslims of the Russian empire. The new grouping, once fully materialized, will be geographically, religiously and culturally nearer and dearer to the down-trodden Muslims of the Russian empire, and its implications will be great and far-reaching. Central Asia, one of the world's oldest inhabited areas and the home of an ancient and highly developed civilisation, was until 1989-90 viewed as a faraway God-forsaken place of no serious interest to anyone. Today Iran, Turkey and Pakistan, as well as Saudi Arabia and the Gulf states, are wooing the five former Soviet republics of Central Asia while the major powers—United States, China and the-newly born Russian Federation—are watching the far-reaching developments in the area with interest and concern. The newly independent states of Central Asia were once a part of the legendary 'silk road' between China and the west until the Portuguese discovered the sea route to India in 1498, effectively closing the area's economic and intellectual development. Czarist Russia and then the Soviet Union tried to crush its Islamic identity. When the Soviet Union was heading towards disintegration, the Muslims of the communist empire raised their voices against the ruthless suppression and oppression of their cherished way of life based on the tradition of Islam.

Taking note of the revolutionary changes, the regional countries (Iran, Pakistan, Turkey) revived their old regional organisation the RCD (Regional Council for Development). Very soon they tried to expand the RCD into a larger economic cooperation organisation (ECO) to face the challenges of emerging international order by enhancing the level of cooperation and also addressing the problems of conflicts and tension in the region, as stated by Pakistan's prime minister in his inaugural address at the foreign minister's meeting of the ECO countries in Quetta on February 6-7, 1993. The ECO today consists of the three original members of the RCD—Iran, Pakistan, Turkey—and Afghanistan and five Central Asian republics—Kazakhstan, Uzbekistan, Tajikistan, Turkmenistan, Kyrgyzistan and Azerbaijan. The first meeting of the ECO was mooted in Tehran. Then in November 1992, Afghanistan and the Central Asian Republics were formally inducted into it and the next meeting took place in Quetta in February 1993. It is too early to predict the future shape and role of this new organisation. However, it has already raised eyebrows in New Delhi, Moscow, Washington and some other Western countries and great interest in Beijing, while Iran and Pakistan are working around the clock to make it as a source of their bargaining strength. At the moment it is primarily engaged with economic cooperation and development within the ECO and with the outside world. There is great potential in this vast region for both economic and political benefits and for the world of Islam it has very great significance. The total number of the Muslim population of the

ECO countries is quite significant in the world of Islam; this organisation may play a vital role even more significant than the Middle Eastern Muslim countries. The fifty million Muslims of the Central Asian republics have joined the Muslim countries of Iran, Afghanistan, Turkey and Pakistan with common hopes and aspirations. No doubt there is still a long way for the ECO to go before it can play its proper role. Its ways of development will be slow, but it is destined to be a major regional force with global implications.

ECO Summit

We reproduce below a thoughtful analysis of the ECO after its summit meeting in July 1993 at Istanbul, Turkey, from a prominent English-language daily newspaper of Bangladesh (the Dhaka *Morning Star*, 28 July 1993), a country which is also considering joining the ECO:

> The leaders of the ten Economic Cooperation Organisation (ECO) nations proposed building transport and telecommunication network to connect members of the trading bloc. The regional pact—ECO—whose aim is to remove trade barriers, consists of Turkey, Iran, Pakistan, Uzbekistan, Kyrgyzistan, Afghanistan, Azerbijan, Kazakhstan and Tajikistan. The two-day ECO summit which began its deliberations in Istanbul dealt at length on trade and other related issues. In his address President Suleyman Demirel dwelt upon the necessity to build a network of telecommunications and express ways, air routes, sea routes and railroads. He rightly warned, 'should we fail to embark immediately on these measures, the organisation will gradually wither away and lose an historical opportunity.' Turkmenistan's President Sapamurad Niyazov proposed construction of new highways linking his country with Uzbekistan, Afghanistan, Pakistan, Iran and Turkey. The absence of highways in the region has made construction of road systems a priority. Niyazov also urged wider use of the Caspian Sea, which borders four member nations for sea transportation.
>
> The new roads would give landlocked members of ECO, including Afghanistan and former Soviet Central Asian Republics, vital access to the sea. Kabul asked Pakistan to provide her with a free port for its transit trade. And therefore, Afghan President Burhanuddin Rabbani felt allotment of such a free port will prove of immense value to the overall regional transit trade. The two day summit has set the agenda for future

cooperation among the members. The trading block with a population of 300 million with headquarters in Tehran has immense possibilities of expanding regional trade. The three old members—Turkey, Iran and Pakistan—are in strategically vital positions to render requisite aid in building telecommunications, road and infrastructures which have been collectively emphasised by the ECO leaders.

Sustained efforts both at the official and private levels are required by the ECO members in the process of economic transformation. A steady progress in this task would understandably result in mutual economic benefits for both the old and new members of the regional trade pact. Their priority should now be on effectively building transport and telecom networks to stimulate economic growth.

The expansion of ECO has opened a new vista for the new Asian republics and as such, for realising the global trade pattern, effective measures are required by all to give this expanded regional trade body a new look and dimension.

With geographical contiguity, it is hoped the process of economic ties and collaboration among the member states will be hastened with exchange of expertise in different other sectors of economy.

Notes

1. Flora Lewis, 'Upsurge in Islam', *New York Times*, 28-30 December 1979.
2. See the text of President Zia's speech at the thirty-fifth session of the UN General Assembly, 1 October 1980: UN General Assembly, Official Record of the Eighteenth Plenary Meeting, p. 336.
3. *Pakistan Times*, Islamabad, 31 January 1980.
4. See 'Explosion in the Muslim World: A Round Table on Islam' (whose participants included Dr Bruce Lawrence, Dr Wilfred C Smith, Dr Leonard Binder, Professor Majid Khaduri, and Professor Nikki Keddie), *New York Times*, 11 December 1979; and Peregine Worsthorne, 'Meeting the Islamic Threat', Sunday Telegraph, London, 17 December 1978.
5. Edward Said, *Orientalism*, New York, 1979.
6. *Dawn*, Karachi, 24-30 November 1979.
7. UN Official Records, *op. cit.*, p. 341.
8. Amin Saikal, 'Islam: Resistance and Reassertion' in *World Today*, London, November 1987.
9. R Stephen Humphreys, 'The Contemporary Resurgence in the context of Modern Islam' in Ali E Hillal Dessouki (ed.), *Islamic Resurgence in the Arab World*, New York, 1982, 67.
10. Daniel Pipes, 'Oil Wealth and Islamic Resurgence' in *ibid.*, 45.
11. See Wilfred C Smith, *Pakistan as an Islamic State*, preliminary draft, Montreal, 1951, 25.
12. Ronald R MacIntyre, 'Saudi Arabia', cited in Mohammad Ayoob (ed.), *Politics of Islamic Reassertion*, New York, 1981, 13.

13 J O Voll, *Islam: Continuity and Change in the Modern World*, Boulder, 1982, 347.
14 Khurshid Ahmed, 'The Nature of the Islamic Resurgence' in John L Esposito (ed), *Voices of Resurgent Islam*, New York, 1983, 222.
15 The full text of the ten-point programme is given in Gerald De-Gaury, *Faisal, King of Saudi Arabia*, New York, 1967, 147-51.
16 Malcolm C Peek, 'Saudi Arabia: Islamic Tradition and Modernization' in Philip Stoddard et al (eds), *Change and the Muslim World*, New York, 1981.
17 *Ibid.*
18 Farouk A Sankari, 'Islam and Politics in Saudi Arabia' in Humphreys, *op. cit.*, 145.
19 *Time*, 12 June 1989.
20 William O Beeman, 'The Ayatollah has set Forces in Motion' in *The Sun*, Baltimore, 11 June 1989.
21 Rouhollah K Ramazani, 'Iran: The Islamic Cultural Revolution' in Stoddard *et al.*, *op. cit.*, 41.
22 For details see Shahrough Ahhavi, 'Iran: Implementation of an Islamic State' in John L Esposito (ed.), *Islam in Asia: Religion, Politics and Society*, New York, 1987, Chapter 2.
23 Abdul Huq (leader of the Afghan resistance groups) 'Afghanistan Won't be a US or Soviet Puppet', *New York Times*, 9 June 1989.
24 Cited by Ashraf Ghani, 'Afghanistan: Islam and Counter-Revolutionary Movements' in Esposito, *op. cit.*, 79.
25 Ibid., 89.
26 See Richard S Newell, 'Islam and the Struggle for Afghan National Liberation' in Cyriae K Pullapilly (ed.), *Islam in the Contemporary World*, Cross Road Books, 252.

Chapter IX
Islamic Fundamentalists: Is Islam a Threat to World Peace?

We shall deal, in our concluding chapter, with some serious challenges and issues facing the Islamic *ummah* and the risks, real or myth, of a conflict between the world of Islam and the West, in particular, the only serving superpower, the USA.

Since, the ending of the East-West cold war as a result of the collapse of the 'Evil Empire', the USSR, we quite often hear of a new global conflict between the Islamic world and the West.[1]

In recent years, particularly since the Gulf War of 1991, there have been deliberate attempts to vilify and misinterpret Islam and its fundamental principles and ideology. It has been asserted in the US press that the war between communism and the West is about to be replaced by a war between the West and Muslims. In the previous chapter, we have described the current resurgence of Islam. One aspect of this powerful reawakening among Muslims seems to be clear: its main urge is the rejection of what is regarded as alien to Islamic values leading to a vigorous search for renewed strength from Islamic ideals and principles. There is a new realisation in the world of Islam that the era of the last two centuries, during which the Muslim world had been oppressed, suppressed, colonised, remained backward and lost its initiatives, has, at last come to an end and a new era of unity and inward strength based on the broad teachings of Islam has dawned on the Islamic community.

Islamic unity is not, however, directed against any country or any bloc. Islam is a religion of peace. It preaches tolerance, universal brotherhood and it does not permit its ideology to be imposed on others by force, just as it does not want other ideologies to be imposed on Muslims. Islam believes in the principle of peaceful coexistence. As Dr Zbigniew Brzesinki, President Carter's National Security Advisor, points out, there is really no reason why Americans should be hostile toward an Islamic renaissance. It is a religious phenomenon rooted in certain basic values which are not alien to the Christian tradition; yet, instinctively, many Americans are perplexed by this development.

The present resurgence of Islam and the reawakening among the Muslims of the world is a welcome phenomenon. It should be regarded as a revitalising force that could bring peace to a weary world and hope to a distraught humanity. It is not a religion that forces itself on others. The Quran explicitly reminds us: 'There is no compulsion in religion.'

In spite of the fact that Islam is a religious phenomenon rooted in certain values which are common to the broad ideals of Judeo-Christian ethics, it is depicted as anti-Western, a religion of intolerance, a creed of violence and terrorism, uncompromising, bent on conquering the non-Muslim world by *jihad* (holy war). Some actions of violent groups such as the 'Army of God' (*Jund Allah*) and 'Party of God' (*Hizbullah*) are misinterpreted as the work of the entire Islamic world. The so-called threat of 'Islamic Fundamentalism' is most unfortunate and potentially dangerous for the emerging world order after the collapse of the Soviet Union. The vast majority of Muslim countries cherish and value closer and friendly relations with the West, in particular with the United States. They are engaged in a major process of modernisation, technological, scientific, educational and economic development; Islam, in its true spirit and meaning, is perfectly compatible with modernisation.

When the Muslim world wants to recover its glorious past, it has nothing against any other religion or group. Islam is a religion of peace; it preaches tolerance, universal brotherhood and it does not permit its ideology to be imposed on others by force. Islam believes in the principle of live and let live. Coercion is strictly forbidden in Islam. If any individual or group indulges in acts of violence or terrorism, they are not true followers of Islam. Islam is noted for strict adherence to the rule of law.

The Next Battleground

Islam was destined to become a world religion and to create a civilization which stretched from one end of the globe to the other.

Already during the early Muslim caliphates, first the Arabs, then the Persians and later the Turks, set about creating a classical Islamic civilization. Later, in the 13th century, both Africa and India became great centres of Islamic civilization and soon thereafter Muslim kingdoms were established in the Malay-Indonesian world, while Chinese Muslims flourished throughout China.

Islam is a religion for all people from whatever race or background they might be. That is why Islamic civilization is based on a unity which stands completely against any racial or ethnic discrimination. Such major racial and ethnic groups as the Arabs, Persians, Turks, Africans, Indians, Chinese and Malays, in addition to numerous smaller units embraced Islam and contributed to the building of Islamic civilization.

The Islamic world remains today a vast land stretching from the Atlantic to the Pacific, with an important presence in Europe and America, animated by the teachings of Islam and seeking to assert its own identity. Despite the presence of nationalism and various secular ideologies in their midst, Muslims wish to live in the modern world but without simply imitating blindly the ways followed by the West. The Islamic world wishes to live at peace with the West as well as the East but at the same time not to be dominated by them. It wishes to devote its resources and energies to building a better life for its people on the basis of the teachings of Islam and not to squander its resources in either internal or external conflicts. It seeks finally to create better understanding with the West and to be better understood by the West. The destinies of the Islamic world and the West cannot be totally separated and therefore it is only in understanding each other better that they can serve their own people more successfully and also contribute to a better life for the whole of humanity.[2]

In spite of the peaceful nature of the Islamic civilization, Professor Samuel Huntington of Harvard University predicts a cultural conflict and a conflict of civilization between the world of Islam and the West. He elaborates his views by pointing out the following:

> a) We are moving out of the era where the nation state is the central focus, although obviously it will remain the leading entity on the world scene.
> b) The conflicts among civilizations will be increasingly central: the West and Islam, Islam and Hindu civilization in India, Islam vs. Slav Orthodox Russian civilization, China and Japan as civilizations. These are going to be the major entities among which international relations will take place.
> c) A civilization is the broadest level of cultural identity a person

has. Civilizations to a large extent are defined by religion. It is a much more absolute distinction than others. A person could be half French and half Arab, but it would be rather difficult to be half Catholic and half Muslim. This has been most obvious in Islamic countries.

d) Islam is the most strict religion in the world outside of Christianity. There is no separation between religion and politics. Also, there is the feeling that the Muslim world has been abused by the West, exploited, and that some form of renaissance is under way. The conflict will take many forms. Yet one does not want to think of this as the great apocalyptic world war between Islam and the West.

e) All the Middle Eastern Islamic states are increasing their military strength. There is this Confucian-Islamic connection between China and North Korea on one hand and Middle Eastern states like Iran, Iraq, Syria and Libya on the other. It is primarily a military connection, where the Confucian states provide weapons and weapons technology.[3]

The Islamic Fundamentalists

Professor Daniel Pipes of the Foreign Policy Research Institute in Philadelphia speaks a lot about the so-called 'Fundamentalist Muslims and their attitude towards the two superpowers' (USA and the demised USSR), their perception of the conflict between Islam and the West and similar issues in a lengthy article in *Foreign Affairs*. Before we discuss the conflicts of the Islamic fundamentalists and others and the alleged 'dangers' or 'threats' posed by 'Islamic fundamentalists', let us examine who the 'Islamic fundamentalists' are? Obviously there cannot be a universally accepted definition of 'fundamentalists'. Broadly speaking the word 'fundamentalists' may be categorized into two main groups: (a) as the word is understood or at least should be understood in accordance with the proper teaching and guidelines of Islam and (b) the term as is now widely used describing the current conflicts, real or imaginary, between Islam and the West.

In accordance with Islamic fundamental principles as we have discussed in Chapter I of this work, we may call a follower or *mu'min* a (genuine) Muslim the one who believes and practises unconditionally and unequivocally 'The Five Pillars of Islam': faith in one God: Allah; five daily prayers; almsgiving (*zakat*); fasting in the month of Ramadan; and the pilgrimage, once in a life time, to Makkah. We tried to analyze the true significance and spirit of these fundamentals of Islam. They are not merely rituals. They are of self purification and for acquiring the virtues as enjoined in the Quran and as practised by the Prophet of Islam, Muhammad, as the 'Quran in Practice'. We may repeat here the brilliant description of their significance by Charles Le Gai Eaton:

> When in accordance with the first Pillar of his religion, the Muslim makes the Confession of Faith he attaches himself to the essential and puts aside all that is—in appearance—other than God, and he acknowledges the truth brought by the messengers. When, in accordance with the second Pillar, he prays—whether in a mosque or on the desert sands, in a Western city or in the polar regions—he places himself at the centre of all possible worlds, for God has promised that He will be present wherever His name is mentioned, and the place where He is present is necessarily central in every dimension.
>
> When, in accordance with the third Pillar, this Muslim pays the poor-due and observes the obligation of loving-kindness towards his fellows, he acknowledges the rights of other creatures—made in the same image as himself—and recognizes that God, who is close to him, is close also to them. When he fasts, in accordance with the fourth Pillar, he detaches himself from the locality in which he is temporarily housed, the better to prepare himself for his everlasting home.
>
> And when, as a pilgrim, he stands before the Ka'ba in Mecca (after circling it seven times), the centrality, already prefigured by his orientation when he prayed far off, is made actual. Clothed only in two pieces of plain, unsewn cloth, he has left behind him the characteristics which identified him in this world, his race, his nationality, his status; he is no longer so-and-so from such-and-such a place, but simply a pilgrim.
>
> Beneath his bare feet, like mother-of-pearl, is the pale marble of this amphitheatre at the centre of the world, and although he is commanded to lower his eyes when praying elsewhere, he is now permitted to raise them and look upon the Ka'ba, which is the earthly shadow of the Pole or Pivot around which circle the starry heavens. Although Paradise may still seem far distant, he has already come home.[4]

If any Muslim believes in these principles he or she cannot, we strongly believe, indulge in acts of violence, terrorism, hijacking or any kind of action which goes against the universal principles of truth, justice, peace and universal brotherhood. If anybody in actual practice commits any such violation of human rights, he or she may be anything—nationalists, patriots, or believer in any 'ism'—but certainly he or she is not a true follower of Islam. In fact, by committing any such activities, he ceases to be a follower of the true spirit of Islam. Islam at the cost of its reputation, we may say, is a religion of peace, justice, tolerant of other religions, of universal brotherhood and peace. So our definition of a true Muslim or Islamic Fundamentalist is completely different from what is currently used in the Western and non-Muslim world, whether by a serious scholar, or politicians, or by any news media.

Islamic fundamentalists have been described and defined in many other ways. Thus Yousuf M Choueiri in his *Islamic Fundamentalism* says:

> Islamic Fundamentalism is a vague term, currently in vogue as a catch-phrase used to describe the militant ideology of contemporary Islamic movements. It is, however, adopted in this book to refer to Islamic systems of thought and political movements that emerged from the eighteenth century onwards in countries as far apart as Saudi Arabia, Indonesia, Nigeria and India.
>
> Whereas the term 'fundamentalism' has an obvious Protestant origin, denoting the literal yet creative interpretation of the Bible, it is here redefined, for lack of a better word, in order to convey a less rigorous connotation. Its direct meaning is assumed to indicate a certain intellectual stance that claims to derive political principles from a timeless, divine text.

He continues:

> However, not all movements designated 'Islam' are necessarily right-wing or fascist. In Egypt, for example, Hasan Hanafi, Professor of Philosophy at Cairo University, leads a school of thought that calls itself 'the Islamic Left'. This particular instance only goes to show that political classifications have become a world-wide phenomenon, bypassing local cultures or purely religious beliefs. It also serves to draw attention to the multifaced attributes and specifications of Islamic ideologies.[5]

We may cite yet another interpretation of Islamic or Muslim fundamentalism:

> In times of crisis and historic change, some social groups look to the past to find ways to cope with the present. In the Middle East, dissatisfaction with the present and fear about the future

have led some groups to develop a restorationist image of society. The theme most often associated with this view of history and society is what is generally called Muslim fundamentalism. The gist of this ideological current is that neither Arab nationalism nor Arab socialism has been able to deal with the challenges facing the Arab world. The only way to resist fierce attacks from the outside is to go back to the pure roots of Islam. Restoring faith and discipline, with the values associated with them, and rekindling the fervor that characterized early Islam are considered key to a revival that will restore dignity to people of the region.

Muslim fundamentalism was invigorated by the success of revolutionary Islam in Iran. It was also strengthened by the ability of Islamic groups to force Israel out of southern Lebanon. Above all, however, Muslim reaction focused on declining social mores, and unrestrained westernization, and the spread of drugs, alcohol and sexual promiscuity.[6]

Professor Daneil Pipes of the Foreign Policy Research Institute in Philadelphia wrote about 'Fundamentalist Muslims between America and Russia' before the final collapse of the Soviet Union. His contention was that between America and Russia, 'Fundamentalist Muslims' had more in common with the latter. He elaborated his theme in a lengthy article in *Foreign Affairs*. His theory was:

> Muslim fundamentalists offer a most peculiar interpretation of superpower relationships, derived from an awareness of what many in the West overlook. Cultural similarities between the United States and the Soviet Union far outweigh the differences between them. By looking beyond political disagreements, fundamentalist Muslims see how much alike the two are. If American and Soviet citizens alike have difficulty recognizing themselves—or for that matter, each other—as they are portrayed by fundamentalist Muslims, this eccentric assessment motivates a significant body of opinion through the Muslim world.
>
> Both powers are perceived as having similar plans for imperial expansion, continuing the scramble for colonies among the European states a century ago. 'Before, it was the British that brought us misfortune,' says Ayatollah Ruhollah Khomeini, 'now it is the Soviets on the one hand, and the Americans on the other.'
>
> Arguments between the two powers over freedom, equality, democracy and so on, have little relevance to fundamentalist

> Muslims. Violence is a legitimate tactic for preventing close relations with either superpower.
>
> Fundamentalist Muslims base their views on public and private life, indeed their entire existence, on the sacred law of Islam, the *Shari'ah*. This massive body of regulations, drawn from precepts found in the Quran and other Islamic writings, covers everything from the most public aspects of life—a penal code based on corporal punishment, taxes in accordance with Koranic levies, second-class citizenship for non-Muslims living under Muslim rule—to the most intimate, such as personal hygiene and sexual relations. Fundamentalism offers them an instrument with which to fend off frightening European influences and preserve accustomed ways. Hashemi Rafsanjani, speaker of the Iranian parliament, has stated what every fundamentalist believes: 'Islam is important because it is capable of defeating Western culture.'
>
> They portray Western civilization as aesthetically loathsome, ethically corrupt and morally obtuse. They whisper dark run modes of conspiracy, claiming that the West spreads its culture to weaken the Muslims and steal their resources. They ignore the West's economic and cultural achievements, harping on its unemployment and pornography. To discredit secularist and reformist Muslims, fundamentalists call them lackeys of the Western powers. Fundamentalists discern a strong crusading component to US foreign policy. 'The U.S. attitude is motivated by several factors, but the most important, in my view,' writes Umar at-Talmasani, the Egyptian fundamentalist leader, 'is religious fanaticism . . . This attitude is a continuation of the crusader invasion of a thousand years ago.'
>
> In sum, the more attractive an alien culture, the more fundamentalist Muslims fear it and fight it. A leading Iranian mullah declared that the main objective of the Islamic revolution is to 'root out' American culture from Muslim countries.[7]

US foreign policy towards the Middle East has become a real sore point for Muslims in general and for the so-called Muslim fundamentalists in particular. Analysing the American political process and US Middle East policy, Findlay writes: 'In respect to the Middle East policy, our government is not a superpower—not even a minor power—in its captivity to the pressures by a lobby devoted to the interests of a foreign government. Muslims have become increasingly aware of the power of the Israeli lobby, which to them appears to have "hijacked" the American government and subverted it to Israeli interests.'[8] Other Americans who have experienced the power of the lobby share their view. To some Washington experts it is quite evident that America is unable to execute an independent American foreign policy in the interests of the United States. As previously stated, former Assistant Secretary of State Richard Murphy grumbled that American policy is controlled by Israel and its allies, whose approval is necessary before any action can be taken. Identifying Jordan as a friend in need of American assistance against outside aggression and terrorism, he acknowledged that this assistance can be provided only when we are able to persuade Israel that the security of Jordan is in Israel's interests.[9] Donald McHenry, former US Ambassador to the United Nations, expressed a similar opinion when he acknowledged that the Israeli lobby prevents the United States from freely pursuing its own national interests in the Middle East.[10]

Of all the problems in the region, none inflames public opinion more than the inability of Arab governments to put an end to the suffering of the Palestinians under Israeli occupation. It is indeed a measure of how important and potentially explosive this problem is that it hovers at all times over any discussion of the Gulf crisis.

The majority of people in the region blame the continuation of the problem on the United States. The latter is seen as Israel's protector because it guarantees financial and political support and refuses to pressure Israel to come to the negotiating table.[11]

Professor John L Esposito has rendered great services to Islam by explaining the Islamic message in his various books. In the latest, *The Islamic Threat: Myth or Reality* (1992,) Esposito raised the questions:

> Are Islam and the West on an inevitable collision course? Are Islamic fundamentalists medieval fanatics? Are Islam and democracy incompatible? Is Islamic fundamentalism a threat to stability in the Muslim world and to American interests in the region? These are critical questions for our times that come from a history of mutual distrust and condemnation.[12]

The answer to these type of queries which agitate the minds of many is: the Islamic world wishes to live at peace with the West as well as the East but at the same time not to be dominated by them. It wishes to devote its resources and energies to building a better life for each people on the basis of the teaching of Islam and not to squander its resources in either internal or external conflicts. It seeks finally to create better understanding with the West. The destinies of the Islamic world and the West cannot be totally separated and therefore it is only in understanding each other better that they can serve their own people more

> successfully and also contribute to a better life for the whole of humanity.

We feel tempted to quote Esposito's thoughtful and perceptive remarks about the alleged Islamic threat:

> The West often reinforces the equation of Islam with danger or threat, viewing the Islamic world with catchwords like 'militant Islam,' 'Islamic fundamentalism,' and 'terrorism'. Our selective memory then blocks our ability to appreciate the other side of the equation—the sources of Muslim images of the West in turn as the 'real' threat to them. Many in the Arab and Muslim world view the history of Islam and of the Muslim world's dealings with the West as one of victimization and oppression at the hands of an expansive imperial power. Thus many counter that it is 'militant Christianity' and 'militant Judaism' that are the root causes of failed Muslim societies and instability: the aggression and intolerance of Christian-initiated Crusades and the Inquisition; European colonialism; the breakup of the Ottoman empire and artificial creation of modern states in Iraq, Lebanon, Syria, Iran, Jordan, and Palestine; the establishment of Israel; Israel's occupation of the West Bank and Gaza and its invasion and occupation of Lebanon; and the extent to which oil interests have been the determining factor in support for autocratic regimes.
>
> Today we are witnessing a new historical transformation. Countries in the Muslim world, as in the former Soviet Union, Eastern Europe, and other parts of the world, are undergoing a process of political liberalization or democratization that was prevented in the past by colonialism and more recently by authoritarian governments. Risks exist, for there can be no risk-free democracy. Those who fear the unknown—what specific Islamic movements in power will be like or how they will act—have a legitimate concern. However, in principle if we condemn government repression of the opposition, cancellation of elections, and massive violation of human rights, then the same concern must apply to many current regimes, such as those in Tunisia and Algeria, where the results of the Arab world's first free parliamentary elections have been denied and the winners imprisoned. The track record of these governments on political participation and pluralism and respect for human rights we know already.
>
> As some dream of the creation of a new world order, and many millions in North Africa, the Middle East, Central Asia,

> and southern and South East Asia aspire to greater political liberalization and democratization, the continued vitality of Islam and Islamic movements need not be a threat but a challenge. For many Muslims, Islamic revivalism is a social rather than a political movement whose goal is a more Islamically minded and oriented society, but not necessarily the creation of an Islamic state. For others, the establishment of an Islamic order requires the creation of an Islamic state. In either case, Islam and most Islamic movements are not necessarily anti-Western, anti-American, or anti-democratic. While they are a challenge to the outdated assumptions of the established and to autocratic regimes, they do not necessarily threaten American interests. Our challenge is to better understand the history and realities of the Muslim world. Recognizing the diversity and many faces of Islam counters our image of a unified Islamic threat. Our image of a unified Islamic threat lessens the risk of creating self-fulfilling prophecies about the battle of the West against a radical Islam guided by our stated ideals and goals of freedom and self determination. The West has an ideal vantage point for appreciating the aspirations of many in the Muslim world as they seek to define new paths for their future.[13]

We firmly believe that any movement of Muslims based on the true spirit of Islamic principles or ideals cannot be a threat to the world; nor are there any reasons to haunt ourselves with a new global conflict between the world of Islam and the West, replacing the East-West Cold War. We shall conclude with a note of optimism and hope by referring a recent policy statement on Islam by the US government. Assistant Secretary Edward Dijerejian told the US Congress on 12 May 1993:

> Islam, one of the world's great religions, is not our enemy. What we do oppose is extremism and fanaticism, whether of a religious or secular nature. We part company with those who preach intolerance, abuse human rights or resort to violence in pursuit of their political goal.

Islam, we may add, is in agreement in opposing this violence and abuse of human rights as mentioned by Dijerejian.

Notes

1 William Pfapt, 'Help Algeria's Fundamentalist', New York, 28 January 1991, cited in J L Esposito, *The Islamic Threat: Myth or Reality*, New York, 1992, 3.

[2] See *Islam: A Global Civilization*, prepared by the Islamic Department of the Embassy of Saudi Arabia, Washington D.C.
[3] Samuel Huntington, 'The Next Battleground', *Time*, 28 June 1993.
[4] Charles Le Gai Eaton, *Islam and Destiny*, New York, 1985, 221-222.
[5] Yousuf M Choueiri, *Islamic Fundamentalism*, Boston, 1990, 9-10.
[6] 'The Middle East: Myths and Realities', special report in *World and I*, New York, 1990, 37.
[7] 'Between America and Russia' in *Foreign Affairs*, summer, 1986.
[8] Paul Finlay, 'The American Political Process and the US Middle East Policy' in *American Arab Affairs*, 16, spring, 1986.
[9] Yvonne Y Haddad, *The Muslims of America*, New York, 1991, 223.
[10] Richard Murphy, cited in *ibid*.
[11] Haddad, *op. cit*. 223.
[12] Esposito, *The Islamic Threat*, 3.
[13] *Ibid*., 211-217

Bibliography

A Brief History and Philosophy of the International Institute of Islamic Thought and Civilization

Abdul Rauf, M, *Islam Creed and Worship*, Washington D.C., Islamic Centre, 1974

Abdul Waheed, Khwaja, *Islam and the Origins of Modern Science*, Lahore, 1978

Abu Sulayman, Abdul Hamid A, *The Islamic Theory of International Relations: New Directions for Islamic Methodology and Thought*, Handen, USA, 1987

Ahhavi, Shahrough, 'Iran: Implementation of an Islamic State' in John L Esposito (ed.), *Islam in Asia: Religion, Politics and Society*, New York, 1987,

Ahmad, Akbar S, *Discovering Islam: Making Sense of Muslim History and Society*, London, 1989

Ahmad, Khurshid, *Towards Understanding Islam*, Leicester, 1979

Ahmed, Khurshid, 'The Nature of the Islamic Resurgence' in John L Esposito (ed),*Voices of Resurgent Islam*, New York, 1983

Al Farsy, Fouad, *Saudi Arabia: A Case Study in Development*, London, 1982

al-Ahsan, Abdullah, *OIC: The Organization of the Islamic Conference*, Handen, USA, 1950

al-Ghazzali, Muhammad, *Our Beginning in Wisdom*, translated by Ismail R al-Faruqi, Washington D.C., 1953

Ameer Ali, Syed, *The Spirit of Islam*, London, 1935, reprinted Pakistan, 1985

Amini, M, *Muslims in the Soviet Union*, New York, 1982

Ansari, Fazlur Rahman, *The Quranic Foundation and Structure of Muslim Society*, vol. II, Karachi, 1977

Arnold, T M, *Preaching of Islam*, London, 1913

Asad, Muhammad, *The Message of The Quran*, Gibraltar, 1987

Asad, Muhammad, *The Principles of State and Government in Islam*, new ed. Gibraltar, 1980

Ayoob (ed.), Mohammad, *Politics of Islamic Reassertion*, New York, 1981

Benningsen, A, and C Lemercier Quelquejay, *Islam in the Soviet Union*, London, 1967

Brohi, A K, *Islam in the Modern World*, 2nd ed., Lahore, 1975

Choueiri, Yousuf M, *Islamic Fundamentalism*, Boston, 1990

Choudhury, G W, *Constitutional Development in Pakistan* (2nd ed.), London, 1970

Choudhury, G W, *India, Pakistan, Bangladesh and the Major Powers: Politics of a Divided Subcontinent*, New York, 1975

Choudhury, G W, *Pakistan's Relations with India*, London, 1968

Choudhury, G W, *The Last Days of United Pakistan*, Bloomington, repr. Karachi, 1993

Choudhury, G W, *The Prophet Muhammad: His Life and Eternal Message*, London, 1993

Current History, Philadelphia, June 1956

Cuyler Young, T, 'Pan-Islamism in the Modern World: Solidarity and Conflict Among Muslim Countries' in Proctor (ed.) *Islam and International Relations*, London, 1965

De-Gaury, Gerald, *Faisal, King of Saudi Arabia*, New York, 1967

Dessouki (ed.), Ali E Hillal, *Islamic Resurgence in the Arab World*, New York, 1982

Donohue, John J, and John L Esposito (eds.), *Islam In Transition: Muslim Perspective*, New York, 1987

Emerson, Donald K, 'Islam in Modern Indonesia', in Stoddard *et al.* (eds), *Change and the Muslim World*, New York, 1981

Esposito, J L, *Islam and Politics*, New York, 1987

Esposito, J L, *Islam, the Straight Path*,, New York, 1989

Esposito, J L, *The Islamic Threat: Myth or Reality*, New York, 1992

Findley, Paul, 'The American Political Process and the Middle East Policy', *American Arab Affairs*, spring, 1986

Fundamental Principles of an Islamic State, prepared by various groups of *'ulama'* in Pakistan, Karachi

Gallagher, Charles F, *The United States and North Africa*, Harvard, 1964

Ghani, Ashraf, 'Afghanistan: Islam and Counter-Revolutionary Movements' in J Esposito (ed.), *Islam in Asia: Religion, Politics and Society*, New York, 1987

Ghaynr, M Arif, 'Muslims in the United States and Visitors', cited in Yvonne Haddad (ed.), *Muslims of America*, New York,

Gibb, H A R, *Modern Trends in Islam*, Chicago, 1945

Goldsmith Jr., Arthur, 'Colonial Period', in Marjorie Kelly, (ed.), *Islam: The Religious and Political Life of a World Community*, New York, 1984

Haberman, Clyde, 'As Islam is Revived, Secular Turks Wince', *New York Times*, 26 March 1989

Haddad (ed.), Yvonne (ed.), *Muslims of America*, New York, 1974

Haddad, Yvonne Y, *The Muslims of America*, New York, 1991

Haque, Mozammel, 'The Need for a Revival of Islam in Africa', *Islamic Quarterly*, London, 3rd quarter, 1992

Haykal, Muhammad Husayn, *The Life of Mohammad*, 1976

Herper, M, and R Israeli (eds.), *Islam and Politics in the Modern Middle East*, New York, 1984

Hodgson Marshall, G S, *The Venture of Islam*, Chicago, 1974

Humphreys, R Stephen, 'The Contemporary Resurgence in the context of Modern Islam' in Ali E Hillal Dessouki (ed.), *Islamic Resurgence in the Arab World*, New York, 1982

Iqbal, Javid, paper entitled 'Islam, Pakistan: Iran and Gulf States' given at the International Conference, Bellago Conference Centre, Lake Como, Italy, 13-18 August 1985

Iqbal, Muhammad, *The Reconstruction of Religious Thought in Islam*, London, 1934

Islam: A Global Civilization, the Islamic Department of the Embassy of Saudi Arabia, Washington D.C.

Ismail, Tareq Y, *Arab Left*, New York, 1976

Ismail, Tareq Y, and Jacqueline Ismail, *Government and Politics in Islam*, London, 1985

Johns, Anthony H, 'Indonesia: Islam and Cultural Pluralism', in J L Esposito (ed.), *Islam in Asia: Religion, Politics and Society*, New York, 1987, ch. 9.

Kessing Record of World Events, UK 1991-93

Khadduri, Majid, *War and Peace in the Law of Islam*, Baltimore, 1955

Khadduri, Majid, 'The Islamic Theory of International Relations' in J Harris Proctor (ed.) *Islam and International Relations*, London, 1965

Kramer, Martin, *Islam Assemblies: The Advent of the Muslim Congress*, New York, 1986

Lapidus, Ira M, *A History of Islamic Societies*, Cambridge, 1988

Le Gai Eaton, Charles, *Islam and The Destiny of Man*, New York, 1985

Lewis, Bernard, 'Politics and War' in Joseph Schacht and C E Bosworth (eds.), *The Legacy of Islam*, London, 1974

Lewis, Bernard, 'The Return of Islam' in *Middle East Review*, No. 12, 1979

Lewis, Flora, 'Upsurge in Islam', *New York Times*, 28-30 December 1979

MacIntyre, Ronald R, 'Saudi Arabia', in Mohammad Ayoob (ed.), *Politics of Islamic Reassertion*, New York, 1981

Marie, Robert, *Ahmed Ben Bella*, translated by Camilla Sykes, New York, 1967

Mawdudi, Abul A'la, *Let Us Be Muslims*, Leicester, 1985

Mawdudi, Abul A'la, *Towards Understanding Islam* (revised edition), Leicester, 1979.

Mayer, Ann Elizabeth, 'Islamic Law' in Marjorie Kelly (ed.), *Islam: The Religious and Political Life of a World Community*, New York, 1984

Metin Kunt, I, 'The Later Muslim Empire' in Marjorie Kelly (ed.), *Islam: The Religious and Political Life of a World Community*, New York, 1984

Mukherjee, R K, *Democracies of the East*, London, 1923

Naqavi, Ali Muhammad, *Islam and Nationalism*, Tehran, 1984

Nasr, Sayyed Hossain, *Ideals and Realities of Islam*, London, 1971

Newell, Richard S, 'Islam and the Struggle for Afghan National Liberation' in Cyriae K Pullapilly (ed.), *Islam in the Contemporary World*, Cross Road Books

Nyang, Sulayman S, 'Convergence and Divergence in an Emergent Community. A Study of Challenges Facing US Muslims', in Yvonne Haddad (ed.), *op. cit.*, New York, 1991

Nyang, Sulayman S, 'Sub-Saharan Africa: Islamic Penetration', in Stoddard *et al.* (eds.), Change and the Muslim World, New York, 1981.

Peek, Malcolm C, 'Saudi Arabia: Islamic Tradition and Modernization' in Stoddard *et al.* (eds), *Change and the Muslim World*, New York, 1981

Perlez, Jane, 'Sudan Leader of Many Hats and Two Worlds', *The New York Times*, 14 March 1989

Piscatori, James (ed.), *Islam in a World of National States*, London, 1988

Pipes, Daniel, 'Oil Wealth and Islamic Resurgence' in Ali E. Hillal Dessouki (ed.), *Islamic Resurgence in the Arab World*, New York, 1982

Pullapilly (ed.), Cyriae K, *Islam in the Contemporary World*, Cross Road Books

Qureshi, I H, *Administration of the Sultanate of Delhi*, London, 1944

Qureshi, I H, *The Concept of Sovereignty and Executive Goverment in Islam*, Proceedings of the All-Pakistan Political Conference, Karachi, 1952

Qutb, Muhammad, 'Islam and the Genesis of the Modern World', in Khurshid (ed.), *Islam: Its Meaning and Message*, Islamic Council of Europe, 1976

Rahman, Fazlur, *Islam*, Chicago, 1977, 2nd ed.

Rahman, Fazlur, *Major Themes of the Quran*, Minneapolis, 1980

Rahman, Fazlur, 'The Message and The Messenger', in Kelly, Marjorie (ed.), *Islam, The Religious and Political Life of a World Community*, New York, 1984

Ramazani, Rouhollah K, 'Iran: The Islamic Cultural Revolution' in P Stoddard *et al.* (eds.), *Change and the Muslim World*, New York, 1981

Rosenthal, E J, *Islam in Modern National States*, London, 1965

Roy, Oliver, 'New Political Elite of Afghanistan' (unpublished), Afghanistan-Iran-Pakistan Workshop, 31 October, 1988, MIT Centre for International Studies

Said, E W, *Orientalism*, New York, 1979

Saikal, Amin, 'Islam: Resistance and Reassertion' in *World Today*, London, November 1987

Schimmel, Annemarie, *Islam: An Introduction*, New York, 1992

Schimmel, Annemarie, *And Muhammad is His Messenger, The Veneration of the Prophet in Islamic Piety*, Chapel Hill and London, 1968

Schuon, Frithjof, *Understanding Islam* (tr. D M Matheson), London, 1976

Smith, W C, *Pakistan as an Islamic State*, Lahore, 1951

Smith, Wilfred C, *Islam in Modern History*, Princeton, 1957

Stoddard, Philip, *et al* (eds), *Change and the Muslim World*, New York, 1981

Trimingham, J S, *The Influence of Islam upon Africa*, New York, 1968

Understanding Islam and The Muslims, Washington D.C., Islamic Affairs Department, Saudi Embassy

van der Mehden, Fred R, 'Malaysia: Islam and Multi-Ethnic Politics', in J Esposito (ed.), *The Voice of Resurgent Islam*, New York, 1987

Voll, J O, *Islam: Continuity and Change in the Modern World*, Boulder, 1982

Watt, W Montgomery, *Muhammad at Madina*, London, 1956

Watt, W Montgomery, *Muhammad Prophet and Statesman*, Oxford, 1961

Yousef Ali, Abdullah, *Meaning of the Glorious Quran*, Cairo, n.d.

Zafrullah Kan, Muhammad, *Its Message for the Modern Mind*, London, 1962

Zakaria, Rafiq, *The Struggle within Islam, the Conflict Between Religion and Politics*, New York, 1989

Index